THE MOSAIC NAVIGATOR

The Essential Guide to the Internet Interface

Paul Gilster

John Wiley & Sons, Inc.

NEW YORK • CHICHESTER • BRISBANE • TORONTO • SINGAPORE

Publisher: Katherine Schowalter
Editor: Paul Farrell
Assistant Editor: Allison Roarty
Managing Editor: Frank Grazioli
Copyeditor: Janice Borzendowski
Book Design & Composition: North Market Street Graphics, Lancaster, PA

Cover Art: *The Arrival of the Body of Saint Mark*
(Anonymous, from St. Mark's Basilica, Venice, Italy)

Library of Congress Cataloging-in-Publication Data:
Gilster, Paul
    The mosaic navigator : the essential guide to the internet interface /
Paul Gilster.
        p.   cm.
    Includes index.
    ISBN 0-471-11336-0 (paper : acid-free paper)
    1. Internet (Computer network) 2. Mosaic (Computer file)
I. Title.
TK5105.875.I57G56   1995
025.04—dc20   94-37772
                                                  CIP

Printed in the United States of America
10 9 8 7 6 5 4 3 2 1

For my father, August E. Gilster,
who would have loved Mosaic

Contents

Foreword

The Mosaic Navigator is a book whose time has come. These days, it seems that half the world is calling the Internet Society, and two of the most often-asked questions are, "How do I use the World Wide Web," and "How do I access Mosaic?" Paul Gilster, in his trademark enjoyable and informative writing style, thoroughly answers these and every other question users might have about Mosaic.

The World Wide Web is a profound change in how people share and discover information. The Web is the result of the work of many people, but none so instrumental as Tim Berners-Lee. (Not many people know that he was an occasional actor at the Little Theatre of Geneva. His vision, enthusiasm, and flair for the dramatic all combined in the WWW.) I was fortunate to be in Geneva when Tim conceived and developed the Web concept and its underlying protocol and language at CERN, the European Laboratory for Particle Physics.

Like so many developments in the Internet global community, Tim's ideas and enthusiasm spread, and soon other groups became active participants, including the Networked Information Resources standards group. And Larry Smarr's NCSA Mosaic team, led by Marc Andreessen, developed the standards and the elegant Mosaic client. As Tim likes to say, "It's a damned elegant front end."

The magic of Mosaic became clear to me the first time I unzipped and used it at home. My 7-year-old son Ryan, sitting at my side, immediately said, "Let me try it, Daddy." In no time he had steered his way to the world's Fractal Art Museum at Rennes in Normandy, France, where together we viewed the continually updated collection of Mandelbrot art "hanging" there, put them on the workstation screen, and printed them.

What's really remarkable is that the Web revolution is just beginning. Traffic on the Web continues to increase at such a rapid rate that present projections estimate it will exceed the world's telephone traffic in three years. Nothing in human communications history has developed at such a pace. Around the world, innumerable Internet access providers are scrambling to provide access over almost every type of transport medium, from CATV to telephone lines to wireless services.

As this book goes to press, Tim Berners-Lee is establishing a World Wide Web Consortium at M.I.T. to foster new developments in human communications. And the new International WWW Conferences bring people together from across the globe. Not to be outdone, the original Mosaic team is in the process of building an even better Mosaic for the masses, so keep the URL **http://www.w3.org** in easy reach—you're going to need it.

It can't be emphasized enough in this world of mass media hype and spoon-fed broadcasting what a treasure the WWW represents as a means for organizations and institutions throughout the world to share information, sell products and services, and support customers or the general public. Perhaps more important is that it offers an entirely new dimension of collective wisdom and experience shared through HTML links to others. Learn, enjoy, wonder, create, and share yourself.

ANTHONY M. RUTKOWSKI
Executive Director
Internet Society
Reston, VA USA
September 1994

Preface

Mosaic has captured the imagination of Internet users worldwide because of its intuitive graphical interface. The beauty of accessing the Internet's **World Wide Web** through a tool like Mosaic is that you can receive on-screen formatting that is similar to that of a printed page, including photographs or graphics and a variety of textual effects. Even audio clips can be included, as can full-motion video. No wonder Mosaic is winning converts right and left; it seems to be the interface of the future.

In this book, I examine Mosaic for the individual computer user. Most such users will be connecting to the Internet through a SLIP (Serial Line Internet Protocol) account, and will thus be limited by the speed of their modems and the nature of their telephone-line connection to the net. This invariably raises issues concerning Mosaic's speed, since the program downloads images one at a time; a page created with multiple images, even small ones, can take quite a while to build itself on the user's screen. The focus here, then, is not only on learning how to use Mosaic, but also on how to customize it for individual use.

Although I have used Mosaic for Microsoft Windows as the core version for this study of Mosaic, I have also included a chapter on installing the program on a Macintosh. The two programs are similar enough in their operations that I felt confident in not making too much of their specific differences. Any Macintosh user should be able to make his or her way through Mosaic with the information presented here, while the more complex installation and configuration issues raised by the Windows version demanded a tighter focus. The chapter on installing the Windows version is by necessity much longer than the comparable chapter for the Macintosh, a fact which will bring a wry smile to the hardcore Mac users I know.

This book divides into sections as follows:

- Chapter 1 provides a broad overview of Mosaic and its place within the community of Internet access tools, while Chapter 2 contains the necessary information about SLIP and PPP (Point-to-Point Protocol) to get the individual user up to speed. A straight dial-up, or shell, account cannot be used to run Mosaic. The program requires the complete Internet connection only SLIP/PPP can provide through a modem.

- Chapters 3 and 4 contain installation instructions for the Windows and Macintosh versions respectively. Installation is not particularly difficult, but adding viewers and configuring the program can be tricky unless the user knows what to do when.

- Chapter 5 is an overview of the **World Wide Web**, introducing the concepts of hypertext and hypermedia and discussing the **Web**'s growth as a system of interlinked information. I also provide background on the protocols that make the **Web** work, and include a brief look at HTML.
- Chapter 6 proceeds through Mosaic's bag of tricks, showing you how the program can be used to access a variety of Internet tools, from **Gopher** to FTP and Telnet.
- Chapters 7 and 8 are devoted to customizing Mosaic. The program is readily adapted to the individual's needs; its menus can be structured to taste, and up to twenty new menus can be created. The user can also create an individualized home page with links to frequently accessed resources; I provide the necessary HTML commands to do this, along with a sample home page. Finally, I examine the **mosaic.ini** configuration file, which can be edited to establish a variety of working parameters.
- Chapter 9 examines the newly developing search tools that scour the **Web** for interesting sites and information. It also examines the question of where Mosaic is going, as a new breed of commercial Mosaics comes to the market.
- Chapter 10 is a travelogue, containing interesting **Web** sites I have visited in the course of writing this book.

I owe thanks to my friend and neighbor David Warlick for the Macintosh screen shots, and for thoughts about the Macintosh versions of Mosaic. David is engaged in developing a **World Wide Web** site for state government here in North Carolina. He and the thousands of people like him around the world who are building **Web** pages are the real heroes of this book. It is their work on which Mosaic draws; without the influx of new destinations on the **Web**, Mosaic would not have achieved the degree of success that it has as an all-purpose access tool. The future of the **Web** and of Mosaic now rests with the content providers who will continue to bring new ideas to this fascinating medium.

And thanks, as always, to my friends at John Wiley & Sons. Paul Farrell, Allison Roarty, and Frank Grazioli have proven valuable colleagues on three books; their insights and numerous tips have contributed materially to the value of each. As for copyeditors, if there is a better one in the business than Janice Borzendowski, I'm not aware of it.

1

Introduction and Background

The Internet has seen nothing like Mosaic. The hot new program has taken the network scene by storm, seizing the attention of users worldwide with its enticing interface. No longer limited to straight text, Mosaic devotees travel an Internet stuffed with photographs, colorful graphics, sound clips, and even movies. What's more, Mosaic's formatting features allow an electronic screen to be manipulated as if it were a printed page, while providing access to old Internet standbys like **Gopher**, FTP, and Telnet. If there is an all-purpose Internet program, Mosaic is it.

What makes this program special is good engineering. Mosaic takes a problem—the fact that millions of new users are coming onto the Internet, only to find it formidable and hard to use—and solves it brilliantly. Science fiction writer Robert Heinlein once said: "Never worry about theory as long as the machinery does what it's supposed to do." The great majority of new Internet users aren't computer scientists or programmers. They have little patience with a computer system that requires them to master tricky commands and numerous parameter settings to get any work done. Mosaic allows them to forget about the theory behind the Internet and let the machinery, in this case a brilliantly conceived program, do what it is supposed to do.

Mosaic at Maximum Thrust

Following this software's trajectory is like watching a Saturn V clawing for sky. Back in the moon shot days, the huge booster would hang over the launchpad for agonizing seconds, matching pounds of thrust against gravity in a contest it seemed unlikely to win. But then, miraculously, it would clear the tower, moving up and downrange, ever accelerating, until it was but a searing pin-point of light, "carrying the fire," to cite the title of Mike Collins's description of astronauts riding their torch to the moon.

Ponder this: 340,000 copies of Mosaic have been downloaded from the National Center for Supercomputing Applications (NCSA). Further consider the fact that Mosaic also can be downloaded from sites other than the NCSA, while a single copy, once installed on a fileserver, may support more than one user. Balance these points against another fact: Mosaic is software in an early stage of development; each new release inclines present users to upgrade. All of this makes estimating the actual user pool difficult. We can talk reasonably of a Mosaic-using population in the hundreds of thousands, but it may be an exaggeration to claim a million or more active users, as some have. The big program is gaining momentum, but it's still hanging in the sky over the launch-pad, its engines at maximum thrust.

What will push it up, downrange, and out is the issue of access. The manifest advantages of using Mosaic, most especially its point-and-shoot interface and its ability to make almost any kind of Internet information available from within a single program, are driving us toward a truly democratic Internet. We are in the preliminary stages of an interface revolution that will change the way we retrieve networked data. Millions currently access the net through standard dial-up, or *shell*, accounts rather than the more specialized and powerful Serial Line Inter-net Protocol (SLIP) or Point-to-Point Protocol (PPP) techniques that make run-ning Mosaic possible over a modem link. But higher-speed modems and dramatically falling connection prices are making SLIP/PPP more affordable than ever before, while those with direct network access at work have already experienced the pleasure of running Mosaic at maximum speed. As the nature of our connections changes, the use of Mosaic will accelerate to escape velocity.

Software and History

But if Mosaic is the tool of the future, it also owes a debt to history. Take small pebbles, bits of cut marble, the occasional piece of glass, or terra cotta; embed these in plaster or putty to hold them in place. The result is one of the most strikingly beautiful of all ancient decorations. In the British Museum, mosaics from the Roman era hang on the walls of a vast stairway leading up to the exhibitions from classical cultures—Greece, Rome, Byzantium. What aston-ishes the eye are the colors, the vibrancy of the royal blues, the turquoises, the roses, and golds. You see similar work at the Roman ruins in Bath, where craftsmen painstakingly laid down, pebble by pebble, glass by stone, floors as lovely and delicate, as anything that has ever been walked on. Floors as kalei-doscopes. We always forget how colorful the ancient world was.

A mosaic called "the grand hunt" was recovered from the ruins of Piazza Armerina, Sicily, where more than 7,000 feet of floor mosaics show us glimpses of life from the latter days of the Roman empire. We see patricians on their horses hunting deer in one unforgettable scene, the faces of both hunter and hunted somehow captured through minute insertions of the small, constituent cubes called *tesserae*. Thin colored stones were cut into shapes to fit each design feature, while molten glass was colored with metal oxides before being poured onto a surface for drying and cutting. Even before Roman times, baked clay pieces were embedded in brick walls to create patterns in ancient Sumeria. The use of mosaics as a decorative tool survives to our own time.

What more apt name, then, for the software tool we examine here? Mosaic is composed of minute objects, too, each painstakingly laid into place. The fact that they are digital—a collection of binary data in infinitely varied form, complex as a strand of DNA—does not change the central equation. The concept remains: The accumulation of tiny details creates beauty and information. We built terrazzoes, and moon landers, and cyberspace cities, stone by stone and byte by byte. Collections of raw materials fused in the core of ancient stellar explosions, we ourselves are testimony to the power of nature to astound the senses.

Now we can take advantage of the labors of the Internet's creators by tapping the digital flow with a software program that renders its most complex negotiations transparent to us. What we receive on the other side is not just data but artistry. A properly designed **World Wide Web** page reveals, through Mosaic, the hand of its creator. We see photographs in full color, hear sounds, view movies. We use our mouse to move through embedded links to other information. A single click takes us to them, where we find another page opening up before us, with its own links to still further flights. The entire framework is self-referential. Mosaic and the underlying **Web** are the first attempt to bring to life an aesthetics of digital networking. At some point, someone suggested that a Roman floor might be beautiful, and someone else said, why not?

The National Center for Supercomputing Applications

In our time, a similar dialogue was carried out at the National Center for Supercomputing Applications. Located at the University of Illinois at Urbana-Champaign, the NCSA is a research center specializing in high-performance computing within an interdisciplinary environment. That synergy was perhaps inevitable, for the development of Mosaic required an ability to tie together diverse kinds of information; more important, it required a vision of what a fully powered Internet access tool would look like if it were to appeal not just to computer scientists but to the entire universe of network users, from academics to home computerists.

The name for what NCSA does is *computational science,* a method of research that combines theory with laboratory experiment within the context of a supercomputer. You can model natural phenomena on such a computer, working with real-time data to tease out otherwise hidden results. Since it opened to the research community in January 1986, NCSA has worked with more than 6,000 users at close to 400 universities and corporations. Among its beneficiaries are educators, scientists, artists, and engineers. Think of them as being linked through networking into what NCSA calls a *metacenter* for computational science and engineering. As conceived by NCSA, this metacenter actually takes in several supercomputing sites: the NCSA itself, the Cornell Theory Center, the Pittsburgh Supercomputing Center, and the San Diego Supercomputer Center. Their common challenge—to make data available no matter where the user is located, and to make it usable no matter what the computing platform.

Mosaic grows directly out of this need. The system is designed to be distributed across a wide-area network; the user of the system is never required to know the actual site of any document he or she needs to access. The conceptual place thus travelled is *cyberspace*, the universe of connected computer communications. A key player in the creation of that space, the NCSA Software Development Group (SDG), uses the software to distribute further information about its own mission and the potentialities of the programs it has created. SDG develops various tools for all major computing platforms, from the IBM-compatible desktop machine to UNIX workstations, Macintoshes, and supercomputers themselves. Much of this software has been placed in the public domain, while other programs are copyrighted but available to the academic and research communities.

NCSA Mosaic is copyrighted but free for academic and research use. As with other NCSA software, it can be obtained through CD-ROM, e-mail server, the U.S. Post Office, and anonymous FTP. Assuming you are already an Internet user, I provide complete directions on how to retrieve and install Mosaic in Chapters 3 and 4.

Those following the Mosaic saga also know that a number of commercial versions of the program are becoming available. In fact, Marc Andreesen, originator of Mosaic, and a large part of the Mosaic technology team from NCSA, have left NCSA to form Mosaic Communications Corp. in Mountain View, California. The company's aim is to provide services and software for commercial activities on the Internet. It is joined by a host of firms now entering the commercial Mosaic arena, including Spyglass, a Savoy, Illinois-based company that recently arranged with NCSA to handle licensing of Mosaic; Spry, the Seattle-based developer that has produced the Internet In A Box product; and Quarterdeck, which plans to bring out a product of its own. We will examine the ramifications of this rapid commercialization in Chapter 9.

For now, the question is, which Mosaic to use? The answer provided in this book is simple: Download and learn about Mosaic using the NCSA version, which is free and provides the whole range of useful features we're about to explore. Get to know about the resources available on the **Web** and the various ways of getting at them through Mosaic. Then, if you are involved in a commercial operation and hope to apply Mosaic to your business, or if you are an individual user who finds particular features useful in one of the enhanced

Mosaics now coming to the market, move to one of them. Most individual users will do well, I think, to learn the ropes with the NCSA version, which is, after all, continually being improved through the efforts of NCSA's team of developers. Many enhancements from commercial Mosaic versions are also likely to flow back to the NCSA.

How Mosaic Works

Given the amount of attention it has generated, the fact that Mosaic is often considered in isolation is surprising. People speak of the program as if it stands apart from the Internet tools which, in fact, it supports.

If you operate through a standard dial-up account using a character-based interface, the various parts of the Internet are laid out before you in separate units. You need to give commands to your service provider's computer to get anything done. Each time you do so, you activate a program. Enter the **pine** command and you call up the mail-reader program of that name. Enter the **trn** command and a program for reading USENET newsgroups appears. Each task, from File Transfer Protocol (FTP) sessions for transferring files, to Telnet connections allowing you to use a remote computer, is handled by a program designed for the purpose. Each of these programs has its own specific set of commands.

The beauty of Mosaic is that its functions include almost all the major features of the Internet. Yes, you can establish a Telnet connection through Mosaic. Indeed, you can do so by invoking the same Telnet program you use normally with a SLIP/PPP account, but Mosaic will pop up the relevant work screen inside your Mosaic session, and you will return to Mosaic when you're through. You can download files using FTP, but instead of operating through memorized commands at a system prompt, you are presented with a Mosaic screen that allows you to use a mouse for point-and-shoot operations, and that shows you the file structure of the remote computer in a logical and easy-to-understand format. **Gopher** is available, and so are USENET newsgroups. And so, of course, is the entire world of linked hypermedia resources made available through the **World Wide Web**.

This is why so many people are excited about Mosaic. *The New York Times's* John Markoff has called it "... a map to the buried treasures of the Information Age." What excites Markoff is his ability to click his mouse on a highlighted word and pop through a hypertext connection to a new Mosaic screen, one containing further information about the concept under discussion. Click on an image and you can summon up everything from travel scenes in Bali to a NASA weather satellite photograph. Click on an audio speaker icon and you can hear music from the highlands of Peru or the voice of Babe Ruth. Museum exhibits are available through Mosaic, as are city directories and catalogs of products for sale. Each day brings new, Mosaic-accessible resources into view.

This is exciting stuff for people used to pushing around character-based displays. Using so-called *terminal emulation*, such displays result when computers pretend to be terminals of the computers to which they are connected. Regular dial-up (non-SLIP/PPP) users have no alternative, but the method inevitably limits their capabilities. Graphics are out, and on-screen formatting is visually primitive.

Mosaic changes all that. Suddenly a range of sight and sound opens up, a wild, digital information bazaar populated by businesspeople, scientists, academics, and home users—visionaries, cranks, and the occasional loudmouth. By building *home pages,* users can create their own Mosaic environments, using a special hypertext language called HTML to convert normal, linear information into a new linked format, one that includes not only textual information but every form of media up to full-motion video.

Underlying the glitter is the **World Wide Web**, a system of networked, hypertextual information developed at CERN, the giant particle physics research center in Switzerland. Tim Berners-Lee, the **Web**'s developer, may not have foreseen how his intricately crafted brainchild would one day supply the muscle behind the full-featured Mosaic overlay. In fact, the wonders of Mosaic occur precisely because it is an overlay, or *browser,* program designed to exploit the resources already set in place by the **Web**. Nothing inherent in the **Web**'s design demands that it be graphical; indeed, there are other **Web** browsers, including several character-based ones like **www** and **lynx**. The latter are fine implementations and do everything that could be expected of a character-based system. They just can't fold in the graphics, the textual formatting, the photographs, and the sounds in as consistently managed a whole. It took Mosaic to turn the **Web** into the revolutionary publishing tool it has become. A Hollywood wag who knew and worked with them both once said this about Fred Astaire and Ginger Rogers: "She gave him sex appeal, and he gave her class." Mosaic and the **Web** are our digital Astaire and Rogers.

Mosaic's Premises

A great interface tool is one that is easier to demonstrate than to explain. Its premises should be self-evident, as indeed Mosaic's are. It should lead users into trying new things, while being supported by a menu system that allows them to recover when they hit the occasional cul-de-sac. Its operations should be consistent, offering available command options in a logical manner and making them accessible by mouse click alone. And it should be not only simple to install, but easy to customize, so that its menus can be tailored to the needs of a specific situation.

Mosaic doesn't yet fulfill all these requirements, but it comes closer to meeting them than any other Internet front-end has ever managed, and it does so while retaining the power inherent in our growing number of networked tools. We could wish it to be faster, for to show us that beautiful photograph of Mount Fuji, Mosaic must retrieve the entire file over the network and then display it by tapping an external viewer program expressly installed for the purpose. The same is true of large audio files; run into the Japanese national anthem on-line and our mouse click may result in long minutes of waiting as the file is pumped, byte by byte, across our network connection.

Frustrating, yes. But the limitation is not Mosaic's; it's the result of the quality of our connections themselves. This is why modem users will need to work with as fast an instrument as possible, preferably nothing less than 14,400 baud (we'll look at minimum equipment requirements in Chapter 3). If anything, Mosaic demonstrates that communications technology has outrun our delivery systems; we could all use high-speed fiber connections into our homes and places of business, which could deliver wider bandwidth than copper wiring and allow Mosaic to spread its wings. The popularity of Mosaic and the growth of the Internet itself will be only two of the driving factors leading to a realization of that goal, but we know that it's coming. Call it the Infobahn, the Information Highway or whatever you please; we're moving toward a wide bandwidth infrastructure that will show Mosaic off at its best.

All that doesn't mean this program isn't ready for prime time, even though it is, admittedly, in its infancy. No, Mosaic can be used today for numerous network tasks, many of which you might not have attempted because of the daunting complexity of the task under any other interface.

The Mosaic Interface

For users coming to Mosaic from the conventional dial-up world, the feel of the software is at first curious, then exhilarating. Character-based connections always place you at a user prompt. Thus, what you see on your screen gives no clue as to what you can do. Here, for example, is the user prompt at Interpath, an Internet service provider in the Raleigh area which I use. This is what I see when I log on:

```
mercury:
```

The word "mercury" is simply the name of the computer into which I have dialed. The colon following it is an icon for the other shoe waiting to drop. This prompt means, "type in a command to use the system." Various service providers customize their command prompts; you might encounter a percent sign (%) as the user prompt, or a dollar sign ($) or a plain colon (:). Whatever the prompt looks like, you need to know which command to type or nothing will happen.

Contrast this with what happens when you call up Mosaic. Instead of a user prompt waiting for you to act, you are presented with a full screen of information. Figure 1.1 shows an example of what this screen may look like. This is, in fact, only one of thousands and thousands of possible Mosaic screens. Because Mosaic ties into **World Wide Web** sites, we can use it to move to any of the sites we specify, each of which will offer multiple screens,

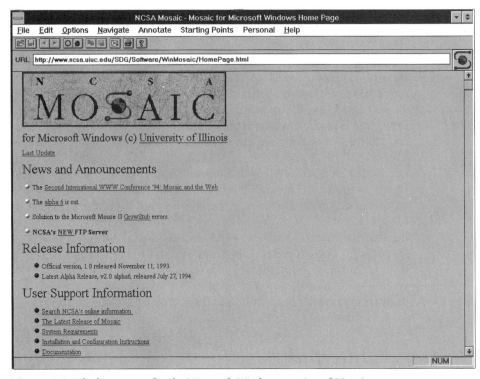

Figure 1.1   The home page for the Microsoft Windows version of Mosaic.

or *pages,* of information. The number of such sites is expanding rapidly as the popularity of Mosaic increases.

Figure 1.1 is, in fact, the home page for the Microsoft Windows version of Mosaic. You can verify this by noting the information at the top of the screen, which shows you at any given time which page you have accessed through the **Web**'s complex and interlinking framework. Below it is the URL: statement, which specifies an address for the document we are examining. URL stands for Uniform Resource Locator; a URL provides complete information about finding a particular resource, no matter what its format, on the Internet. As we'll see, Mosaic allows us to enter any URL to move directly to that site.

You can see in Figure 1.1 that some text is underlined; a color monitor would reveal that the underlined text can appear in a different color than the rest. Both underlining and color indicate the presence of a hyperlink to further information; click on it with the left mouse button to move to that link. You won't go wrong if you make the assumption that curiosity is the best vehicle for exploring the capabilities of Mosaic and the destinations available through the **World Wide Web**. Point-and-shoot makes the entire process a simple one.

When you invoke Mosaic for the first time, the program attempts to lock on to a particular home page. Windows users are shown to the page appropriate for the Windows version, while Macintosh and UNIX users likewise receive a connection to the page specified by NCSA. As packaged by the Center, Mosaic is set up to access one of these pages when you start the program, a useful feature because it allows you to keep up with new versions as well as news from within the Mosaic community. Later, you may choose to customize the system to start with a different home page. We'll even set up a home page of our own in Chapter 8.

Don't be confused by the term *home page*. It simply refers to the top level of information at a particular site. From this level, you can move further into the nested information provided by the **Web** and made available in graphic form through Mosaic. Because the **Web** is a hypermedia application, you can begin at one site and, following links between data, move to any other available page, whether in the same location or anywhere in the world.

The page metaphor is particularly appropriate, for each Mosaic screen can be conceived as a page in a dynamic book, one with an ever-growing number of pages, and the built-in ability to move between them as necessary to find linked information. And like the pages of a book, Mosaic presents information in various forms. Changes in font and typeface can be employed—notice that in Figure 1.1 we are shown a variety of point sizes. But Mosaic doesn't stop with formatting. In Figure 1.2, you can see an example of the program's ability to work with images. Each system designer will choose his or her own presentation, with the flexibility of tapping sound, images, and formatted text.

In this figure we are examining a collection of artwork from Australian National University in Canberra, prepared by Professor Michael Greenhalgh, who is exploring the uses of technology in making such imagery accessible for noncommercial purposes. The small images seen here can be expanded by clicking on any one of them. Mosaic will retrieve the image and display it, using the external viewer program that I have installed to do the job. The image will be presented in a window, which can be sized or moved as necessary. When you choose to receive such images, you will need to wait until the file transfer is complete before Mosaic can display it. This is why a fast modem is necessary, when using a SLIP/PPP account, to work with Mosaic images. A full network connection reduces this problem.

Moving between Sites

In Figure 1.3, I have moved to a site in Britain. You can see the URL at the top of the screen:

```
http://www.ucs.ed.ac.uk/misc/uk/intro.html
```

This is a clickable map of the British Isles, meaning that I can move my mouse to any of the marked sites and click on it to retrieve information. Such maps, increasingly common on the **Web**, make moving between sites a simple,

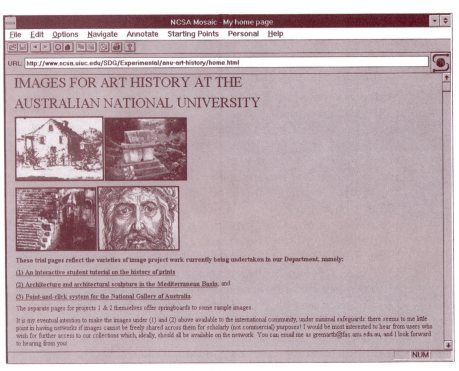

Figure 1.2 A Mosaic page incorporating inline images.

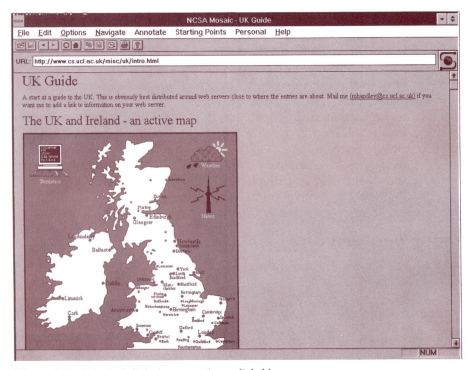

Figure 1.3 A site in Britain incorporating a clickable map.

graphical process. In Figure 1.4, I have clicked on one of the links to the city of Bath, in west-central England.

Mosaic has then delivered a screen of information which offers me choices for further browsing; I can check **Web** servers in Bath, or **Gopher** servers, and more is available by scrolling through the document. In Figure 1.5, I have clicked on the small bus icon at the bottom of the screen. The server I have contacted allows me to take an on-line tour of neighboring Bristol. As you can see, the **Web** can be just the thing for those with a passion for on-line travel.

There are also more prosaic ways of moving about in the **Web**. Examine Figure 1.6, where I have generated two menus. The first is the menu called up by clicking on the Starting Points item at the top of the Mosaic screen. As you can see, this menu includes nested submenus. I clicked on the item called Other Documents to retrieve a list of sites, or as we now know to think of them, pages. In this way, I can move easily between sites by clicking on whichever one I want. Mosaic thus simplifies what the user needs to do to move around the Internet. The sites listed in these menus are provided as the default items when you download Mosaic for the first time. However, the list is entirely customizable, and in Chapter 7 we will talk about how to add sites to your menus. Eventually you can build a Mosaic that is specifically tailored to your own interests.

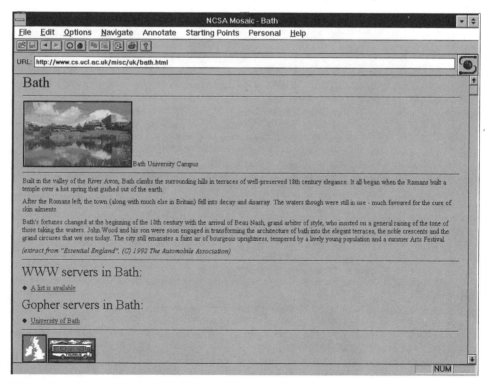

Figure 1.4   The results of taking the hyperlink to the city of Bath.

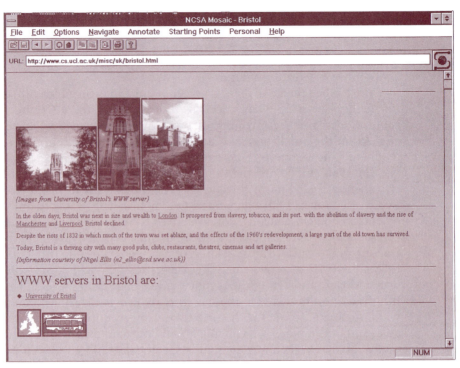

Figure 1.5 Moving to Bristol for a quick tour.

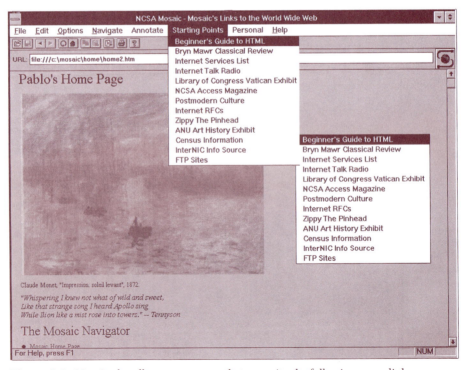

Figure 1.6 Mosaic also allows you to move between sites by following menu links.

Note: Sharp-eyed readers will notice that I have already customized this copy of Mosaic. The Personal menu at the top of my screen is in fact a menu I have added to the program to keep track of sites I use in my daily work.

New **World Wide Web** servers appear all the time, so many, in fact, that it's likely you will find servers covering almost any subject that might interest you. We're still early in the game, so the process of creating the appropriate hypertext documents and putting them into the necessary format (we'll discuss how this is done in Chapter 5), is nascent. Figure 1.7 shows a page devoted to shortwave radio. Note that you are not looking at the complete page, but must use the scroll bar to the right of the screen to move further into the document. Doing so would reveal an enormous variety of information, from radio schedules to news items, propagation forecasts and more.

When we note interesting sites like this, it becomes crucial that we don't have to jot down their addresses and then painstakingly reenter them every time we want to return. In the case of the shortwave radio server, you can see that the address involved is a relatively lengthy one:

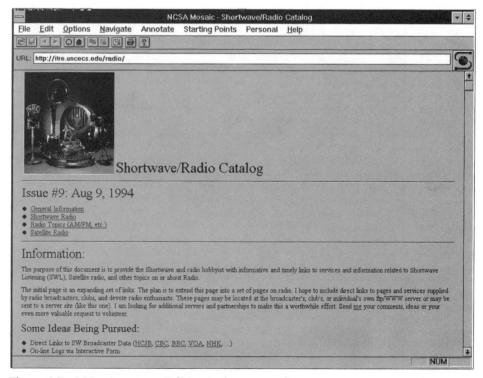

Figure 1.7 A Mosaic page specializing in shortwave radio.

```
http://itre.uncecs.edu/radio/
```

At least, it seems lengthy now; in fact, as we'll soon discover, URLs can be considerably longer, and can be used to specify resources with a great degree of precision as well as consistency across Internet applications. We wouldn't want to have to enter such an address every time we specified a resource, though, so we can use Mosaic's built-in capability to add a particular site to any of its menus.

Each of the items on the Other Documents menu is a site that has come with the particular version of Mosaic I am using, established by NCSA in the original package. These sites are places the NCSA programmers thought would be useful as well as typical; they show off the power of Mosaic. But any and all of them can be eliminated; any **Web** site you prefer can be substituted with your new list alphabetized by using Mosaic's Menu Editor. You are able to create up to twenty menus in this way for your own use.

Adding a menu item is easy. Suppose we were examining a particular site and wanted to refer back to it.

Figure 1.8 shows what happens when I pull down the necessary menu. I am looking at the InterNIC InfoGuide, a splendid source of Internet informa-

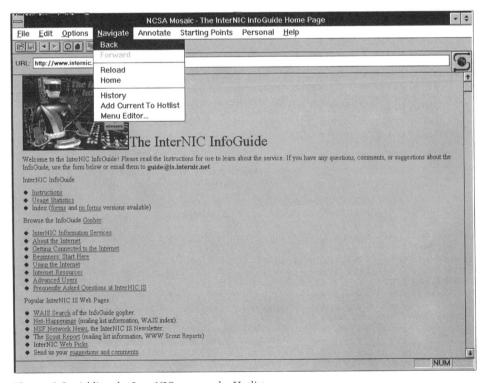

Figure 1.8   Adding the InterNIC page to the Hotlist.

tion that I plan to use for later reference. I have pulled down the Navigate menu, where you will note the penultimate item, Add Current to Hotlist.

By moving the highlight to this item and clicking on it, I can add the URL of the current document to any menu I choose. To send Mosaic back to that document, all I have to do is access the appropriate menu and click on the item.

To the Heart of the Web

Let's now use Mosaic to contact the place where the **World Wide Web** began, the CERN research center in Switzerland. There are a variety of ways to get there. First, we could find the site by pulling down the Starting Points menu and taking the World Wide Web Info option. That would, in turn, lead us to an item called Web Overview. Clicking on it would take us directly to CERN.

Easy? Sure, but what if we've removed that item from our menus? In that case, we can always enter a URL directly by choosing the Open URL . . . item on the File menu, and then type in the URL in question:

```
http://info.cern.ch/
```

In Chapter 7, we will examine how to use the Mosaic menus to move to new URLs and perform many other functions. For now, though, simply take a look at the **Web**'s birthplace, as interpreted through Mosaic. Figure 1.9 shows you the home page at CERN and the associated pages linked to it. We see the by now familiar Mosaic interface interpreting **World Wide Web** data; you've probably already looked at this site through a character-based browser like **www**. If you will examine Figure 1.10, showing the **www** browser in action, you can see that the benefits of the Mosaic interface are more than purely graphical. The character-based **www** requires you to enter a number to tell the system which hypertext link you would like to follow. This can be cumbersome, although **www** implements the system clearly. But the graphical, point-and-shoot nature of Mosaic clearly wins on aesthetic grounds.

Using Mosaic to Retrieve Files

As mentioned, Mosaic contains a variety of specific tools. Among the most useful is its FTP capability. When you use Mosaic to manage an FTP, or File Transfer Protocol, session, you bring additional graphical benefits to a process that, in the text-based environment, can be confusing and to some extent unforgiving. When you run a directory display with a conventional dial-up connection to the Internet, you will be presented with a great deal of information that may be superfluous to your needs. You learn about the various *permissions* available for a given file, those UNIX parameters that tell who can access what, along with other information about file size and date.

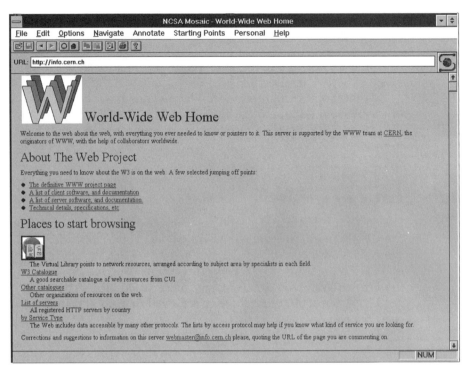

Figure 1.9 The home page at CERN, birthplace of the **World Wide Web**.

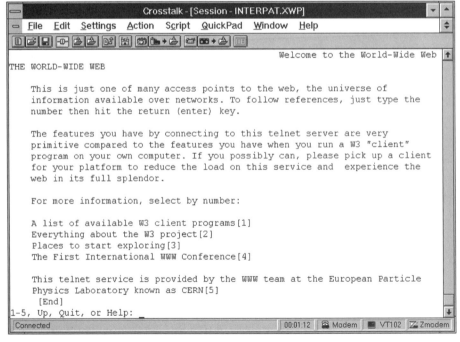

Figure 1.10 The **www** browser shows the limitations of a character-based interface.

Put Mosaic to work, however, and the situation changes. In Figure 1.11, I have opened a connection to an FTP site and have paused to examine a directory. The URL tells me where I am:

`ftp://oak.oakland.edu/pub/msdos/`

In non-URL lingo, this means I have connected to the FTP site **oak.oakland.edu**, and have accessed the *pub/msdos* directory.

Note how clean the screen display is. At the top of the screen is the directory name (it is set in a larger typeface, a trick a character-based connection would be unable to pull off). Below that is a useful statement, underlined and colored in blue, that says Up to Parent Directory. Thus, we receive a clickable command that would otherwise, in a character-based environment, have called for a written one such as **cd ..** to achieve the same result. Each of the underlined terms below this link is a subdirectory, which we can likewise reach with a click.

Note, too, that Mosaic presents us with icons to help us visualize what we will be seeing. Directory icons are different from file icons. Mosaic's graphical capabilities can be a useful guidance tool, helping us to find the information

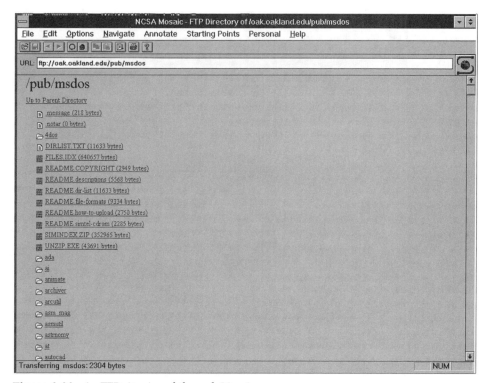

Figure 1.11 An FTP site viewed through Mosaic.

we need and navigate among the files. And remember that Mosaic isn't just for fancy screen displays. It can also do the work of retrieving the file we need.

If we do choose to retrieve a file, the process couldn't be simpler. We tell Mosaic to save the file to disk by clicking on the relevant menu item (full instructions on how to do this will be presented in Chapter 6). Then we click on the file name, which will call up a menu giving us options on where to save the file and what to name it, along with default suggestions.

Figure 1.12 shows this process in motion. There, I have gone into the *pub/msdos/astrnomy* subdirectory from my original position in *pub/msdos*, and have clicked on the file **astro202.zip** to retrieve it. I can now place the file wherever I choose. Obviously, I was not required to enter any difficult-to-remember commands, such as telling the server I wanted to transfer a binary file by entering **binary** at a prompt before I began the transfer, or instructing it to **get astro202.zip**.

Mosaic to Gopher in Style

Gopher is easy to use anyway. The whole idea behind the **Gopher** project that originated at the University of Minnesota was to make **Gopher** a way for stu-

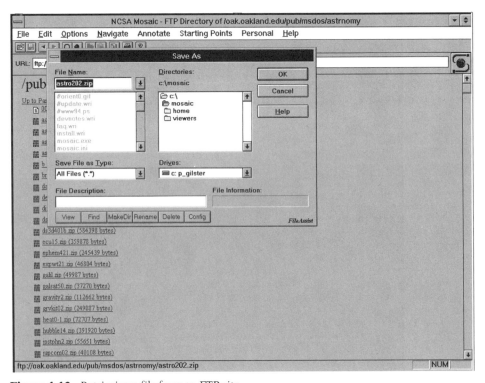

Figure 1.12   Retrieving a file from an FTP site.

dents and faculty, people without broad computer backgrounds, to use the resources available through the campus network. To do this, the developers set up **Gopher** as a menu system. All you had to do to use it was to move an on-screen marker down to the item you wanted and then press the Return key.

Mosaic adds to this picture the graphical interface features we've already demonstrated with other tools. In Figure 1.13, we're looking at a **Gopher** maintained by The Internet Wiretap in Cupertino, California. Again, we're in an environment where we can point to what we want, with the underlining and color variations telling us that we can click on any of these items to extract further menus. And once again, we are in the presence of icons, which show us what kind of item we are dealing with. The first item, for example, is a document that can be read by clicking on it. The rest of these items contain submenus stuffed with further information. We can click on text files in these submenus to read them on-screen or, if we choose, we can download them directly to our own computers.

Where We're Going

We've only begun to examine the multitudinous possibilities of this remarkable software. We haven't looked at Telnet yet, or called up a USENET news-

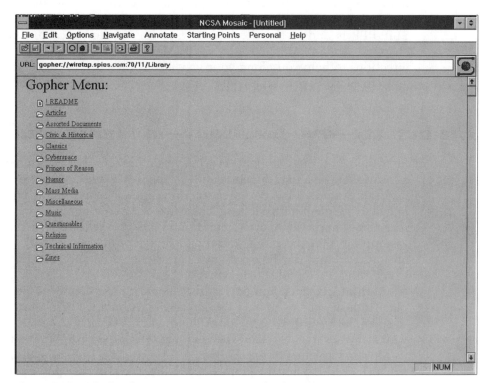

Figure 1.13 A look at how Mosaic presents a **Gopher**'s menus.

group, or tinkered with Mosaic's initialization file. Nor have we done anything but nicked the surface of the **World Wide Web** system, with its thousands of intercommunicating information structures. We will learn, as this book proceeds, to examine not just the imagery built in to a particular Mosaic page, but also to retrieve larger images and display them. We will learn how to configure Mosaic to work with graphics software to make this possible, and how to add other file viewers to do such things as play audio files and even compressed full-motion video, not to mention converting files in formats like PostScript into material we can read on-screen, with all of their formatting intact.

And we will learn that the ability to customize Mosaic's menus is but one of its options. We will work with **mosaic.ini**, the special file that Mosaic consults to determine how it is to proceed, and learn how to make changes that can make our Mosaic sessions more productive. We will tour the capabilities of this powerful program in reaching various Internet tools, with plentiful examples of the use of each. And we will go on a sightseeing tour that will take us through some of the **Web**'s most exotic locales.

I know you are in a hurry to get the program up and running, so we will cut directly to the chase. The first thing you must have available to run Mosaic is a SLIP or PPP account on the Internet (or else a full network connection). Mosaic won't run over a standard dial-up, or shell, account; if this is the kind of access you currently have, the good news is that it will cost you less than ever before to upgrade your account to SLIP/PPP. Chapter 2 explains what SLIP/PPP is and offers alternative ways for you to proceed. The following chapters explain how to locate the key Mosaic files and install them, with full directions to help you along your way. From then on, we will tweak the program until we have customized it into a personal user environment.

The Ecstasy—and the Agony—of Multimedia

First though, a final thought on what this all means. No book on Mosaic can afford to ignore a paradigmatic shift in the way we use computers. Mosaic is itself an example of it. We are becoming increasingly reliant on sound and image to supplement basic text. The wave of Mosaic publicity in newspapers, magazines, and even television and radio has proceeded uncritically, with the assumption that the more sound and imagery, the better. Isn't it intuitively obvious that multimedia experiences are richer than purely textual ones? You would think so, to judge from what we read.

Multimedia can claim powerful advocates; indeed, almost the entire computer industry seems to have embraced the technology that Mosaic shows off so splendidly. But I wouldn't be doing my job if I didn't close out this chapter with some observations, and speculations, about the nature of multimedia and its Mosaic implementation. We pay a certain price, in bandwidth, in time, in network overload, for the glories of Mosaic. We also may pay a price in terms of accessibility, and the ongoing development of the intellectual process as mediated by computer networks.

Don't get me wrong. I am an unabashed fan of Mosaic, even if some multimedia applications from other developers leave me unimpressed. But for this tool to continue to develop in the right direction, we must proceed with caution. We must ask ourselves what it is we hope to achieve with it, and what the results of our work are going to be. A strain of critical examination will, I hope, run through this book as a counterpoint that may make your experience of Mosaic richer. What would a Bach fugue be without its exquisite contrapuntal variations? Like Bach's work, Mosaic is too rich an environment to leave in the hands of media hypsters and short-sighted enthusiasts. A serious look at Mosaic will suggest that its impact is cultural, for it may emerge as a major factor shaping the way we look at information. And any time you start tinkering with a culture, you had better do it right.

2

The Nature of the Connection

Despite its complexity, Mosaic is a remarkably easy program to install. The trick lies in getting the right version of the program to begin with. To do this, we will travel in Chapter 3 to the computer holdings of the National Center for Super-computing Applications in Urbana-Champaign, Illinois, where Mosaic origi-nated, and where work on the program continues. There we can choose between the Macintosh, Windows, or UNIX versions of Mosaic. Chapters 3 and 4 will demonstrate how to retrieve the appropriate files, unpack them, and install the program on your hard disk. We will then perform the basic setup procedures and begin the process of putting your copy of Mosaic through its paces.

But before we can proceed, there is a fundamental issue to be discussed. What kind of connection to the Internet is required to make Mosaic workable? This is perhaps the most confusing issue of all for newcomers; they have heard that a program exists that eliminates the necessity of remembering commands to maneuver through the Internet. Many have downloaded the program, unpacked and installed it, only to be confronted with a cryptic message and an apparently lifeless network connection when they tried to click it into life. Thus we begin with the question of connectivity, a primary concern for any would-be Mosaic user.

If you are currently accessing the Internet through a modem and dialing into a UNIX-based service provider, then this chapter is for you. Mosaic can't work with your modem unless you're running a SLIP or PPP account, and the following pages explain what SLIP/PPP is and how you can get it. If your cur-rent Internet account is at your place of work over an office network tying directly into the Internet, however, you will not need to worry about SLIP/PPP, and can safely move into the next chapter, which describes how to install Mosaic.

The actual SLIP/PPP installation is beyond the scope of this book. Instead, I present a number of alternatives for finding SLIP/PPP software and getting help in its implementation. Several books now on the market include diskettes with SLIP/PPP sampler software, and a fine shareware program called Trumpet Winsock is available for Microsoft Windows. Whether you use a Macintosh or an IBM-compatible PC, SLIP/PPP can best be brought up and running by, first, establishing an account with an Internet service provider, and second, using that provider's help in installing the necessary software. A good service provider should be willing and able to help you through the installation process. In many cases, providers offer a book/diskette combination which will be familiar to their help desk staff. Use the information and software provided and you shouldn't have any trouble. If you are an adventurous soul, you can always try to implement SLIP on your own through the Trumpet Winsock program, but first-timers are advised to stick with their provider's recommendations and try to establish, as much as possible, a generic SLIP/PPP environment.

Kinds of Internet Connectivity

If life were simple, there would be one method for connecting to the Internet. Like CompuServe or DELPHI, the Internet would be accessible through a modem. The modem, connecting to your computer's serial port and interposing itself between computer and telephone network, is your way to translate the binary workings of your computer into the analog workings of the telephone system. Think of a modem as a translation device; it turns digital data into sound.

If you listen to a modem at work over a telephone line, you hear a series of tones. The modem is turning data into a kind of music at one end, letting that music flow through the phone lines, and be translated back into digital data by the modem at the other end. We've become familiar with modems in the past decade and are beginning to take their use for granted. For many users, they represent the high end of communications, allowing them to connect to remote databases, leave electronic mail, and join and participate in discussion groups on commercial on-line services.

The key to understanding Internet connectivity is to realize that there are several different ways to gain access. Two of them involve modems, the third does not. In this book, I am assuming that you want to use a modem to make your connection; my job, then, is to show you how to change your Internet connectivity to make the modem work as it should with Mosaic. If you do not use a modem to connect to the Internet, it means you are tying in directly, probably at work, where your office's computers are networked together and reach the Internet by sending their traffic through a computer called a *router*. Let's examine the three options.

Dial-Up (Shell) Connectivity

Because the Internet is so new, we are still engaged in a search for the best terminology to describe certain concepts. I will use the term *dial-up* to refer to the most basic kind of Internet account. When you sign up with a service provider for a dial-up account, you are being granted access to one of the provider's computers. At the time you open your account, you will be given a telephone number to call, a user ID to identify you to the computer, and an initial password. You will be instructed to change your password once you get established on-line, so that no one else can know your password and use your account.

Another common term for the same kind of account is a *shell account*. The UNIX command interpreter is called a *shell;* think of it as the interface you work with when you interact with UNIX on-line (most such accounts use UNIX as their operating system). There are a wide variety of UNIX shells available (some of the most common are the C Shell, known as **csh**, and the Bourne Shell, or **sh**); each of these shells provides an interface that accepts your commands and performs the actions you specify. Your job is to log in to the UNIX host computer and type UNIX commands in this shell environment. I prefer the term *dial-up* because some services, like DELPHI or America Online, offer connectivity to the Internet but do not employ a UNIX shell to do so.

Whatever the term, dial-up or shell account, we are not limited in the kind of software we use to connect to the system. Any communications package—Procomm Plus, Zterm, Crosstalk, Crosstalk for Windows—can do the trick. Most modem users already have such a program, which they have been using to contact local bulletin board systems (BBS) and commercial on-line services like CompuServe or America Online. They may well be using these systems to move files between home and office computers. Our typical dial-up connection works much the same way; we dial a number by setting it up as a directory entry in our communications software, and then use a user ID and password to log on to the remote system.

Dial-up connectivity provides a particular kind of access to the Internet. Once you have called your service provider, you will sign on and be confronted with a prompt or, in some cases, a menu providing options available to you. Most of the time, the computer you are dialing into will be using the UNIX operating system, which is the most common operating system used on the Internet. And your dial-up account gives you the ability to run whatever programs are available on your service provider's computer.

Let me say this again: What is available with your regular dial-up account is the ability to run programs on the other computer, the one you have reached by dialing in. You are thus dependent upon your service provider to put programs on its computer for your use. These programs can do numerous things on the Internet. The **pine** program, for example, allows you to send and receive electronic mail. The **trn** program lets you read and post messages to any of the more than 8,500 newsgroups available over USENET. The Telnet program lets you connect to remote computers on the Internet and use their resources.

The crucial distinction between dial-up and other accounts is this: When you use a dial-up account, your own computer is not actually on the Internet; it uses terminal emulation to fool the service provider's computer into thinking it is a terminal of that computer. The method works, usually by using the VT-100 terminal emulation designed for Digital Equipment computers, and can provide you with access to numerous Internet tools. But your own computer, acting as a terminal, is reduced to relatively simple operations. A terminal is completely dependent on the computer to which it is connected. The processing power inside your own computer is largely ignored in this setup. Instead, you use your service provider's machine to do the work.

Another ramification of this situation is that, when you use terminal emulation, you are not actually connected to the Internet. That is, your computer does not enjoy a direct Internet connection. The protocols that make the Internet work, called TCP/IP (Transmission Control Protocol/Internet Protocol), are not set up on your computer. Instead, the computer your service provider uses is the one handling the actual Internet data packets. When someone sends you electronic mail, that mail does not go directly to your computer, but to your service provider's machine. You must then dial in to receive the mail.

What exactly is this TCP/IP all about? Without getting too technical, let's just say that it represents ways of packaging data and sending it over the Internet. Each data packet contains full routing information, and the various packets that make up a single document, which are sent out over the net, can be reassembled at their destination to form the complete text, even if they arrived at the site by different routes and completely out of their original order.

Think of dial-up or shell connectivity, then, as your ability to piggyback on somebody else's machine to get your work done. Because it is less demanding and does not pass data packets directly to you from the Internet, dial-up is usually the least expensive connection alternative. If you use a commercial on-line service like CompuServe or America Online, you are using dial-up connectivity. The same is true if you use any of the rapidly multiplying number of Internet access providers around the world. When you send Internet mail or receive messages from an Internet mailing list, you are the beneficiary of actions you have initiated on your service provider's system, not your own.

This has a crucial effect on what you can do on the Internet. Mosaic requires a direct network connection, which is to say, the program needs to use the processing power inside your computer to do its work. It also requires direct passage of Internet data packets between the net and your machine. Put another way, Mosaic requires your machine to have its own Internet address. This is why a commercial on-line service can't help you; there is no way, for example, for a DELPHI or a BIX to provide you with Mosaic, because the nature of the dial-up connection presumes a character-based interface and terminal emulation. No TCP/IP data packets flow between you and these providers.

This problem, incidentally, exists not only for Mosaic but for numerous other programs. The Internet operates through a *client/server* relationship. Think of a *client* as a program that runs on your computer. The *server* is the program running on a remote computer that interacts with the client. The two interact by means of a *protocol*. In the case of the **World Wide Web**, the client program running on your machine sends a request over the Internet to the server, using an underlying communications protocol known as HTTP, or *HyperText Transport Protocol*. These operations occur transparently to the user; what you see on the screen is simply the characteristic Mosaic interface interpreting data it is receiving through the **World Wide Web**.

When you use a dial-up or shell account, the nature of your connection means that you can only use the client programs your service provider has made available on its machine. But if you have a direct Internet connection, you can use whichever client programs you choose. You can find software that suits your taste and operate accordingly.

Numerous client programs exist to perform the basic Internet chores, everything from electronic mail to FTP (File Transfer Protocol) to **Gopher** and other browsing and searching tools. A direct network connection gives you the opportunity to choose which you find the most effective. And because the software will run on your own machine, it can be more complex, graphical, and feature-laden. You will come to see Mosaic as something like the ultimate client program, one that combines almost all major Internet functions into a single interface. Ed Krol said it best in *The Whole Internet User's Guide and Catalog* (O'Reilly, 1994, 2nd Ed.): ". . . if you could only install one piece of network navigating software on your system, Mosaic would be the one to choose." Later, as your expertise grows, you may find specialized programs that handle a specific task better than Mosaic, but first you should consider how much Mosaic allows you to do and master its capabilities.

The SLIP/PPP Connection to the Internet

If you need direct Internet access to use Mosaic, how do you achieve it? For people with modems, the answer is SLIP (Serial Line Internet Protocol) or PPP (Point-to-Point Protocol). SLIP/PPP is a way that your modem can access the Internet without having to piggyback on your service provider's computer. The difference is that, when you use SLIP/PPP, the TCP/IP data packets travel between you and the Internet, because TCP/IP is itself loaded on your machine. SLIP/PPP software will use this TCP/IP connection to turn your computer into a full-fledged member of the net, complete with network address.

To run Mosaic, then, you must have a SLIP/PPP connection to the Internet or better (we'll discuss what "better" means in just a moment). Several years ago, this would have been a tall order. In my area, the difference between dial-up and SLIP/PPP accounts was expressed financially. Not long ago, I could choose to spend $30 a month for 75 hours of Internet access in a straight dial-up context, or $175 per month for a SLIP/PPP connection to the net. This kind of disparity is the reason so many people have used only dial-up accounts, and why they become so frustrated when they learn that Mosaic can't work without a SLIP/PPP connection. The high tariff effectively kept SLIP/PPP in the hands of businesspeople and their companies.

But the explosion in the number of Internet access providers has meant that SLIP/PPP prices have fallen dramatically. My own service provider, Raleigh-based Interpath, charges $30 per month for straight dial-up, while SLIP/PPP costs $35 per month. That extra $5 a month is not asking a lot when you consider how much more network power you will receive with SLIP/PPP. For many users, the best reason of all to get a SLIP/PPP account is Mosaic itself. Once they understand the issues, they choose SLIP/PPP and find themselves entering a different kind of environment, one with point-and-shoot interfaces, drop-down menus and mouse-driven commands, an environment much like the graphical environments for both PC and the Mac that have become more or less the industry standard.

Your first job on the road to Mosaic, then, is to open a SLIP/PPP account. Doing so should pose few difficulties; most service providers today make SLIP/ PPP available. Where problems still occur is in installation. SLIP/PPP software is getting easier to install, but even relatively intuitive implementations, like Internet Chameleon from NetManage, still require you to enter considerable amounts of information. This is why your choice of service providers is critical. Look not only for the best price, but also for the service provider who is most capable of providing you with support when you need it. A good help desk can guide you through the thorniest of SLIP/PPP installation problems.

Like SLIP, PPP supports the TCP/IP protocols over a dial-up telephone line and can thus deliver the same kind of connectivity, although there are those who believe that PPP is the more elegant solution. Growing interest in PPP may cause it to become the method of choice over SLIP in the future, but whether that happens, the essential issues remain the same. Both SLIP and PPP are ways to move Internet data packets over telephone lines, and both allow you to run client programs on your own machine as you interact with the Internet. At the moment, though, SLIP is more widely available.

Using SLIP/PPP software instead of your regular communications program, you dial in to your Internet service provider's computer. But once you have made the connection, your machine is now a part of the Internet. As opposed to being a relatively passive recipient of data, it is now fully operational, sending and receiving data using TCP/IP data packets through an Internet access point made available by your service provider. The major ramification of this is that your machine now owns its own IP address. Mail, for example, can be addressed directly to your machine, not to your service provider's computer for you to pick up later.

And there is another, perhaps unexpected, benefit. Several different connections can be run at once through a SLIP/PPP connection. For example, I subscribe to a number of USENET newsgroups, but don't always manage to check into them as frequently as I would like. Consequently, when I sign on with my SLIP newsreader, I often find myself waiting while an apparently end-less stream of message titles is passed across the connection. I could watch the process unfold and daydream, but if I'm busy, I want to proceed with my work. Perhaps there is an FTP site I'd like to extract a file from. With SLIP/PPP, I can engage the FTP client program and run the FTP session, transferring the file to my machine, *at the same time that the USENET session is in progress.*

This is major magic; we don't need to know how it works, only that TCP/IP and SLIP/PPP can somehow untangle all the data being sent and received over a single telephone line and manage to carry through each session to a success-ful conclusion. Yes, you'll lose performance on the session operating in the background to some extent, but you have maximized your time. And it is cer-tainly useful to keep the various applications you may need to use available as icons, to be called up whenever they are needed.

And don't forget a final benefit of using SLIP/PPP. With a shell account, every time you want to retrieve a file by FTP or have it sent to you from **Gopher**, you are engaged in a two-step process. First, you give the appropriate commands to get the file, which is then transferred to your service provider's computer. Second, you use your communications software to download that file to your own machine. With SLIP/PPP, this two-step process is eliminated. The file you want from an FTP site comes directly to your computer, as soon as you activate the retrieval. Mosaic, as we will soon see, is a remarkably effective FTP engine, just as it makes it possible to view and retrieve files on any **Gopher**.

Think of SLIP/PPP as having three layers of software with which it must work. First, there is the underlying TCP/IP software, which manages data in terms the Internet understands. Second, there is the separate SLIP/PPP soft-ware, which actually makes the connection to your service provider's access point and allows you to establish the necessary network connection. Finally, there are the client programs, which are the basic tools you use to perform net-work operations like FTP, Telnet, and electronic mail. Getting all three layers to work together can be something of a challenge, depending on the kind of equipment you use. But as we'll soon see, this situation is rapidly improving.

Full Internet Access

SLIP/PPP provides you with everything you need to run Internet sessions over your telephone line while maintaining your own Internet address and running client programs on your own computer. To move into the truly fast lane of con-nectivity, you would need full Internet access. Here, rather than dialing a tele-phone number to activate your computer's access to the Internet, you are working with leased, high-speed fiber-optic lines. Large organizations such as research laboratories, corporations, and universities maintain wide-band-width data channels from the Internet to their own organizations, connecting to the net through specialized computers known as *routers*. In this way, a sys-tem administrator can serve the needs of a wide spectrum of users, distributing Internet resources throughout the organization. No dial-up process is required; the Internet link is available on these machines 24 hours a day.

Using SLIP/PPP in an office network, on the other hand, you dial in to a machine known as a *terminal server*. This computer receives your incoming modem data and moves it onto your service provider's local area network (LAN). The provider's LAN, like that of any major network, is connected to the Internet by a router. You have wound up moving your data out and onto the Internet by router just as you would with a full Internet connection, but you are adding an extra step to the process (and limiting your performance in terms of speed) by moving your data through a modem and a telephone line.

Dedicated access, then, makes for higher speeds in data transfer, a real bonus when using images and audio files, as Mosaic is wont to do. Rather than using a modem to establish the connection, dedicated access uses a *network interface card* (NIC)—which in most cases is an Ethernet card—inside your computer. The card is then connected to the office LAN, either by coaxial cable or twisted pair telephone wiring. The LAN is itself connected to the Internet. Because of the nature of this connection, the password you use with a SLIP/PPP account and its accompanying user identification number are unnecessary. The company receives an overall bill for its monthly use.

Naturally, with a full Internet connection, it is possible to run any client software you choose on your own machine, just as you can do with SLIP/PPP. Mosaic and all the other client programs are available, and the material in the rest of this book is as suitable for those with full Internet access as for those with SLIP/PPP accounts. Given the nature of the Internet's growth, however, I am operating under the assumption that you are either moving to a SLIP/PPP account to run Mosaic or that you already have SLIP/PPP. This describes the multitude of individual users now connecting to the net, as well as the small to medium-sized businesses for whom the Internet has yet to become a strong enough factor in their operations to justify the expense of a leased line and full Internet access.

Incidentally, if you are a SLIP/PPP user, you should take any chance you have to see Mosaic operating over a full network connection. The wider the bandwidth, the faster Mosaic works, and it can be a revelation to move effortlessly between image, text, and sound files with almost imperceptible delays. A SLIP/PPP connection to the network can't deliver that kind of performance due to the limitations of the technology; in particular, we are held back by the ability of our modems to transfer data. This can make the program at times frustratingly slow—we begin thinking twice about clicking on large image files, for instance—but there are solutions to this problem that we will discuss later in this book.

Implementing SLIP/PPP

Whether you run a Macintosh or an IBM-compatible PC, SLIP/PPP connectivity is now easier to achieve than ever before. Many providers now make software packages available that handle the necessary TCP/IP connectivity. Your service provider should always be your first point of reference; obviously, your connection is best monitored through a close relationship between you and the provider's help staff (and this is one more reason why you want to be sure to pick a provider whose help desk is first-rate). Because installation can be tricky, SLIP/PPP is best set up using a service provider's instructions; the provider can then answer questions as they arise.

SLIP/PPP Books Bundled with Software

I have already mentioned Internet Chameleon, from NetManage. My own service provider, Interpath, gives new SLIP/PPP users an older version of Internet Chameleon called Chameleon Sampler, which is bundled with many Internet books. I used Michael Fraase's *Windows Internet Tour Guide* (Ventana Press, 1994) to set up Chameleon Sampler, working with the included software until I understood basic SLIP/PPP concepts before upgrading to the full Internet Chameleon package.

The benefit of a book/disk combination is that the book can help you work through the thornier points of using the software, and even with the Chameleon Sampler, installation does pose certain conceptual difficulties. MS-DOS users are not left out of the picture, either; Fraase has also published *The PC Internet Tour Guide* (Ventana Books, 1994), which implements the University of Minnesota's UMSLIP and Minuet software, thus providing the same SLIP/PPP benefits in the DOS environment. And for the Mac user, *The Mac Internet Tour Guide* (Ventana Books, 1994) offers software and guidance for those first making the SLIP/PPP connection (although the MacTCP software and necessary SLIP/PPP drivers are not included). Each of these books works with the particular subset of tools made available on the enclosed disk. Later, you can search out your own set of commercial shareware or public-domain tools to handle the same functions.

I mention Fraase's books first because I found setting up the SLIP software relatively simple following his suggestions, and because many service providers are making these books available as their starter kits for new users. But there are other implementations. Adam Engst's *Internet Starter Kit for Macintosh* (Hayden Books, 1994) includes MacTCP, Apple's implementation of TCP/IP software for the Macintosh. Engst has also written *Internet Starter Kit for Windows* (Hayden Books, 1994), which includes the Chameleon Sampler and several other tools. Other books charting these waters and providing bundled software include *The Internet Unleashed* (SAMS Publishing, 1994; various authors) and *Navigating the Internet*, Deluxe Edition, by Richard Smith and Mark Gibbs (SAMS Publishing, 1994). Both of these come with the Chameleon Sampler package.

In evaluating any book/diskette combination, bear the following in mind. You will need a SLIP or PPP network driver along with the TCP/IP software to access your SLIP/PPP account. You should also evaluate the book's diskette in terms of client programs. It isn't critical that you wind up using each and every one of these programs, but they will be the tools that get you started in your SLIP/PPP activities. You will definitely need an FTP client so that you can retrieve Mosaic, as we will do in Chapter 3. The alternative would be to retrieve it through FTP in an existing shell account; if you already have such an account, by all means feel free to get the files through it.

Acquiring SLIP/PPP Software on Your Own

If you buy Internet Chameleon on your own, you will receive the necessary tools plus a number of additional features, such as a USENET newsreader, a **Gopher** client, and other software not included in the Chameleon Sampler package. If you are using one of the major national Internet providers, the software is preconfigured for you; otherwise, you will need to set up a custom installation. Internet Chameleon supports both SLIP and PPP, but don't assume that Internet Chameleon is your only choice. The number of SLIP/PPP software packages is growing rapidly. The following, starting with Internet Chameleon, is a brief look at the possibilities. These packages, incidentally, are all-in-one solutions; they contain both client programs and the TCP/IP and SLIP/PPP software necessary to connect to the Internet.

Internet Chameleon.   This product contains complete TCP/IP software for Windows along with client programs for electronic mail, FTP, **Gopher**, Telnet, and USENET. Contact:

> NetManage, Inc.
> 20823 Stevens Creek Blvd.
> Cupertino, CA 95014
> Voice: 408-973-7171
> Fax: 408-257-6405
> E-mail: **sales@netmanage.com**

Trumpet Winsock.   Peter Tattam's Trumpet Software International has developed this shareware product. The package includes the TCP/IP software implementation and the necessary driver to handle SLIP connections, along with several other Internet shareware applications (I particularly like Trumpet's newsreader for USENET).

Internet archives change as directories are modified, new files are added, and old files deleted. At the time of this writing, Trumpet Winsock was available on-line through the following site:

> Address: **ftp.utas.edu.au**
> Directory: */pc/trumpet/winsock*
> File Names: **twsk10a.zip** (includes the TCP/IP protocol stack); **winapps.zip**
>   (includes client programs)
> There is a $20 shareware fee.

WinGopher Complete.   A complete **Gopher** implementation, this package also includes the necessary TCP/IP software to get you up and running on the Internet. A **Gopher** client is simply a program, in this case run in the Windows environment, that brings a wealth of additional features to the standard **Gopher** interface you may have worked with over a UNIX-based dial-up connection. The results are immediately obvious: The WinGopher software moves you into a graphical world, running with the same basic functionality of any Windows program, and allowing you to take advantage of point-and-click interface technology rather than entering commands. WinGopher is unique in offering the TCP/IP software tools along with a single client program. Chameleon, for example, provides a full range of tools, although its **Gopher** implementation is not nearly as powerful as WinGopher's. This package also provides an introductory offer from an Internet access provider to get you on-line swiftly. Contact the developer of WinGopher at:

NOTIS Systems, Inc.
1007 Church St.
Evanston, IL 60201-3665
Voice: 800-556-6847
Fax: 708-866-4970
E-mail: **wingopher@notis.com**

Internet In A Box.   Perhaps none of the products on today's market has caught the attention of the public quite so much as Internet In A Box. The software is being developed by Spry, Inc., whose business is developing Windows-based TCP/IP software. The documentation comes from O'Reilly & Associates, which publishes a wide range of books about UNIX and the Internet, including Ed Krol's *The Whole Internet User's Guide and Catalog* (the latter is included in the Internet In A Box package). The reason for the interest is that Internet In a Box is being billed as a complete Internet solution and, moreover, one that already contains a version of Mosaic (Spry's AirMosaic), along with the necessary TCP/IP software to run a PPP session. The Windows version of Internet in A Box is already available; the Macintosh version will follow. Contact the developers at:

Spry, Inc.
316 Occidental Avenue South, Suite 200
Seattle, WA 98104
Voice: 800-777-9638
E-mail: **info@ibox.com**

TCP/Connect II.   InterCon Systems Corporation makes this product available in both Macintosh and Windows versions. The basic Internet applications are here, along with the TCP/IP tools and other programs to support both SLIP and PPP sessions. MacTCP, the standard TCP/IP product for the Macintosh, is supplied by Apple Computer; Intercon's InterSLIP or InterPPP software then

provides the features that MacTCP needs to make TCP/IP work over the telephone lines. Be aware, also, that Apple will make MacTCP available in its System 7.5 operating system; TCP/IP capability will thus be shipped with all new
Macs at no extra cost (although without, of course, the various client programs
InterCon provides). Contact the company at this address:

InterCon Systems Corporation
950 Herndon Parkway
Herndon, VA 22070
Voice: 703-709-5500
Fax: 703-709-5555
E-mail: **sales@intercon.com**

VersaTerm and Versatilities. These two products for the Macintosh
from Synergy Software in Reading, Pennsylvania, include a complete set of
client programs, from e-mail to FTP to a USENET newsreader, in addition to
SLIP/PPP software. Versatilities is a suite of connectivity utilities you will
find helpful in organizing and managing your Internet sessions. You can
contact the company at:

Synergy Software
2457 Perkiomen Ave.
Reading, PA 19606
Voice: 215-779-0522
Fax: 215-370-0548
E-mail: **maxwell@sales.synergy.com**

The Internet Membership Kit. Ventana Press, publishers of Michael
Fraase's various Internet books containing SLIP/PPP software, also makes
available a complete Internet kit—one for Microsoft Windows, one for the
Macintosh—to provide SLIP/PPP access to the net. The kit not only includes
the relevant Fraase book and related software, but also a copy of Harley Hahn's
Internet Yellow Pages and a form for setting up an account directly with an
access provider. I used the Ventana product to set up the SLIP account I
accessed to write this book. To contact Ventana:

Ventana Media
P. O. Box 2468
Chapel Hill, NC 27514
Voice: 919-942-0220
Fax: 919-942-1140
E-mail: **info@vmedia.com**

Compatibility Issues

Macintosh owners need have few concerns about the compatibility of the client programs—like Mosaic—that they choose to run, and the underlying TCP/IP software that it works with. This is because Apple Computer is the supplier of the MacTCP software that enables TCP/IP on the Mac; any developer hoping to write a client program will create it to work seamlessly with this interface. Mosaic fits this bill easily.

Microsoft Windows users, however, are in a more problematical environment. For them, the key term is *Winsock*. Winsock stands for Windows Sockets Interface, which is becoming a standard that specifies how Windows-based Internet programs will work with the TCP/IP software that runs the SLIP/PPP session underlying them. Each TCP/IP vendor includes a file called **winsock.dll**, a proprietary product that has been optimized to work with the vendor's software.

The beauty of the Winsock standard is that the developer of a client program must only master the Winsock interface to enable his or her program to run; it is not necessary to untangle the differences between each vendor's TCP/IP protocol stack to make each product workable with that stack. From the TCP/IP software developer's standpoint, his or her **winsock.dll** file differs from that of all competitors, but both the developer and the competition ensure that their TCP/IP products implement the Winsock interface. Any Winsock-compliant application will encounter the same interface as it hooks into the Winsock software "sockets."

We have thus seen growth in Winsock-compliant software, on both the commercial and shareware fronts, as developers have realized its advantages. Mosaic is a Winsock-compliant application, which means it can run over any of the TCP/IP software implementations for Windows. You can call Mosaic up using Peter Tattam's Trumpet Winsock, a shareware TCP/IP implementation. Or you can use Internet Chameleon, from NetManage, Inc., to do the same thing, just as you can use InterCon Systems Corporation's product. Any TCP/IP application created with the Winsock standard in mind can be used this way.

Not all vendors support the Winsock standard, however; thus, there are client programs that will not function except in conjunction with the TCP/IP software supplied by that vendor. But it is heartening to note that Winsock is gaining momentum, which should bring order to the client program scene.

Shareware and Freeware SLIP/PPP Sites

As your experience with SLIP/PPP grows, you will naturally want to be on the lookout for new software and upgraded versions of your current programs. Although sites around the Internet often carry such materials, as an **archie** search will quickly reveal, there are certain sites that have proven consistently reliable in handling SLIP/PPP materials and, in particular, files related to Mosaic. You can choose from among the following FTP locations:

Address: **ftp.rtd.com**
Directory: *pub/tcpip*

Look particularly for a Frequently Asked Questions (FAQ) document about PC and Macintosh TCP/IP implementations. At the time of this writing, the file name was **pcnfsfaq.zip**.

Address: **sunsite.unc.edu**
Directory: *micro/pc-stuff/ms-windows/winsock*

European users may want to try these FTP sites:

Address: **ftp.demon.co.uk**
Address: **ftp.york.ac.uk**

And don't miss the primary site for Mosaic, which we'll contact shortly to retrieve the actual program.

Address: **ftp.ncsa.uiuc.edu**
Directory: *PC/Mosaic or Mac/Mosaic*

Be warned: The NCSA site is heavily trafficked and, at certain times of day, can be almost impossible to access. Try your session after working hours at the site (it is in Urbana-Champaign, Illinois, and thus on central time in the U.S.—Greenwich mean time plus six hours during daylight savings time; GMT plus five hours during central standard time).

There is also a useful FAQ document about TCP/IP on IBM-compatible equipment to be found at the following site:

Address: **netcom1.netcom.com**
Directory: *pub/mailcom/IBMTCP*
File Name: **ibmtcp.zip**

USENET Newsgroups Helpful in Mastering SLIP/PPP

To keep up with documentation on SLIP/PPP, consider joining several USENET newsgroups. The following list gives several from which you may want to choose. (Bear in mind with these and any other network addresses given in this book that the Internet is in a state of constant flux. The best way to keep up with changes to archival sites and the location of key files is to monitor particular **Web** sites, as we will discuss in the final chapter.)

comp.os.ms-windows.networking.tcp-ip
comp.protocols.tcp-ip
comp.protocols.tcp-ip.ibmpc
comp.protocols.nfs
comp.sys.ibm.pc.hardware.networking
comp.sys.mac.comm
alt.winsock

And be on the lookout for new newsgroups, which appear all the time. More specific newsgroups for Mac users, for example, seem almost certain to develop.

Equipment Requirements for a SLIP/PPP Connection

Now that we've located our software sources for SLIP/PPP (and remember to talk first to your service provider, who may well offer a package specifically customized for his or her operations), we're ready to consider the hardware we'll need to make this connection work. You will need a 386 or better machine to make SLIP/PPP operate in the PC environment, or a Macintosh running System 7 if you're an Apple person. But since our ultimate goal is to run Mosaic, let's listen to what the developers at the NCSA recommend. They specify the following:

For Microsoft Windows-equipped computers:

Windows 3.1 running in enhanced mode

The **winsock.dll** file and Microsoft Win32s software (We'll discuss this in Chapter 3 as we actually install Mosaic.)
An absolute minimum of an 80386SX machine with 4 MB of RAM

NCSA recommends an even more substantial configuration: an 80486 with at least 8 MB of RAM. From my own experience, I can attest to the wisdom of the latter minimum; 4 MB of RAM really isn't adequate for the kind of performance you'll want.

For Macintosh computers:
System 7 or later
MacTCP 2.0.2 or later (NCSA recommends version 2.0.4 or later.)
4 MB or more of RAM
A hard disk

Incidentally, you can order the MacTCP product just discussed direct from Apple as part of a product called "The TCP/IP Connection." To do so, contact Apple Catalog Sales at 800-795-1000. The single user cost is $59; the order number is D1785.

We're not through with equipment specifications yet. The speed of your modem will have quite an effect on how useful Mosaic will be as an Internet access tool. Yes, you can run Mosaic over a 9,600 bps modem connection, but having tried it, I can tell you from experience that the faster the modem, the better. The bare minimum for this kind of work is a 14,400 bps modem. Prices on such modems have plummeted in recent months, as a look through any computer periodical will show. I have seen internal 14,400 modems selling for less than $100 by mail order, while the price of 28,800 bps units is now comfortably below $200. Given prices like these, it simply doesn't make sense to put up with the unnecessary delays caused by slower equipment.

The Pleasures of Built-in TCP/IP

One of the perils of writing software is waiting for the other shoe to drop. As the Internet spread in popularity from the top down (from large organizations like research laboratories and universities to small business and the individual desktop user), SLIP/PPP began to take on a new prominence. People using dial-up or shell accounts began to show an interest in the graphical client programs available through SLIP/PPP. And a fascination with Mosaic has pushed interest in SLIP/PPP over the top, causing price wars between service providers. SLIP/PPP is now available for not much more than the price of a shell account.

We've looked at several companies that are offering complete SLIP/PPP solutions to Internet access, and there will doubtless be more as this market expands. It was inevitable that the major software houses would become involved somewhere along the line. Quarterdeck Office Systems, for example, has licensed Mosaic and plans to offer a connectivity product of its own. Apple Computer has released its revised operating system, System 7.5, with TCP/IP software already included; users of earlier versions can upgrade to the new software, and all new Macs will be sold with System 7.5 installed. Finally, giant Microsoft Corporation intends to include TCP/IP and PPP software tools in the first release of its major Windows upgrade, Windows 4.0. Code-named Chicago, the new Windows is on the horizon as we go to press.

The broader ramification of all this is that the Internet will be accessible through SLIP/PPP connections to a far broader range of people than ever before. Depending upon the success of the various companies in implementing the TCP/IP software, and drawing on the experience of numerous users in installing previous TCP/IP tools, these firms may also make getting up and running on the net easier to achieve. SLIP/PPP, notoriously difficult to configure, may eventually become commonplace, even if it is always best to have a service provider with a good help desk ready to assist.

But smaller firms are unlikely to exit from this market just because a Microsoft or an Apple Computer has weighed in. The Internet Society, which coordinates and encourages network engineering projects in the United States, now estimates that the growth of the Internet has reached 100 percent per year. We could be looking at as many as 100 million users by late in the decade. Advances in the telecommunications infrastructure guarantee that broader bandwidth access to business and the home is in the cards. With vast numbers of potential users being bombarded by media attention to the Internet and the so-called Information Highway, we can expect entrepreneurs to continually release new SLIP/PPP products, each with its own twist. At the same time, the coalescence of standards like Winsock will continue to make client programs portable between different SLIP/PPP implementations. This means that a client program written by one company won't necessarily have to be run on the TCP/IP software that company produces.

Macintosh users already have a consistent interface to the TCP/IP software. As we've seen, Apple Computer is the only supplier of the basic MacTCP software. This means that any Internet client program written for the Macintosh will be written with MacTCP in mind, so that compatibility is not an issue. With both the Mac and Windows moving toward compliance to a single standard, it is likely that we are experiencing the most difficult period for SLIP/PPP installation right now. Things are clearly getting better all the time.

Your job as a potential SLIP/PPP customer is to weigh the advantages of the various products to see which best meet your needs. The first necessity is to get up and running. The second is to continually monitor improvements in software as the technology advances. Just a few years ago, the idea of driving a modem at 28,800 bits per second would have seemed ludicrous; today, it is almost commonplace. The occasional frustrations you will encounter with Mosaic are a temporary thing; the next generation of products in the SLIP/PPP arena, and certainly the one after that, will ensure that your investment of time and money now will result in SLIP/PPP and Mosaic becoming indispensable access tools for the net.

Onward to Mosaic

Having located and installed the necessary SLIP/PPP software, you are ready to proceed by downloading and installing Mosaic. In Chapter 3, you will acquire a copy from the National Center for Supercomputing Applications and install it onto your hard disk, using SLIP/PPP to activate your network connection and bring Mosaic to life.

But before we proceed, a brief recapitulation. Let's take an overview of what SLIP/PPP has done for your Internet connection. Rather than using someone else's direct connection to the Internet, SLIP/PPP has enabled you to create a direct connection of your own. Your computer is now on the Internet. The TCP/IP software on your machine works by connecting to a SLIP/PPP server that provides a connection to the Internet over the telephone line. Unlike a direct connection to an office LAN and thence to the net via a router, SLIP/PPP does not require special driver software to deal with a network interface card, which simplifies the installation procedure. Trumpet Winsock, for example, contains all necessary SLIP support built in to its **tcpman.exe** program; the all-in-one packages we discussed contain all SLIP/PPP functions you will need to run Mosaic.

And SLIP/PPP provides the same capabilities—albeit at somewhat slower speed—that a direct connection through a network card offers. The client programs like Mosaic, which we use to get work done on the net, take no notice of whether our connection is through SLIP/PPP or a network card. Make no mistake about it, SLIP/PPP puts you on the net and allows you to extract maximum power and utility out of your own machine and the software you load onto it. It's now time to prove the point by going out to retrieve Mosaic. Chapter 3 tells you how to download and install the Microsoft Windows version of the program. Chapter 4 explains how to download and install the Macintosh version.

3

Downloading and Installing Mosaic for Microsoft Windows

Ready to install Mosaic on your system? This chapter explains how, and operates under the assumption that you have already established a SLIP or PPP account with an Internet service provider. If you maintain only a dial-up, or shell account, Mosaic will not function on your system. Although you will be able to call up the program, the only resources it will be able to locate will be files on your own computer, rendering it useless as a network tool.

The SLIP/PPP account, then, is crucial for anyone who wants to use a modem to run Mosaic. If, on the other hand, your company provides access by linking your office network directly to the Internet through a router, SLIP/PPP will not be needed. Because your connection already passes data packets directly between the Internet and your network, the essential connection has already been established. Such people can proceed immediately to download and begin working with the Mosaic software. This chapter shows how it's done.

As you embark upon this process, realize that you are hardly alone. The National Center for Supercomputing Applications reports that its server has been seeing remarkable levels of use. In February 1994, for example, NCSA reported 1,153,843 connections to the Mosaic server. As of May 1994, more than 340,000 copies of Mosaic had been downloaded. The *Internet Business Report* notes that in April 1994, the total number of accesses to NCSA files was more than 6 million, a number that is impressive but overstated as an indicator of total Mosaic use, since most users will access more than one file in the course of a Mosaic session. Throughout the summer of 1994, interest built as more and more **Web** servers came on-line.

No one can say for sure how many Mosaic users there are, especially since Mosaic devotees tend to download new versions as they appear, thus increasing the total number of downloads, but it seems reasonable to assume a number closing on half a million as we go to press. As you will see, this level of interest is good for the growth of Mosaic, but it can pose challenges for anyone trying to access the NCSA server during peak hours of use. In later chapters, we'll look at what you can do to help with this problem by customizing your copy of Mosaic.

Where to Find Mosaic

As mentioned, there are numerous commercial implementations of Mosaic on the way. But the best way to begin working with the software is to download the generic product, which is free for the individual user. The National Center for Supercomputing Applications developed Mosaic, and its computers remain the place for you to find the most recent versions. We will use File Transfer Protocol (FTP) procedures to retrieve the package.

A Word on Addresses and Directories

The Mosaic FTP site is a stable address, but the directory structure inside any site is always subject to change. I will give you the directories needed to find each version of Mosaic at the time of this writing, but if you access the site and find that these directories have been changed, the best way to learn where to go is to examine the initial FTP screen, which often tells you what you need. Run a **dir** command to see the subdirectories available, and look for any that contain the word *Mosaic* or else the name of your computer platform; that is, PC, Macintosh, and so on. Also look for any files called README or some variation thereof; these provide information on recent developments.

The NCSA Server

Here is the address we want to reach:

ftp.ncsa.uiuc.edu

The directory we need to access is */Mosaic*. From this directory we will be able to move to the subdirectory that contains the version of Mosaic we need. Mosaic is available in versions for the Macintosh, for Microsoft Windows, and for the X Window System. Here are the directories for each:

- For the Microsoft Windows version of Mosaic, the directory is *Mosaic/Windows*. The file name as of this writing is **wmos20a6.zip**; the numbers may have changed by the time you access the package, but the latest version will always be available. The file is compressed using the PKZIP utility from PKWARE, Inc., and will require the company's PKUNZIP to uncompress it.

- For the Macintosh version of Mosaic, the directory is *Mosaic/Mac*. The file name at the time of this writing is **NCSAMosaicMac.103.sit.hqx**. This file is compressed with the StuffIt utility and then BinHexed to save disk space. To unpack it, you will need StuffIt Expander or a comparable decoding program. Download the program as an ASCII, rather than a binary, file.

- The X Window System version of Mosaic is found in the *Mosaic/Unix* directory. Executable binaries are found in the *Mosaic/Unix/binaries* directory, where versions exist for IBM, Digital Equipment, Sun Microsystems, Silicon Graphics, and workstations from other major manufacturers (the binary files can be uncompressed using the **gunzip** *file_name* command). The complete source code distribution is found in a subdirectory here.

Downloading Mosaic for Microsoft Windows

The NCSA FTP address itself contains the term *ftp*. To reach it from a shell account, then, our command would be as follows:

ftp ftp.ncsa.uiuc.edu

Use **anonymous** as your login name, and your e-mail address as your password.

What you will see when you download Mosaic will depend upon how you are accessing the system. I will show you the operation from two perspectives. First, I will retrieve the software using a standard dial-up, or shell, account. I do this because the transaction will be more obvious to those of you who are used to shell, rather than SLIP/PPP, accounts. By seeing how it proceeds through a familiar interface, you should then be able to relate the procedure to what you see when using SLIP/PPP. Then, I will show you the same process using a client program and SLIP/PPP connection to the Internet.

Logging On at NCSA

Here is what the system looked like when I logged on recently through a shell account:

```
% ftp ftp.ncsa.uiuc.edu
Connected to zaphod.ncsa.uiuc.edu.
```

```
220 zaphod FTP server (Version 6.23 Thu Apr 8 06:37:40 CDT 1993) ready.
Name (ftp.ncsa.uiuc.edu:gilster): anonymous
331 Guest login ok, send e-mail address as password.
Password:
230-
230-Welcome to NCSA s anonymous FTP server! I hope you find what you are
230-  looking for. For questions regarding NCSA software tools, please e-mail
230-  softdev@ncsa.uiuc.edu.
230-
230-The mail archive-server is fully operational. Requests go to
230-  archive-server@ncsa.uiuc.edu and send problem reports to
230-  archive-manager@ncsa.uiuc.edu
230-
230-Note to HyperFTP users: If you log in, and cannot list directories
230-  other than the top-level ones, enter a - as the first character of your
230-  password (e-mail address).
230-
230-If your ftp client has problems with receiving files from this server, send
230-  a - as the first character of your password (e-mail address).
230-
230-If you re ftp ing from Delphi, please remember that the Delphi FTP client
230-  requires you to enclose case-sensitive directory and file names in double
230-  quote (") characters.
230-
230-
230-Please read the file README
230-  it was last modified on Tue Jul 23 15:40:50 1991 - 1097 days ago
230-Please read the file README.BROCHURE
230-  it was last modified on Sat Sep 12 18:30:42 1992 - 680 days ago
230-Please read the file README.FIRST
230-  it was last modified on Sun Oct  3 17:45:17 1993 - 295 days ago
230-Please read the file README_Dialin
230-  it was last modified on Wed Sep  2 14:21:17 1992 - 690 days ago
230 Guest login ok, access restrictions apply.
ftp>
```

The system leaves you at the *ftp>* prompt, ready to transact your business, the changing of directories and downloading of Mosaic.

If you are using SLIP/PPP to download Mosaic, what you see on screen will depend upon the FTP software you are using. However, no matter what kind of computer you work with, the SLIP/PPP client will be more graphical than the character-based interface just shown. In Figure 3.1, I am using Net-Manage Chameleon as my SLIP/PPP software, running the FTP client program that comes with the package.

I have entered the necessary address and made the connection. The Net-Manage client shows the directory structure available at NCSA's server in a relatively intuitive manner, with scrollable fields and the ability to click on a particular directory to move directly to it. I can use the scrollbar in the remote

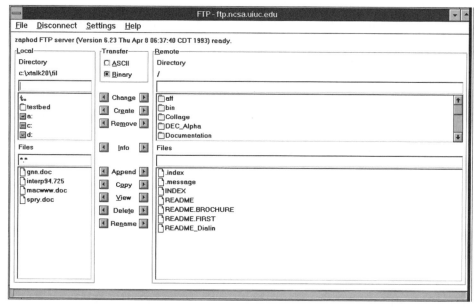

Figure 3.1 SLIP provides graphical features that terminal emulation lacks.

directory box to move to the *Mosaic* directory, clicking on it to call up a listing of files there. To actually download the file with this software, I would select it with my mouse and use the Copy button, making sure that my client program was set up for a binary file transfer, according to the on-screen buttons.

When the NCSA Server Isn't Available

The heavy user load placed on NCSA's FTP server understandably causes a log-jam at certain times of day, when too many people are trying to access the system at once. If you try to log on at one of these times, you will encounter a message giving you a range of other possibilities. Here is an example of what the session might look like with a shell account:

```
% ftp ftp.ncsa.uiuc.edu
Connected to zaphod.ncsa.uiuc.edu.
220 zaphod FTP server (Version 6.23 Thu Apr 8 06:37:40 CDT 1993) ready.
Name (ftp.ncsa.uiuc.edu:gilster): anonymous
530-Sorry, there are too many users online at this time. Please try again later.
530-If you are looking for NCSA Mosaic software you can try one of the following
530-unofficial mirror sites.
530---------------------------------------------------------------------------
530-USA:
530-  site:        sunsite.unc.edu
```

```
530-  location:     /pub/packages/infosystems/WWW           (all versions)
530-Australia:
530-  site:         miriworld.its.unimelb.edu.au
530-  location:     /pub/clients/                            (all versions)
530-Europe:
530-  site:         ftp.luth.se
530-  location:     /pub/infosystems/www/ncsa                (all versions)
530-
530-  site:         ftp.sunet.se
530-  location:     /pub/mac/Mosaic                          (mac version)
530-                /pub/pc/windows/www/Mosaic/              (pc version)
530-                /pub/www/Mosaic                          (X version)
530---------------------------------------------------------------------------
530-If you are looking for HDF software please try the following mirror sites.
530-USA:
530-  site:         ulabibm.gsfc.nasa.gov    (EOSDIS users only, please)
530-  location:     /pub/HDF
530-
530-  site:         opus.ncsa.uiuc.edu       (All Others)
530-  location:     /pub/dist/HDF
530---------------------------------------------------------------------------
530 User anonymous access denied.
Login failed.
ftp> bye
221 Goodbye.
%
```

As you can see, there are a number of other sites that make Mosaic available. A *mirror site* is simply one that makes the same collection of software available that you would find at the central site. You can use any of these for downloading, but this book assumes you are retrieving Mosaic through the NCSA server at the University of Illinois at Urbana-Champaign. You should be able to do so by attempting the data transfer when it is early in the morning or late in the evening at the site. Perseverance pays.

Downloading the Software through a Shell Account

Downloading Mosaic through a shell account is a matter of entering the basic **get** command followed by the file name. Again, be aware that version numbers change constantly; it may well be that by the time you read this, the file name has subtly changed. As I write, the current version number for the Windows version of Mosaic is 20a6, indicating that this is the fifth version of *alpha* release 2.0; the file name is **wmos20a6.zip**. By designating the release as *alpha*, incidentally, NCSA is telling us that not all the bugs have been worked out of the software; this version is still in its developmental process. The downside of this is that we will run into the occasional system crash. The upside is that we can participate in developing and testing Mosaic, having a real say in how the software develops through messages to the developers.

You may see the file listed as **wmos20a9.zip** or something similar. The changes in number may be confusing, but just remember that the latest version will always be the one available in the NCSA directory. The file name for the Windows version will always include the letters *wmos*, short for Windows Mosaic. The compressed file will include, in addition to the actual program, various documents from the NCSA.

Note that the Windows version is in "zipped" format, compressed to save on disk storage space (we will need to use PKUNZIP to uncompress it once we have it on our own machines). The file is binary in nature, so our first order of business is to tell the remote system that we want it to go into binary mode. (With the Macintosh version, it is not necessary to do this. The Mac file is ASCII in nature, and, as specified in the next chapter, should be downloaded with ASCII as the remote system setting).

We can now give the transfer command:

get wmos20a6.zip

What we see should resemble the following:

```
% get wmos20a6.zip
200 PORT command successful.
150 Opening BINARY mode data connection for wmos20a6.zip (272503 bytes).
226 Transfer complete.
local: wmos20a6.zip remote: wmos20a6.zip
272503 bytes received in 96 seconds (2.8 Kbytes/s)
ftp>
```

With a shell account, the file has wound up on our service provider's computer. We can then use **sz** or **sx** to transfer the program to our own machines. My command would be **sz -b wmos20a6.zip**, for example, or **sx -b wmos20a6.zip**.

Downloading the Software through SLIP/PPP

The FTP client program we use with SLIP/PPP also lets us download the file, but with considerably less work. In Figure 3.2, for example, I am again using NetManage Chameleon to perform the task. Notice that the command to set the remote system into binary mode is managed here by clicking on the appropriate field, found at the top center of the screen and labelled as *Transfer*.

The actual file download is simply a matter of clicking in the right places. To do it with NetManage Chameleon, all I need to do is to highlight the file I want to transfer. Whatever directory I am in, the files in that directory are shown in the lower Files field on the FTP screen. By highlighting one and then

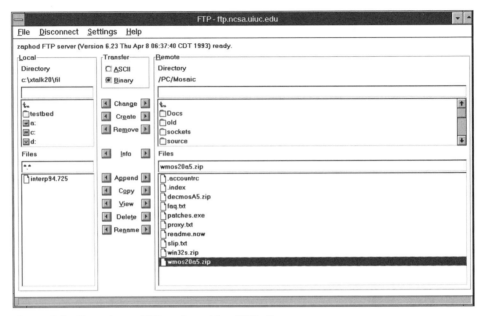

Figure 3.2   Managing an FTP session with a SLIP client.

clicking the Copy button, I move the file to my own computer through the SLIP connection. Macintosh FTP clients use a similar point-and-shoot interface to perform the same functions.

Downloading Win32s for Microsoft Windows

One way or another, we have downloaded Mosaic. But don't log off yet. Although we now have the compressed Mosaic file, we also need another file if we're setting up the system to run the Microsoft Windows version of Mosaic (Macintosh users won't need it). This is a compressed file containing the Win32s software. Windows 3.1 and Windows for Workgroups are 16-bit operating systems, but as of version 20a3, Mosaic for Microsoft Windows has been a 32-bit application. Win32s is needed to allow 32-bit applications like Mosaic to run in the 16-bit environment. The program, developed by Microsoft, is available to licensed users of Windows 3.1 and Windows for Workgroups. As of this writing, the latest release is version 1.1.5.

It is possible that Win32s already exists on your system. This would be the case if you already run other 32-bit Windows applications. To find out if you have the software, look at your directory system. If there is a \windows\system\win32s directory, then the software is there. It is a good idea, however, to upgrade to the latest version. It improves the performance of 32-bit applications and also adds significantly to their stability.

> **Note:**   Windows NT is a 32-bit operating system and, according to advance information, so is Windows 4.0, which had not yet been released at the time of this writing. If you are using Windows NT or Windows 4.0, you will *not* need the Win32s software. Win32s is only necessary for users of Windows 3.1 and Windows for Workgroups.

To get the Win32s software at NCSA, look in the *Mosaic/Windows* directory, where NCSA has packaged the software with an accompanying document and made it available in compressed format. The file name is **win32s.zip**. Download it to your machine using the same procedures already described.

At present, the version of Win32s to use is 1.1.5a. Although this may have changed by the time you read these words, you should always be able to find the latest version of the file at the NCSA site. Be aware, too, that Microsoft makes the file available on its anonymous FTP server; you can find the file in the */developer/DEVTOOLS/WIN32SDK* directory. The address there is **ftp. microsoft.com**.

You should now have two files: **wmos20a6.zip** and **win32s.zip**. You are ready to proceed.

Retrieving Compression and Decompression Tools

With Mosaic on your system, the next step is to unpack it and put it to work. As mentioned, the Macintosh version requires Stuffit Expander or a comparable decoding program. The Windows version, a "zipped" file, requires PKUNZIP. These common utilities are readily located throughout the Internet and other on-line services. If you don't already have a copy, you can download one from the following site:

oak.oakland.edu

Connect to it using standard FTP methods and move to the *pub/msdos/zip* directory. You can also find the PKWARE utilities on the NCSA server.

The file name at the time of this writing is **pkz204g.exe**. This is a self-extracting file, meaning that all you need to do to unpack **pkz204g.exe** is to put the program in its own directory and enter the command **pkz204g.exe**. The program will unpack itself and be ready for use. It is a good idea to put the directory in which you have placed the PKUNZIP program in your path statement so you can use the command in any directory on your hard disk.

To use PKUNZIP to unpack a zipped file, simply give the command **pkunzip** *file_name* at the DOS prompt. (You can do this simply by invoking the DOS shell from within Windows and running PKUNZIP there. In this case, the command would be **pkunzip wmos20a6.zip**.) To unzip the Win32s package, the command is **pkunzip win32s.zip**. But don't do any unpacking yet. First, you have to set up the proper directories.

Installing Mosaic for Microsoft Windows

The basic system requirements for installing Mosaic on a Microsoft-Windows system are these:

- You should have Windows 3.1 or Windows for Workgroups loaded and running.
- You should have the Win32s software installed and configured.
- Your system should be connected to the Internet through at least a SLIP/PPP connection. A straight shell account will not allow you to use Mosaic.

Creating Directories for Mosaic and Win32s

Any installation procedure should be logical and methodical. To successfully get Mosaic running, take one step at a time. The first necessity is to create the proper directory structure on your hard disk. You will then unpack the software in the proper place and proceed with the installation itself. Once you have Mosaic and Win32s ready to go, swinging them into full Internet action is relatively trivial. But the groundwork has to be laid first.

Your next step should be to create a subdirectory on your system where the Mosaic program will be placed. The name of this subdirectory is up to you, but for the purpose of this learning process, let's name it *\Mosaic*. From the DOS prompt, you could do this from your root directory with the command **mkdir mosaic**. But it will probably be easier to proceed from the Windows File Manager, by dropping down the File Menu and then choosing the Create Directory option. In Figure 3.3, I have pulled the menu down and am about to move the highlight to Create Directory.

Choosing Create Directory will cause a dialog box to pop up asking for the name of the directory you wish to create. Simply enter the name of the directory and click on the OK button to create the new directory.

You will also need a directory for the Win32s software—remember, Win32s must be installed before Mosaic can work under Windows 3.1 and Windows for Workgroups (the software is unnecessary if you are running Microsoft Windows NT).

Creating this directory is managed slightly differently, however. First, you need to move the **win32s.zip** file into an empty directory. The name of this directory isn't critical, as the software will create its own new directories in the next step of this process. I decided to use my *\testbed* directory, where I try out new programs and manage operations like this one. You can create such a

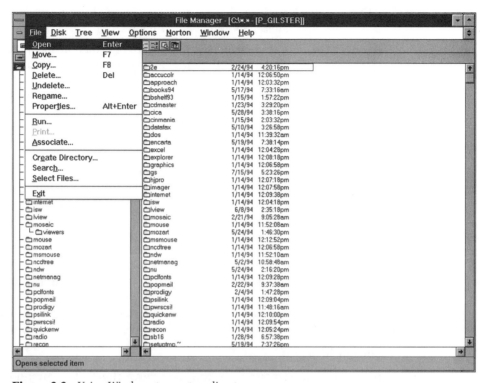

Figure 3.3 Using Windows to create a directory.

directory with the **mkdir testbed** command from the root directory at the DOS prompt, or else create it using Program Manager. Place **win32s.zip** in the *testbed* directory and you will be ready to proceed.

Unpacking the Mosaic Software

You'll now unpack both Mosaic and Win32s. Make sure the **wmos20a6.zip** file is in your *Mosaic* directory (copy it there if necessary), and then run the PKUNZIP program. The command is **pkunzip wmos20a6.zip**. Because PKUNZIP is a DOS program, we will want to activate the Windows DOS shell to run the program there. You can do this by choosing the MS-DOS prompt icon from the Main program group in Program Manager. Once you have finished with your command, you can return to Windows by giving the **exit** command, followed by pressing the Enter key.

If you examine the contents of your *Mosaic* directory at this point, you should find the following files:

wmos20a6.zip file   The original compressed file.

devnote.wri   Notes regarding the current version of Mosaic.

faq.wri	A useful, if very terse, list of Frequently Asked Questions about Mosaic for Microsoft Windows.
install.wri	A document from NCSA with information about the installation procedures. Use this to supplement information found in this book, particularly if the version number of Mosaic has changed since this book was printed. Be advised: NCSA documentation is sparse.
mosaic.exe	The Mosaic program itself. A program that is ready to run is also known as an *executable*.
mosaic.ini	A file that Mosaic uses to configure and initialize its operations.
update.wri	An update document about what is happening with Mosaic at NCSA; it contains version enhancements and bug fixes.

Unpacking the Win32s Software

Now we need to unpack Win32s, which turns out to be a slightly different procedure. Move back into the DOS shell by clicking on the MS-DOS icon in Program Manager's Main program group. Move to the \testbed directory in which you have placed the **win32s.zip** file. There, give the following command:

> **pkunzip win32s.zip**

When the unpacking process is complete, give the **exit** command, and press Enter to return to Windows. Examine the directory in question and you should find the following files:

win32s.zip	The original compressed file.
readme.txt	A file of basic help information about unpacking and setting up Win32s.
w32s1_1.bug	A brief document explaining known bugs in Win32s.
w32s115a.zip	Another zip file, this one containing Win32s version 1.1.5a. We will now use this second zip file to create the directory structure we need for Win32s and to unpack its files (and as before, be aware that these numbers may have changed slightly by the time you read this, as Microsoft releases updated versions of the software).

You can now go back to the MS-DOS prompt and unzip the second zipped file. The command is as follows:

> **pkunzip -d w32s115a.zip**

Note the **-d** switch after the initial command. This tells the PKUNZIP program to restore whatever directory structure it finds in the zipped file. This will make your job easier, as the **w32s115a.zip** file contains all the information necessary to set up the correct directories.

When you run the command above, a large number of files will be unpacked from the compressed file, and two new subdirectories will appear beneath the *testbed* directory. They will be *testbed\disk1* and *testbed\disk2*, and they will be used to finish the procedure. From Program Manager, move to the File menu and select the Run . . . option. In the dialog box that appears, place this command:

c:\testbed\disk1\setup

This launches the Win32s setup program, as shown in Figure 3.4.

From here on, the procedure is simple. The Microsoft software walks you through the installation. It will place some Win32s files in your *Windows\systems* subdirectory and others in a new *Windows\systems\win32s* subdirectory that it creates. And it will also offer you the chance to install a card game called Freecell, which is a 32-bit program that serves to check that the Win32s software is loaded properly. I advise you to go ahead and load this program, as it's quite good.

And don't forget about your original unzipped files. With Win32s installed in the proper subdirectories, there is no reason to keep the files in the *testbed* directory or its *testbed\disk1* and *testbed\disk2* subdirectories any longer. After the Win32s setup procedure restarts Windows, which it needs to do to make Win32s active, you can go back and delete these unnecessary files and subdirectories.

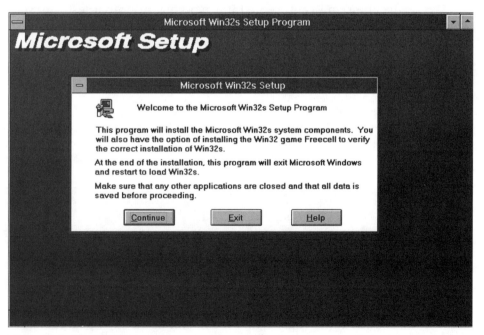

Figure 3.4   The Win32s setup program.

Win32s, at this point, is ready to go, and you can proceed with what you have been waiting for—the installation and running of Mosaic.

Configuring Mosaic

Mosaic uses a critical file called **mosaic.ini** to perform its functions. You will come to know this file very well indeed later in this book as you alter it to create a Mosaic customized for your own use. For now, you need to make sure that **mosaic.ini** is in the right place and ready to be used. A common installation mistake is to make changes to the wrong copy of this file, only to find that any changes you make during a Mosaic operating session are not preserved the next time you start the program. Let's avoid that.

You need to copy the **mosaic.ini** file into the directory where Microsoft Windows is found. In a standard installation of Windows, this directory is \windows. And if you will leave a copy of **mosaic.ini** in your \mosaic directory, you will always have a clean copy to fall back on in case you decide to start from scratch. Mosaic will not make changes to any copy of **mosaic.ini** but the one in the \windows directory (or the directory in which Windows is installed, if you have renamed it).

You also need to make a few small changes to **mosaic.ini** right off the bat. The number of changes you could make to customize your copy of Mosaic is huge; in a later chapter, we will go through the file in considerable detail to do just that. But for now, only a few things need to be done to enable you to test the program to ensure that it is working. After that test run, you will want to find a number of viewer programs that allow us to work with different kinds of files. But more about that in a moment.

Editing mosaic.ini

mosaic.ini is an ASCII file, and is best edited in an ASCII editor like Windows Notepad. In Figure 3.5, you see **mosaic.ini** as called up in Notepad. For the purposes of this discussion, you will not need to modify any part of **mosaic.ini** other than what I specify. Later, we will fine-tune the file to suit your user environment.

 Note: The file you want to edit is the copy of **mosaic.ini** that is in your \windows directory. Remember, the **mosaic.ini** left in the \mosaic directory is there as a backup, a clean copy of **mosaic.ini** in case you want to return to the defaults as set by the NCSA and reconfigure.

Notice in Figure 3.5 that the file consists of a large number of fields, each followed by an equal sign (=). You will be able to make changes to the file by altering the material to the right of each equal sign.

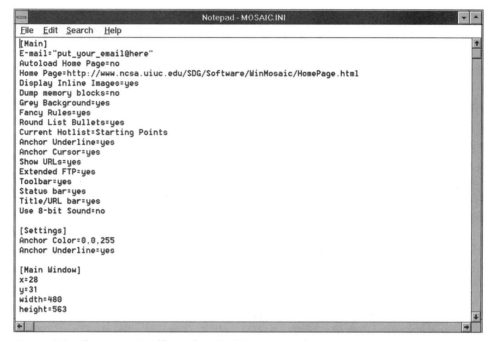

Figure 3.5   The **mosaic.ini** file can be edited in any text editor.

Setting Up Your E-Mail Address

The first line, for example, under the [Main] heading, reads as follows:

```
E-mail="put_your_email@here"
```

This is the place for your first insertion. You will want to put your own Internet e-mail address in this field (note that the NCSA developers have made it clear what to do by the way they have structured the statement, a method that will show up throughout the **mosaic.ini** file).

My address, for example, is **gilster@interpath.net**. I will, therefore, alter the **mosaic.ini** statement to read:

```
E-mail="gilster@interpath.net"
```

Note that I have left the quotation marks around the address.

It is important to make this change to **mosaic.ini** because Mosaic includes a feature that allows you to send e-mail to its developers, and your address is necessary for this to function. Your address is also used in the annotation feature we will examine in a later chapter.

Establishing Home Page Functions

A home page is simply a document on the **World Wide Web** that Mosaic will display every time you open the program. We'll discuss home pages, including background information on how the **Web** works, in Chapter 5. For now, note that as downloaded from the NCSA, Mosaic is set up to retrieve a specific home page. You can verify this by checking the next line in the **mosaic.ini** file:

```
Autoload Home Page=yes
```

This is immediately followed by a related statement:

```
Home Page=http://www.ncsa.uiuc.edu/SDG/Software/WinMosaic/HomePage.html
```

The Home Page= line gives us a URL, an address that Mosaic can use to connect to if we have set it up to go directly to a home page. If you were to start Mosaic with the setting set to no, however, Mosaic would not immediately go over the Internet to make the connection; instead, the program would run, but you would need to manually initiate your opening session with a remote server.

We are going to keep this setting as it is; I show it to you now to pave the way for a change in the Home Page that we will use as our base, one that we will set up in Chapter 8. For now, just be sure the Autoload statement is set to yes, as follows:

```
Autoload Home Page=yes
```

Mosaic will now open, every time you launch it, by connecting to the URL specified, which is a Home Page on the NCSA server that has been set up for Mosaic users.

You should become familiar with the NCSA site, because this is where the latest information about Mosaic is made available. But you should also bear in mind that with the huge increase of interest in Mosaic, this site is becoming very heavily used. Most copies of Mosaic are set up to connect directly to NCSA as the first part of any Mosaic session. The strain on the server shows; there will be times when you cannot connect to this Home Page when you launch Mosaic. The performance of the program is unaffected by this, but the strain on the NCSA system is such that we will want to lighten it later by changing the Home Page= statement to another address. Setting up a different Home Page allows you to choose any site on the **Web** as your introductory page. We will do that after you get a look at the NCSA site.

Displaying Inline Images

There is one other item you should look at before running a quick test of the Mosaic installation. This is the line reading as follows:

```
Display Inline Images=yes
```

Inline images are transferred whenever you go to a document containing them, unless you set this statement to no. As opposed to full-sized graphics or photographs, inline images are generally small and can be accommodated by Mosaic without the addition of any viewer programs. For this test, I recommend leaving this statement as it is, unless your network connection is extremely slow. If you set the value to no, Mosaic will replace any inline images it finds with an icon. You could then click on the icon with the right mouse button, at which point Mosaic would retrieve the image.

Later in your use of Mosaic, you may well want to consider changing this value to no (this can also be done from within the program, by the way). The reason: Over a SLIP/PPP connection, even with a fast modem, Mosaic can be slow. Turning off the inline images allows you to move between **World Wide Web** pages at a much faster pace and, as just mentioned, you can always click on any image you do decide to see (just remember to use the right mouse button). But for testing purposes now, we will leave the inline imagery available, and let the field remain as set.

Underlining Hypermedia Links

If you are using a black-and-white monitor, you will also want to make sure that another line of the **mosaic.ini** file is set to work with your system. The line is:

```
Anchor Underline=yes
```

This value should be yes to allow those with black-and-white monitors to see the underlining beneath each hyperlink. Without the underlining, and unable to see the color changes that manage the same function, you would not know which items contained links to other documents or data. If you are using a color monitor, this value is optional, as you will be able to see hypermedia links set off by a different color than the surrounding text.

Establishing a News Server

If you would like to use Mosaic to read USENET news, the system has already been configured to tap the University of Illinois NNTP server (NNTP is the Internet's news protocol). Thus, the address you will find listed in the **mosaic.ini** file in the [Services] section reads as follows:

```
NNTP Server="news.cso.uiuc.edu"
```

You can set this to your own news server by supplying the appropriate address. If you are unsure what your news server address is, ask your system administrator.

Now that you have, for the time being, finished editing the **mosaic.ini** file, be sure to exit Notepad and save the changes made to the file. You will come to know this file well as you progress into Mosaic operations.

Adding Mosaic to Windows

You now want to set up Mosaic as an item in a Windows program group, so that you can click on it to call it up. The procedure is simple: Go to Program Manager and highlight the program group to which you would like to add Mosaic. From the Program Manager File menu, select New, which will pop up a dialog box. Choose Program Item followed by ok. This will open the Program Item Properties box, as shown in Figure 3.6.

In this example, I have added appropriate information, and the icon for Mosaic will now appear in the chosen program group. Where you put Mosaic is up to you, but I have found it easiest to set it up inside my SLIP/PPP software program group. For the purposes of this book, I am using NetManage Chameleon, so Mosaic is established as an icon within its program group. Figure 3.7 shows the icon along with the other icons of the NetManage group.

A Mosaic Test Run

We still have to find viewers for various Mosaic functions, but for the moment, let's make sure the program works. After the configuration process, the test run is simple. Connect to your SLIP/PPP account and click on the Mosaic icon. If all goes as it should, you should quickly see the Mosaic for Microsoft Windows Home Page, as shown in Figure 3.8.

There still are things to do; in particular, there are types of files you can't use until you set up the correct viewers. But you're finally on-line with Mosaic, so take a few minutes to play around and get a feel for the software.

Notice the underlined items, which appear in blue if you're using a color monitor. As mentioned before, these are your hypermedia links to other data. In Figure 3.9, for example, I have moved the cursor to the item *University of Illinois*, which appears immediately under the NCSA logo at the top of the screen. By clicking on this item, I can move directly to the linked document.

Next look at the tiny house icon on the icon bar at the top of the screen. By clicking on it, you can move directly to a Home Page; in the case of the Windows version, this is the Home Page we just looked at in Figure 3.8. I show this to you now so that you will realize how malleable the Home Page settings are. Had you chosen to leave the Autoload Home Page= item set to no, you would still have been able to move directly to this Home Page with a mouse click.

Notice, too, that there is a scroll bar at the right of the screen. Documents that are longer than one page can be easily moved through by clicking on the bottom of the scroll bar; a click at the top of the bar moves you back up the page. The symbol at the top right of the screen, the tiny globe inside the stylized figure S, is the Mosaic symbol. You will notice that as Mosaic accesses documents, the globe rotates, and the animated symbol changes. Document title and Document URL information are provided at the top of the screen (we discuss URLs in Chapter 5).

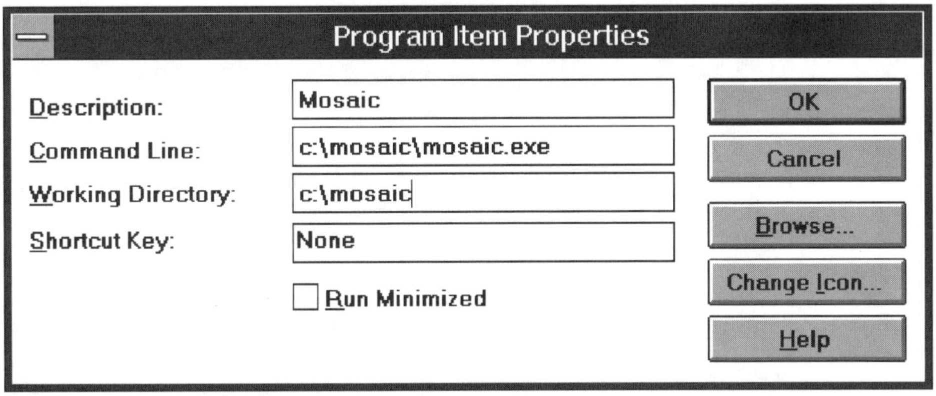

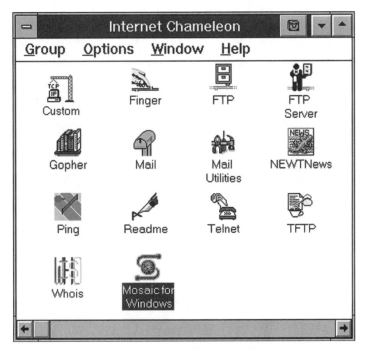

Figure 3.6   The Program Item Properties box in Windows.

Figure 3.7   My NetManage group, along with Mosaic's icon.

Go ahead and enjoy Mosaic for a bit. The program is virtually irresistible, particularly if you are used to a character-based interface to the Internet. When you are through, pull down the File menu and choose Exit to leave the program. Then move to the next section, because we still have to find the necessary file viewers to get Mosaic completely operational. There, we will also perform some customization which should make the program more suited to your individual needs.

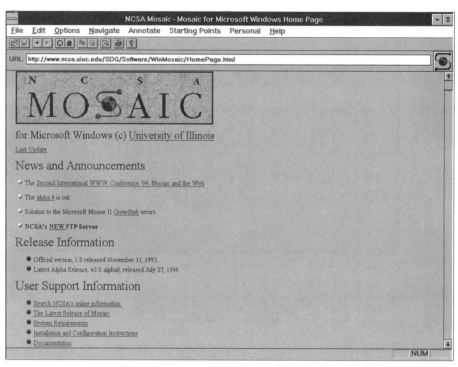

Figure 3.8 The Mosaic for Microsoft Windows home page.

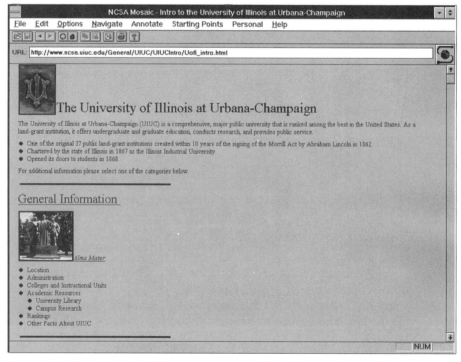

Figure 3.9 The University of Illinois page, retrieved by clicking on its hyperlink.

Tip: Large documents sometimes take a long time to transfer. If you begin the transfer process and change your mind, clicking on the Mosaic icon in the upper right corner of the window will stop the process.

If Mosaic Doesn't Connect

NCSA technical support can help with problems, but its developers need to know what is happening when you try to load the program. Therefore, consider problems in the following light:

- If Mosaic refuses to run, the problem is probably related to the Winsock DLL file (**winsock.dll**). Remember, Mosaic is compliant with WinSock 1.1, and requires that the **winsock.dll** file be compliant as well. Simply check to make sure your installation is WinSock 1.1-compliant. If you worked through the SLIP/PPP options outlined in Chapter 3 to set up your account, you should not run into this problem. In any case, the **winsock.dll** file from Trumpet Software discussed in that chapter can always be accessed at the **ftp.utas.edu.au** site; the directory is */pc/trumpet/winsock*.

- If Mosaic runs but will not connect to the Home Page, NCSA recommends you try the following, which will provide information on what is happening:

  Try to open a file on your system by pulling down the File menu and selecting Open Local File.

  Try to open a different URL by selecting the File menu and picking the option Open URL. You could choose any URL for this purpose, but NCSA recommends trying this one:

```
http://www.ncsa.uiuc.edu/General/UIUC/UIUCIntro/UofI_intro.html
```

  Try to reach a remote FTP site and open a file there. Do this by going to the File menu, selecting Open URL, and entering an FTP address. NCSA recommends you try this URL:

```
file://ftp.ncsa.uiuc.edu/Mosaic/Windows/faq.txt
```

Technical Support for Mosaic for Microsoft Windows

Technical support for Mosaic for Microsoft Windows is provided at this address: **mosaic-win@ncsa.uiuc.edu**. NCSA's Software Development Group encourages comments and reports about problems, but also recommends that users check the information on-line to see whether a particular problem has already been reported. To do so, check this address:

```
http://www.ncsa.uiuc.edu/SDG/Software/WinMosaic/HomePage.html
```

Assuming the problem you are encountering has not already been reported, you can send mail to the developers through Mosaic itself. Use the Help menu, taking the Mail to Developers . . . option to write the message. Click Send to send it.

Bear in mind that the development team can most profitably spend its time working on real problems, so don't complicate the already crowded schedules of these programmers with requests for interesting places to see on the net or other material readily found elsewhere. Also be patient; the NCSA team receives a huge number of messages daily and answers each in turn.

Finding and Installing Viewers

People who work with Mosaic for the first time assume that the program's most intriguing features—its way with graphics, for example, or its ability to serve as an all-purpose navigation tool—are all built in to the package. As you've just seen from your introductory session, Mosaic does provide a great deal of functionality in its generic form, but to truly tap its powers, you will now need to find and install several other programs. This is because Mosaic uses external viewer programs to view particular file types. A JPEG (Joint Photographic Experts Group) image, for example, must be displayed through a program external to Mosaic, and the same is true of large GIF (Graphics Interchange Format) files, movies using the MPEG standard, and other files. Such files cannot be handled inside the Mosaic program, but the right viewer can call them up, as long as you point Mosaic to it.

We will use the **mosaic.ini** file to make the necessary adjustments, telling Mosaic where to find our file viewers. We will also need to set up directories for these viewers, and will use Mosaic itself to retrieve the viewers. In this way, you will get a little practice with the program, and will also wind up with a more or less fully configured Mosaic.

Finding Viewers

Let's now go back into Mosaic. Launch the program as before, by initiating your SLIP/PPP connection and then clicking on the Mosaic icon once SLIP/PPP is running. As Mosaic is currently configured, you should once again find yourself in the Mosaic for Microsoft Windows Home Page. This time, however, use the scroll bar to move to the bottom of the page. Using your mouse, click on the lower side of the scroll bar to move the page down. What you see should resemble Figure 3.10.

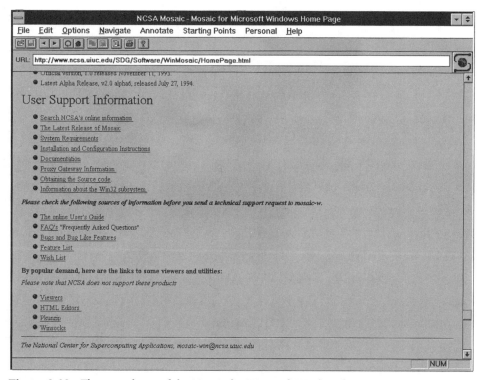

Figure 3.10 The second part of the Mosaic for Microsoft Windows home page.

Notice the very bottom of the image. There, you see hyperlinks to several interesting destinations. One is marked Pkunzip; we could retrieve the latest version of the PKWARE decompression product there. Another is marked Winsocks, which tells us this would be a good place to look for the shareware Winsock product. But the one we want is labelled Viewers. Move your mouse to it and click once, using the left mouse button. You should see the screen shown in Figure 3.11.

Here we have our first chance to explore the wider capabilities of Mosaic. We are going to use the program to access several viewers that NCSA has made available on its server. I would advise you to get each of the following programs:

Lview   A freeware viewer that allows you to see GIF and JPEG image files.

MPEGPLAY   Another shareware product, this one (by Michael Simmons) lets you work with full-motion video files.

WHAM   Waveform Hold and Modify plays sound files for those with properly equipped sound cards.

GhostScript   A program that lets you view PostScript files. Handy indeed, as there are numerous PostScript files available on the Internet.

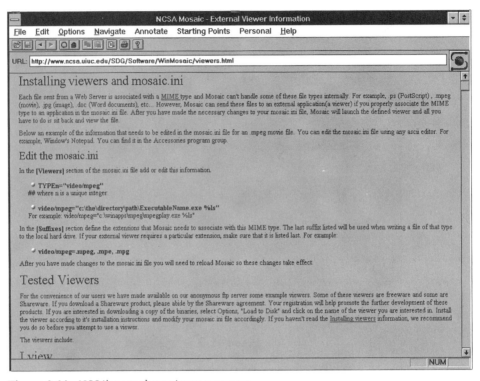

Figure 3.11   NCSA's page about viewer programs.

As you can see, these viewers are independent products. NCSA did not create them, a fact you should remember if you run into trouble with any of them. Support questions for the viewer program itself should always go to the shareware author or company.

About viewers in general: The programs listed are not the only possible viewers. It is your choice which viewer you use, but those listed here are made available through the NCSA site because they have been found to work well with Mosaic. The directory *Mosaic/Windows/viewers*, on NCSA's FTP server at **ftp. ncsa.uiuc.edu**, is the place to look for other viewers, and NCSA is always considering new possibilities. You can use the Mail to Developers item on the Help menu to contact the developers at any point with a suggestion about new viewers.

Creating Directories for Viewers

As with anything having to do with your hard disk, the best idea is to aim at optimum organization. We already have a *\mosaic* directory, where we keep the program itself (everything but the configured **mosaic.ini** file, which we maintain in *\windows*). Now let's create directories for the viewers we are about to download.

Note: You can set up these directories in any way you choose. I am going to show you a system that works for me. The important thing about directories is that they be set up in logical manner, so you always know where to look for your information. Once we have set up the directories and downloaded the files, we will then alter **mosaic.ini**, telling it where to find these files. So consider what I do simply a suggestion.

I plan to download Lview, WHAM, MPEGPLAY, and GhostScript, and all of these are viewers. So first I will create a directory called *\mosaic\viewers*, either from the DOS prompt or by using Windows File Manager. And, to keep the various files of the viewers separate, I will then create subdirectories for this directory in the following way:

c:\mosaic\viewers\lview
c:\mosaic\viewers\mpegplay
c:\mosaic\viewers\wham
c:\mosaic\viewers\ghostscr
c:\mosaic\viewers\ghostvw

(Bear with me on the latter; I set it up for a program related to the GhostScript PostScript viewer called Ghostview; more on this in a few moments.) Armed with this directory structure, I can now proceed to retrieve the viewer programs themselves.

Downloading the Viewers

Now for the fun part. Notice that each of the programs in Figure 3.11 is underlined, indicating it is hyperlinked to something else. In fact, when you click on one of these items, you launch the necessary FTP connection to retrieve it. No need to type in a lengthy FTP address and then proceed with a bunch of hard-to-remember commands.

But first, a mini-lesson in Mosaic use. To download one of these files, the first thing you need to do is to go to the Options menu at the top of the Mosaic screen and look for the Load to Disk option. Click on it; this is a toggle switch that will stay on until you click it off. You need to do this to allow Mosaic to transfer the file directly to your hard disk. Figure 3.12 shows the menu in question. Note that I have already clicked on the Load to Disk option; a check mark has appeared next to it.

Now I can move the cursor to the Lview item and click on it. A dialog box should appear, as shown in Figure 3.13. Mosaic is asking me where I want to place the file. The name of the file is already suggested (although I could change it if I chose): **lview31.zip**. I could put it in any directory I desire, but I will choose the *lview* subdirectory and place it there by clicking on that directory.

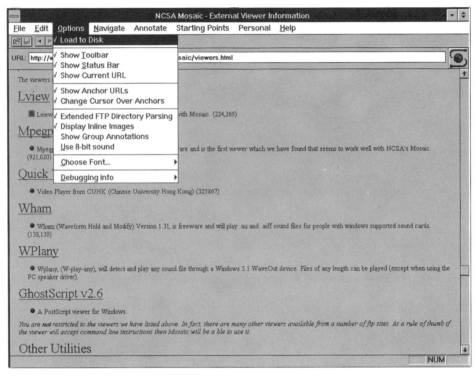

Figure 3.12   Mosaic's Options menu, with the Load to Disk option toggled on.

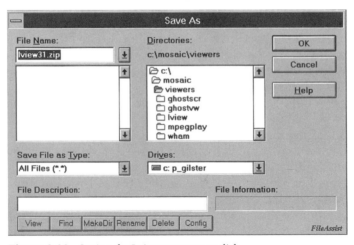

Figure 3.13   Saving the Lview program to disk.

If we are lucky and the server isn't too busy to handle us at the moment, we should soon see the Mosaic logo in the right-hand corner of the screen come to life, while at the bottom of the screen updates will appear about the progress of the file transfer. When the transfer is complete, we will have the Lview program (in compressed format) in a suitable area of our hard disk.

I mention server overload because it is possible that you will receive a message that you can't connect to the FTP server. If this occurs, simply try again in a few minutes, or try at a different time of day, when the workload at the site may be lessened (after business hours in Illinois, say, although with the world-wide nature of Internet activity, it is getting harder and harder to specify a time when computers are less busy).

Let's now move through the rest of the list of viewers. Click on each viewer (leaving on the Load to Disk toggle in the Options menu the whole time). When you are given a choice of where to put each file, be sure to click on the subdirectory to which you would like it to go. Thus, the MPEGPLAY program, which is transferred as a file called **mpegw32e.zip** at the time of this writing, should go into the *c:\mosaic\viewers\mpegplay* directory. In each case, the download will proceed directly to your computer (remember, this is SLIP/PPP, not a shell account; there is no intermediate step along the way). In this manner, download WHAM as well.

A brief aside about GhostScript, before you download it. You will need to disable the Load to Disk toggle switch before clicking on the GhostScript item because, rather than initiating the download, the GhostScript link takes you to a separate page with information about the program. It also tells about Ghostview, an interface program necessary to make GhostScript work under Windows. The latter and full information about it will appear when you click on GhostScript. You can then retoggle the Load to Disk switch to download each of those files. The fact that there are two parts to the GhostScript download explains why I set up two directories earlier when preparing my hard disk for the incoming file viewers.

Viewer Installation

Space constraints make it impossible to give complete installation details about each viewer program. But I will say a few words about Lview, considering it as a representative of the viewer programs we will be working with. The key principle is this: Make sure you print out the necessary documentation after you have unpacked the compressed file viewer. Countless installation problems could be avoided if users would do this, as most of the issues to be resolved are included in the documentation.

In the case of Lview, I proceed to move into the DOS shell from Windows, and go directly to the *c:\mosaic\viewers\lview* directory, where the compressed Lview file is waiting for me. The file name is, at the time of this writing, **lview31.zip**. We know by now that the command to decompress it is simple:

pkunzip lview31.zip

Giving this command at the DOS prompt should result in the creation of the following files on disk:

lview.hlp	The Lview help file.
lview31.exe	The executable program file.
readme.1st	Information about Lview.
wecjlib.dll	A file necessary in the viewing of JPEG imagery.
whats.new	Updated Lview information.

The program is easy to use. All we need to do is to tell the **mosaic.ini** file where Mosaic should look for it. Let's now proceed to another editing session with **mosaic.ini**. We will need to set up **mosaic.ini** for each of the viewer programs we have downloaded.

Configuring Mosaic for Viewer Programs

Call up **mosaic.ini** once again in the Notepad editor, again making sure that you use the **mosaic.ini** file in your *windows* subdirectory, rather than the backup copy in *mosaic*. Now go to the [Viewers] section of the file. Notice the first part of this section, which reads as follows:

```
TYPE0="audio/wav"
TYPE1="application/postscript"
TYPE2="image/gif"
TYPE3="image/jpeg"
TYPE4="video/mpeg"
TYPE5="video/quicktime"
TYPE6="video/msvideo"
TYPE7="application/x-rtf"
TYPE8="audio/x-midi"
TYPE9="application/zip"
```

Listed here are file types in MIME, or multipurpose internet mail extensions, form. MIME is a way of incorporating various file types into electronic mail, of interest to us here only because the file types are those we will be likely to encounter as we make our way around the **World Wide Web** with Mosaic. By including this information, the **mosaic.ini** file can tell Mosaic whether it is necessary to launch an external viewer to view a particular file.

Below this section in the [Viewers] area is listed the following:

```
application/postscript="ghostview %ls"
image/gif="c:\windows\apps\lview\lview31 %ls"
image/jpeg="c:\windows\apps\lview\lview31 %ls"
```

```
video/mpeg="c:\winapps\mpegplay\mpegplay %ls"
video/quicktime="C:\WINAPPS\QTW\bin\player.exe %ls"
video/msvideo="mplayer %ls"
audio/wav="mplayer %ls"
audio/x-midi="mplayer %ls"
application/x-rtf="write %ls"
application/zip="C:\WINDOWS\APPS\ZIPMGR\ZM400.EXE %ls"
rem audio/basic="notepad %ls"
telnet="c:\trumpet\telw.exe"
```

This section specifies which viewer should be used for which file type. Although it looks like gibberish, in fact the method here is straightforward. You want to enter your information here to point to the viewer programs you have established. If you don't make the necessary changes, Mosaic will return an error message when it tries to access a file in one of the formats listed.

Take a look at TYPE2 and TYPE3, for example. TYPE2 is an image file in GIF format; TYPE3 an image file in JPEG. Both of these are standard methods of digitizing imagery; we will find numerous examples of such files on the Internet. The viewer program we have downloaded which can handle both types is Lview. We therefore need to tell Mosaic how to find our Lview program.

Currently, there is a listing next to the entries image/gif= and image/jpeg=. These are dummy listings; they point to directories that may or may not be there, depending on how we have structured our hard disks. Note how they are set up:

```
image/gif="c:\windows\apps\lview\lview31 %ls"
image/jpeg="c:\windows\apps\lview\lview31 %ls"
```

If you have placed the Lview program in a *c:\windows\apps\lview* directory, this setting will not need to be changed. But as you'll recall, I found it more logical to set up subdirectories under my *mosaic\viewers* directory. By creating a directory for each of the viewers under *\mosaic\viewers*, I kept my hard disk logically structured. To reflect my setup, I needed to change the entries in **mosaic.ini** to read as follows:

```
image/gif="c:\mosaic\viewers\lview\lview31 %ls"
image/jpeg="c:\mosaic\viewers\lview\lview31 %ls"
```

Now every time Mosaic runs into a GIF or JPEG file that I want to see, it uses the Lview program to call up the file. An example of this is shown in Figure 3.14. Here we see an image superimposed upon a Home Page, this one from Mt. Wilson Observatory in the San Gabriel mountains near Pasadena, California. Among other information, Mt. Wilson has maintained an archive of interesting photographs from the spectacular collision between the comet Shoemaker/Levy and Jupiter. To see one, the reader simply clicks on an underlined text description. The image is transferred and then Mosaic uses the Lview program to display it.

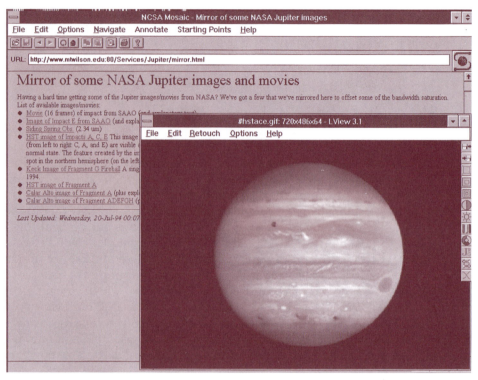

Figure 3.14   An image viewed through the lview program.

The image shown in Figure 3.14 is not from Mt. Wilson itself, but from the Hubble Space Telescope; it illustrates three impact sites as dark spots on the lower part of the image. A range of display options are also provided by the Lview software; these are visible in the palette of icons to the right of the Jupiter image. With these, contrast, brightness, and other features can be controlled. You can see, then, that the partnership between Mosaic and its viewer software can be productive indeed. The more powerful the viewer, the more powerful the total Mosaic experience.

Of course, Lview isn't the only program we downloaded. We now need to add the other viewer programs to the **mosaic.ini** file to make them effective. The procedure is the same as we used for Lview. We will find the appropriate line in the **mosaic.ini** file and then replace the default statement with the path and executable program we intend to use. The following line, for example, could be changed:

```
video/mpeg="c:\winapps\mpegplay\mpegplay %ls"
```

We would like to define the path to our **mpegplay.exe** file by simply changing the directories:

```
video/mpeg="c:\mosaic\viewers\mpegplay\mpegplay %ls"
```

and the job is done.

As you can see, there is a wide range of viewer possibilities listed under the TYPE statements at the top of the [Viewers] section in the **mosaic.ini** file. For now, I would recommend that you concentrate on the Lview program to make sure you can call up images as necessary. You can include other viewers as they become necessary. The last thing you want to do when just embarking upon your Mosaic experience is to become bogged down in loading viewers that you may seldom need. The programs we have downloaded should tide you over for the time being (just remember that each requires that the **mosaic.ini** file be edited to reflect the path to the appropriate executable). And remember, too, to read the documentation for any viewer you plan to add before trying to set it up. GhostScript, for example, is more finicky than most and works best with a separate \gs directory. Printing out and reading the installation instructions before making any changes to the **mosaic.ini** file is the best course of action in such cases.

What happens if you don't need a particular viewer that is listed in the **mosaic.ini** file? Nothing. You don't have to delete this material from the file or make any changes to it. The only time you need to change the **mosaic.ini** file with regard to viewers is when you want to add a viewer and show the path to it.

Using WHAM for Audio Files

When setting up WHAM (Waveform Hold and Modify) to play sound files, you need to make an additional change to the **mosaic.ini** file. If you examine **mosaic.ini**, you will see that there is no place listed for WHAM under the [Viewers] section. We can fix that by doing the following:

1. Go to the section of [Viewers] where TYPEs are defined. There, after TYPE9, add the following statement: **TYPE10="audio/basic"**.

2. Directly below, where the paths to the various viewers are listed, add the following line: **audio/basic="c:\mosaic\viewers\wham\wham.exe %ls"**.

3. Now drop to the [Suffixes] section of the file and add the following information there: **audio/basic=.au**.

Now you have established WHAM as your "viewer" for audio files.

Note that we have used the [Suffixes] section of the **mosaic.ini** file for the first time. This section is set up to tell Mosaic what file extensions mean. For example, the **mosaic.ini** file specifies this information about MPEG files:

```
video/mpeg=.mpeg,.mpe,.mpg
```

This means that Mosaic will recognize any of the listed extensions as referring to an MPEG file, and will automatically load the correct viewer. Most HTTP servers don't need to use this information, as the file types are maintained by the servers themselves. But earlier HTTP server versions may need to refer to this material, which is why it is there. By adding the information about **.au** files to the [Suffixes] section, we have prepared Mosaic to handle files with that extension.

Creating the Telnet Connection

There is one more change we must be sure to make now. Telnet is a key Mosaic application; we use Telnet all the time in our normal Internet work, and we cannot leave Telnet out of the picture. Therefore, find the following line in the **mosaic.ini** file (in the [Viewers] section):

```
telnet="c:\trumpet\telw.exe"
```

Here, again, we must enter the line to reflect our own Telnet program, whatever it might be. I use NetManage Chameleon's Telnet implementation, and have changed the telnet= line to read as follows:

```
telnet="c:\netmanag\telnet.exe"
```

You should alter this line to reflect the path to your own Telnet program. And, of course, be sure to exit and save the changes to **mosaic.ini** when you have made these alterations.

Although it may seem as if **mosaic.ini** is an extremely complicated file, in fact, the number of changes we need to make to customize it is relatively small, and they have important results. The range that **mosaic.ini** provides in allowing us to customize Mosaic is wide; we will examine other options, some of them set up by editing this file, others by making changes to the menus while inside the program, in Chapters 7 and 8.

4

Installing Mosaic on a Macintosh

As with Mosaic for Microsoft Windows, Mosaic for Macintosh undergoes frequent on-line revisions. As of this writing, the latest release of the Macintosh product was version 2.0.0 alpha 6. Any alpha release is essentially a test version; users needing the fully developed, more rigorously tested version of Mosaic for Macintosh can download version 1.0.3, which was released in late January 1994. The choice if yours, but in this chapter, I illustrate the Macintosh take on Mosaic with the earlier version, which is more stable and more widely distributed.

After you've become accustomed to version 1.0.3, you may well want to upgrade. Keeping up with rapid changes in Mosaic is often worth the effort, even if it occasionally results in problems. In particular, the *forms* feature available in Mosaic for X Windows and Mosaic for Microsoft Windows is to be supported in the alpha releases of Mosaic for Macintosh 2.0.0, but it is not available in version 1.0.3. Forms are HTML documents that can be filled in online; they hold great potential for expanding the Internet's commercial marketplace, and will see much future use.

Equipment Requirements for Mosaic for Macintosh

Mosaic for Macintosh is considerably easier to install than its Microsoft Windows-based cousin, but some details must still be attended to for successful installation. In particular, note these equipment requirements. You must meet them to get the system running:

- System 7 or later as your operating system software.
- MacTCP 2.0.2 or later. The developers recommend at least MacTCP 2.0.4 for the best results.
- 4 or more megabytes of RAM. As with the Windows version, the more memory, the better; 8 MB is preferred.
- A hard disk.

Downloading Mosaic for Macintosh

To download the necessary Macintosh files, we use NCSA's FTP address:

ftp.ncsa.uiuc.edu

We can download the program either through a shell account or through SLIP, using a client program running on our own Macs. Here's a quick look at both methods.

Retrieving Mosaic through a Shell Account

Log in at the site as **anonymous**, using your Internet mail address as your password. The first thing to do is retrieve the **README.FIRST** file, which will contain any updated information about retrieving the Mosaic files from NCSA. To get the file, enter the command as follows:

get README.FIRST

You can now give the **bye** command to end your FTP session. Review the **README.FIRST** file for any further information before proceeding. Any changes, for example, to the directory structure at NCSA would be listed here. At present, this file is found in the NCSA root directory.

Now log back on to the site, using the same methods. You will want to move to the Mosaic for Macintosh directory, which is *Mac/Mosaic*. To get there, give this command:

cd Mosaic/Mac

An **ls** command will show you which files are available in this directory. Below are the results of both commands:

```
ftp> cd Mosaic/Mac
250 CWD command successful.
ftp> ls
200 PORT command successful.
150 Opening ASCII mode data connection for file list.
.index
Apple
.accountrc
```

```
FAQ
...
LocalHome.html
NCSAMosaicMac.103.sit.hqx
copyright
NCSAMosaic.1.0.3.README
QuickStart.Txt
GIFS
Documents
Helpers
Related
NCSAMosaicA6.68k.hqx
NCSAMosaicA6.PPC.hqx
226 Transfer complete.
211 bytes received in 0.021 seconds (9.8 Kbytes/s)
ftp>
```

The file you need depends upon which version you choose to download:

NCSAMosaicA6.68k.hqx   Version 2.0.0 Alpha 6 for the 68K Macintosh.

NCSAMosaicA6.PPC.hqx   Version 2.0.0 Alpha 6 for the Power PC platform.

NCSAMosaicMac.103.sit.hqx   The current, fully released version of Mosaic for Macintosh.

Whichever version you choose, remember that the numbers in the file names may have changed slightly by the time you read this.

You will need to find and download one of these files to proceed; the file should be downloaded as an ASCII file. To ensure that you are in ASCII mode, type **ascii** at the prompt:

```
ftp> ascii
200 Type set to A.
ftp>
```

The system responds with *Type set to A,* and you are ready to go. Your command to download the file is:

get NCSAMosaicMac.103.sit.hqx

The file now winds up on your service provider's machine, from which you must download it to your own hard disk.

Note that because of the compression and other file preparation, it will be necessary to unpack Mosaic once it is on your hard disk. You will need to unstuff it by using Stuffit Expander or another data compression program like Compact Pro. Simply drag the Mosaic file over to the Stuffit Expander icon and let the program do its work. You will now have the Mosaic folder on your desktop.

Downloading through a SLIP/PPP Connection

If you are downloading Mosaic through an FTP client program like Fetch or NCSA Telnet, the procedure is simpler because of the graphical nature of the interface. It will be necessary to enter the site information and user ID; the latter, as stated, should be **anonymous**. The password should be your full Internet address.

When you have reached the NCSA site, you will be able to move through the file directories to the *Mosaic/Mac* directory. Figure 4.1 shows you how this directory looks from the Fetch program. Other programs may sport a slightly different look, but the graphical nature of the presentation will be the same.

You simply click on the Get File . . . button and the file transfer will take place. Fetch relieves you of the need to set the file type; it handles this process automatically. With Automatic File Opening enabled, the file will be unpacked automatically. Mosaic will now be available on your hard disk.

Mosaic by Mail

Be advised, too, that if you choose, for whatever reason, not to download the software using the NCSA FTP server, you can also obtain Mosaic through the

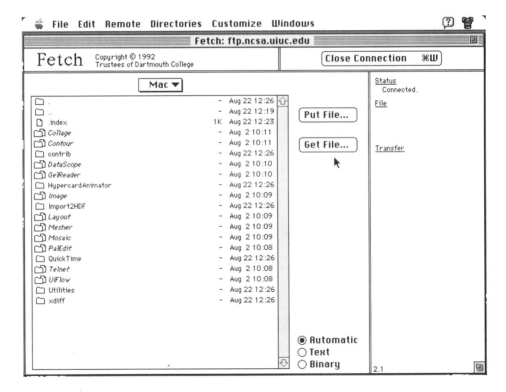

Figure 4.1 Using Fetch to display directory information at NCSA.

U.S. Mail. The NCSA Technical Resources Catalog is available from the following address:

NCSA Orders
152 Computing Applications Building
605 East Springfield Ave.
Champaign, IL 61820-5518
Voice: 217-244-4130
E-mail: **orders@ncsa.uiuc.edu**

Both software and manuals are available for purchase.

Installing and Configuring Mosaic for Macintosh

Installation is a matter of dragging the Mosaic icon onto the appropriate position on your hard disk. If you have used Fetch or a comparable client to download the program, it has already been unpacked; if you've downloaded it through a shell account, you will need to unpack it with Stuffit Expander or a comparable program.

A double click on the Mosaic icon should then allow you to call up the program. What you see on-screen should resemble Figure 4.2. Choose Preferences . . . from the Options menu to call up the screen shown in Figure 4.3.

In the User Name: field, enter your name. Add your e-mail address to the EMail Address: field. Any information you wish to pass along to the developers of the Macintosh version of Mosaic will include this information. You will notice that the Home Page: field already contains an HTTP site. For now, leave this as it is, but later, you will want to return to this menu to change to a new home page. Our goal is to reduce the enormous load on the NCSA server, which is set as the default home page when you first start Mosaic. More on customizing Mosaic in Chapters 7 and 8.

If you now click on Apply, you will be able to save the changes you have just made. But don't leave the Preferences menu just yet.

Configuring Mosaic as Newsreader

You also want to enter information in the Newshost: field of the dialog box. This specifies the Internet address of your local news server. In my case, for example, I would enter the following address for my news server in the field Newshost:

news-server@interpath.net

Your news host may look similar or it may consist of a series of IP numbers. In any case, you can get the information you need to enter here from your local system administrator. You will not need this information if you do not intend to use Mosaic as a newsreader.

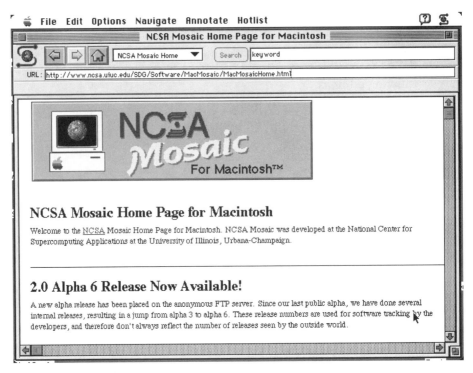

Figure 4.2 The NCSA home page for Macintosh.

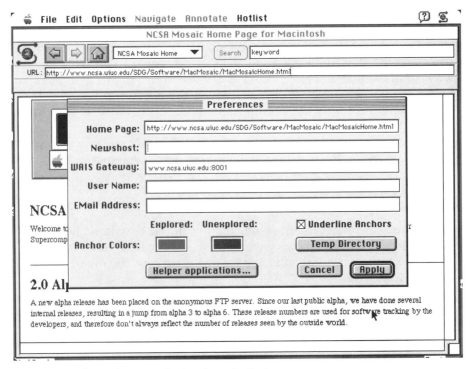

Figure 4.3 The Preferences selection from the Options menu.

Setting Up a WAIS Gateway

Mosaic for Macintosh as currently configured cannot talk directly to a **WAIS** server (only Mosaic for X Windows can do this, although the feature is to be added to the Macintosh version in the future). Instead, the program goes through a gateway that handles the different protocols involved and makes translations between them. This gateway is set up by default as the gateway at NCSA itself. The default is:

www.ncsa.uiuc.edu:8001

which means that the **WAIS** gateway is running on port 8001 at the address listed.

If you want to list a different gateway, you can do so in the space provided. This will not be necessary for U.S. users, but depending on the country you are accessing the Internet from, you may well want to consider changing the gateway to pick one closer to your own location.

The need to use a **WAIS** gateway will eventually be abolished when future versions of Mosaic for Macintosh make it possible for Mosaic to talk directly to **WAIS** servers. The same is true of the Windows version. Currently, the **WWW-WAIS** gateways are frequently inoperative. Users of the X Windows version don't have this problem, because their program is capable of dealing directly with **WAIS** servers.

Changing the Screen Display for PowerBooks

If you are using a PowerBook, it will make sense to change the screen display so that you can maximize your view of each document selected for the smaller screen involved. To do so, you can do two things:

- Hide status messages by going to the Options menu and choosing the Hide Status Messages item.
- Hide the URL field by going to the Options menu and choosing Hide URLs.

Adding to Your Memory Partition

NCSA recommends that users set the Mosaic memory partition to higher levels than the default, which is 2 MB. The thinking here is that documents containing numerous inline images will need more memory than this; too little memory can cause the program to crash. Here is how to change the partition:

1. Ensure that Mosaic is not running.
2. Click on the Mosaic icon in the Finder.
3. From the File menu, choose the Get Info item.
4. In the Get Info window, go to the Preferred Size: field, and change the number to its new value. NCSA recommends 4 to 5 MB.

Setting Up Mosaic Viewers

Like the Microsoft Windows version of Mosaic, Mosaic for Macintosh requires the installation of external viewers to enable you to get the most out of the software. You will also hear these referred to as helper applications. They handle launching the various file types, such as QuickTime movies and audio files. If your use of Mosaic is primarily text-based, you won't need to worry about viewer programs, but if you plan to take advantage of the full multimedia range of Mosaic, viewers become essential.

Here are the basic file types Mosaic for Macintosh can be set up to handle, along with the programs currently recommended for using them:

GIF/JPEG images	JPEGView
TIFF images	GIFConverter
QuickTime movies	SimplePlayer
MPEG movies	Sparkle
AU sound files	SoundMachine
BinHexed files	Stuffit Expander

These are all shareware or freeware programs with the exception of Simple-Player, which is a QuickTime viewer from Apple that comes packaged with QuickTime; it is also available on the NCSA FTP server. The best way to retrieve these programs is through anonymous FTP. If you take a close look at the Mosaic for Macintosh home page, you will see that it incorporates a link called Quick Start. Follow this link and you will learn more about viewers. You can simply click on the viewer you need to download it to your disk. Figure 4.4 shows viewer information from this screen. Or, if you're in the mood to acquire the software through regular FTP, you might try this address:

sumex-aim.stanford.edu

An alternative is:

mac.archive.umich.edu

You will note, if you have any experience using FTP for Macintosh software, that these are major file archives for the computer. Each of the viewer programs comes with the necessary documentation to allow you to install it on your Macintosh. Remember, SimplePlayer is Apple Computer's QuickTime viewer. You can find this copyrighted program on the NCSA anonymous FTP server at **ftp.ncsa.uiuc.edu**.

The Mosaic for Macintosh Screen

Assuming you have installed your viewer programs and set up the few changes needed in the Preferences menu, you are ready to go. As with the Microsoft

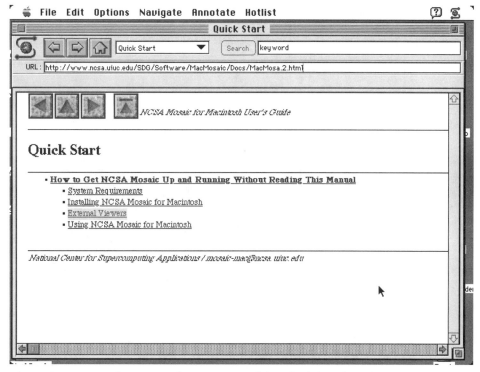

Figure 4.4   You can learn more about viewers and download them from this screen.

Windows version of Mosaic, the basic means of navigation is using the mouse to point at the resource you would like to visit and clicking on that resource. The stylized indicator at the top of the screen tells you that data is being transferred; status messages beneath it explain where you are in the data transfer process. You can use the arrows at the top of the screen to go back to a previous document and then return to the one you were just reading. The small house icon is used to return you automatically to the Home Page set on your Preferences menu.

You will note that the screen display contains normal Macintosh features. As with the Microsoft Windows version of Mosaic, you use the scroll bar at the right of the screen to move up or down within the current document. The horizontal scroll bar moves left or right as necessary for the display of images, while text will generally wrap automatically to fit the screen size. You can alter the window by clicking the zoom box in the top right corner, which enlarges it to a full-screen display. The resize box at the bottom right-hand corner of the screen allows you to change the size of the window as necessary. Figure 4.5 shows an average screen with these features visible.

To find linked data, look for material that is either underlined or set off by a contrasting color on your screen. A nice feature of the Macintosh version is

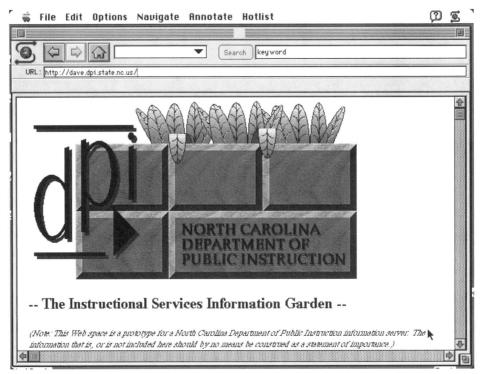

Figure 4.5 A typical Mosaic screen, showing the zoom box in the top right corner and the resize box in the bottom right.

that once you have looked at a particular screen, the links to that document change color, alerting you to the fact that you have already seen the material. Looking twice or more at hyperlinked information is a common aggravation of using the **World Wide Web**, and it's nice to see this ability to make the navigation process more directed. Another way to locate a hyperlink is simply to move the cursor over it; it should turn into a small hand symbol, as shown in Figure 4.6. Look for the symbol at the bottom left of the screen.

The icon bar at the top of the screen is fairly self-explanatory. The title of the window in question is always displayed at the top center of the image; the Mosaic status indicator is the S-shaped symbol containing a small globe to the left that flashes while data is being transferred. Navigation buttons move you from document to document; the one pointing left goes to the previous document, while the one pointing right takes you to the next one. You will see the latter button dimmed unless you have moved back to a previous document first and now have the option to once again move forward. The small house symbol is, as mentioned, a quick way to reach your home page.

By moving to the field next to the house symbol, you can pull down a list of sites you have visited during the current session. To the right of this field is

Figure 4.6   The cursor changes to a small hand symbol as it moves over a hyperlink.

the search button and field, which are used when sending queries for specific text to a searchable index of documents.

Below the search field and at the far left of the screen begins the URL: field, which displays the Uniform Resource Locator of the current document. This field can be turned off using the Options menu if desired. Below the URL field is an area for status messages, which are displayed during document downloads; also, moving the cursor over a hyperlink will cause the URL of that hyperlink to be shown here. Status messages can also be turned off at the Options menu.

Technical Support for Mosaic for Macintosh

NCSA provides technical support for Mosaic through e-mail. You can reach the Macintosh team at this address:

mosaic-mac@ncsa.uiuc.edu

It is easy to use Mosaic itself to send this mail. Under the File menu, choose the Mail Developers option. You will not need to include any information about your system because Mosaic automatically adds the model of your Macintosh, operating system version, and other useful data that will help NCSA's developers isolate your problem. You can also send postal mail to the following address:

Software Development Group
National Center for Supercomputing Applications
605 East Springfield Ave.
Champaign, IL 61820

And don't forget that abundant help exists on-line; in fact, given the rapid state of Mosaic development, the most up-to-date information is invariably to be found in this way. An on-line help manual, a user's guide to HTML and URLs, and a *Frequently Asked Questions* document for Mosaic for Macintosh are all available through NCSA. You can access these links quickly by invoking the Balloon Help menu, then choosing the MacMosaic Documentation option.

Mosaic is not a difficult program to run, either in its Microsoft Windows or Macintosh version. The ideas underlying its operations are logical and consistent across the platforms. Figure 4.7 shows a **Gopher** as seen through Mosaic

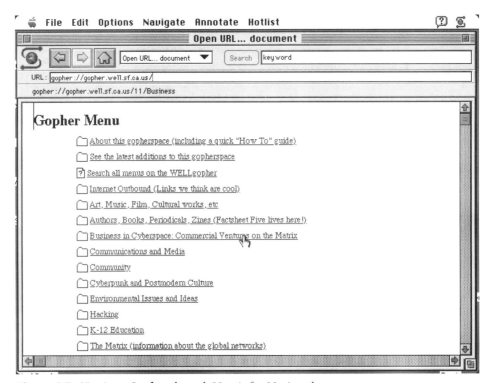

Figure 4.7 Viewing a **Gopher** through Mosaic for Macintosh.

for Macintosh. Notice that the same principles apply here, including using icons to flag files and directories. The third item on the **Gopher** menu list, for example, contains a question mark because it is a searchable index.

Although we will be using the Microsoft Windows version of Mosaic predominantly in this book, translating between the two versions should pose no difficulties. It is more critical to understand what is happening as Mosaic works, and that means understanding the workings of the **World Wide Web**. We turn to that necessary background in Chapter 5.

5

Mosaic and the World Wide Web

In the early days of desktop computing, the first spreadsheet that won over the business audience was VisiCalc. The idea that you could plug numbers into a document and let the computer automatically update all the resulting changes was revolutionary. Businesspeople who had never used computers before began appearing in computer stores asking a single question: "How do I get a VisiCalc?" Not understanding the nature of computers, or their dependence upon software, these potential users didn't know that a computer could become whatever software let it become. If it could be a VisiCalc, it could also be an Electric Pencil, a WordStar, a PowerPoint.

How mutable these machines are, and how reflective of our individual needs, provided we learn how to tailor them correctly. Optimum computer use means understanding the distinction between applications and the processes that drive them. How pointless it would be if we were locked into a particular software program just because we assumed it was the only one our computers could run. And if we fail to understand how our operating systems serve as the intermediary between our computer hardware and our programs, we might easily miss some of the more useful features of those programs. It is hard to tweak and customize a system we don't understand.

Mosaic offers a parallel. Unused to networking, novice users take the same approach to Mosaic that those early office managers took toward VisiCalc. They want Mosaic, because Mosaic is what they have been reading about in the press and seeing demonstrations of at trade shows and on television. And just as VisiCalc users needed to learn about CP/M, the operating system on which their software ran, to optimize their program, so Mosaic users need to understand the **World Wide Web** to get the most out of Mosaic. In this chapter, we look at that necessary relationship. The goal is to make the Mosaic engine more accessible by showing how it works with existing data.

The World Wide Web

Begun as a way of sharing information among physicists, the **World Wide Web** owes its origins to developers at CERN (Conseil Europeen pour la Recherche Nucleair)—the European Particle Physics Laboratory north of Geneva. That the project has moved well beyond this initial audience is made clear by a home page dedicated to explaining the **Web**, wherein it is described as ". . . the universe of network-accessible information, an embodiment of human knowledge." The statement is grandiose but, then, so is the project. Somewhere along the line it became obvious that the amount of information being made available over the Internet was almost ungovernably large, and that the **World Wide Web** offered a workable way of navigating across and through it. The huge growth in **Web** servers in the past two years demonstrates how decisively this idea has caught on.

And well it might. The **Web** is seamless in a way no other network implementation has proven to be. It is, on the one hand, readily crossed and, on the other hand, frustratingly time-consuming. Its vision encompasses all the network tools we are familiar with, from FTP to Telnet to **Gopher** and **archie**. But the **Web** does more than offer a friendly interface to an otherwise inscrutable environment. By providing hypertext and hypermedia links between data, the **Web** also changes our understanding of proximity. The home page we are using at any given time may contain links both to a server down the street and a comparable machine halfway around the world. Our travels between them occur transparently; the object is not to master networking but to obtain information, no matter where it is located.

Timothy Berners-Lee first developed the proposal that would lead to the **World Wide Web** in 1989, although his own work with hypertext as a model had begun as early as 1980. The Oxford graduate wrote the original application on the NeXT computer and developed the communications software that would make the project fly. We can take a look at the many people who have become significant in the fortunes of **WWW** by using Mosaic to retrieve a particular home page. Here is the URL:

```
http://info.cern.ch/hypertext/WWW/People.html
```

You won't find a more talented bunch of programmers and systems designers anywhere. Some are at CERN, but as the **Web** has spread, so have its applications elsewhere on the net, and you will see from examining this page how diverse are its current sources of talent and inspiration.

Background to Hypertext

What exactly is hypertext? Think about how you read a conventional book, like this one. Although it is somewhat different with reference books, you tend to read sequentially. You don't pick up *The Pickwick Papers* and read in random sequence if you hope to understand, much less enjoy, what is going on in the novel. And even with a reference work, you tend to read with a sense of sequential order. Perhaps you skip a chapter that doesn't appeal to you, or that contains information you already understand, but when you do approach a chapter you need, you read in consecutive segments, moving from one section to another, following the structure imposed by the author.

Hypertext provides a different way of approaching such information. Rather than forcing you to read sequentially, it allows you to move between related items of information. This is not a novel concept. In fact, footnotes, bibliographical citations, and indices are all set up in conventional books precisely to allow you to move from one reference to another, following your own information needs. Think of hypertext, then, as a way of making this transition between data points simpler. Rather than turning pages or looking up chapter headings, you point to an item with your mouse and click on it. Finding the embedded information is easy; the mouse click brings it across the network to you.

An Example of Hypertext

Text can be turned into hypertext by setting up links to a given word or phrase and other information. Here, for example, is a passage from Shakespeare's *Othello,* wherein Othello discusses the effects of jealousy with Iago. Let's look at the text and consider what we could do with it if we moved it out of its printed book format and into the hypertext environment. I am going to set up hypertext links that will be shown by underlining; read on for the meaning of the links. We can click on a link to see the underlying information.

```
Oth. Why? why is this?
Think st thou I ld make a life of jealousy?
To follow still the changes of the moon
With fresh suspicions? No! to be once in doubt
is [once] to be resolved. Exchange me for a goat,
When I shall turn the business of my soul
To such exsufflicate and [blown] surmises,
Matching thy inference.  Tis not to make me jealious
To say my wife is fair, feeds well, loves company,
Is free of speech, sings, plays, and dances [well];
Where virtue is, these are more virtuous.
Nor from mine own weak merits will I draw
The smallest fear or doubt of her revolt,
For she had eyes, and chose me. No, Iago,
```

```
I ll see before I doubt; when I doubt, prove;
And on the proof, there is no more but this
Away at once with love or jealousy!¹
```

The text seems straightforward enough; Othello is arguing that he is not, in fact, a jealous man (at this point, Iago has been feeding him a steady diet of questionable observations about Desdemona, his wife, in hopes of enraging him). But the text, being Elizabethan English, could use some support; modern readers will find terms they don't understand. We can provide that support with hypertext.

Our initial italic emphasis falls upon the first word, Oth.—an abbreviation for Othello. Here we might provide the act, scene, and line information for the passage. We can then click on the link to pop up a window with the information inside. We could also include basic plot information in that link, synopsizing the tale of Desdemona's wedding to the Moor Othello, a general in service to the state of Venice, and telling how the marriage was manipulated and destroyed by a jealous soldier, Iago.

Look at line 5. There the word once is not only underlined, but is also in brackets. The underlining, again alerting us to the presence of a hypertext link, points up the nearness of further information. Here the link might be to a quote from the introductory remarks by G. Blakemore Evans, the editor of this edition of Shakespeare, about how he chose to mark particular textual questions in the edition. Clicking our mouse, then, on [once], we might call up the following passage from his preface:

```
When the copy text, however, resisted all reasonable
attempts to make sense of it, readings from another early
printed text or from other editions have, of course, been
admitted, but in all such cases the emendation has been
placed in square brackets to warn the reader that the text
at this point is open to question. ²
```

The word "once," then, is bracketed in this edition because there is some question as to its validity; its usage is inferred rather than proven. Of course, we can capture this information through a conventional footnote; the information we gain is not made greater by hypertext, but it is made easier to locate, since we don't have to page through a paper edition to track down footnotes at the ends of chapters.

With a hypertext editor, we can create links wherever we choose. When we run into an awkward word like "exsufflicate," we can create a hypertext link to its meaning, which seems to be "blown-up" or "inflated," although literary scholars aren't completely sure on the point. When we come to the name "Iago," we can open up an information link that would explain to someone who hadn't read *Othello* who Iago was. The reader then learns that this is a soldier who has been bypassed for promotion by Othello in favor of young Cassio. And that the plot of the play hinges on his revenge, as he creates the impression that Desdemona is involved romantically with Cassio, which causes Othello to strangle her in her bed.

The choice of links is ours. Notice, too, that we are not limited to a single set of links. Should we choose to open a link explaining who Iago is, we could also embed links within that explanation to further information, providing background about Iago, or about his literary role as an emblem for jealousy and how critics see him in our time, and so on. Each set of links could lead us further and further into our subject, allowing for a homing in of interests that is more difficult with conventional texts.

Starting with a single passage from *Othello*, we could theoretically advance into a presentation of opposing critical views, or an explication of life in Venice during the era of the play, or perhaps a page showing literary sources that Shakespeare used in his work. There is no limit on how deep we could go with the appropriate links, other than the patience of the people who produce them.

Hypertext links must be carefully created. Any time we are examining a hypertext document, we are looking at information the way the editor of that document wants us to see it. Although hypertext gives us the initial impression of being a wide-open exploration of data, one we can tailor specifically for our own use, it is in fact just as arbitrary as any traditional text, in that the choice of links has been managed by an editor using hypertext tools. The process of building hypertext documents, arduous and time-consuming, is one that will be eased by the development of further tools to automate the process, but the human choices behind the links will always determine how useful a particular hypertext document will be.

Now take a look at straight hypertext as found on the **World Wide Web** and viewed through Mosaic. In Figure 5.1, we are looking at a home page called Books On-line, Listed by Author. Each of the books is underlined and, if you were using a color monitor, each would also appear in blue; both forms of marking indicate the presence of a hyperlink. Clicking on *Beowulf* yields the document seen in Figure 5.2.

This is straight hypertext, meaning we are looking at single links to deeper information. The *Beowulf* text itself contains no further links. The only navigation possible at this point is to go back to the initial on-line books page, from which we can choose another book. Hypertext can serve as an intelligent table of contents that takes us directly to where we need to go and back again.

The Onset of Hypermedia

Hypertext, originally billed as a new way of reading books and other forms of text, will probably always have a useful function in information navigation. But the big news of the past two years, corresponding to the growth of the **World Wide Web** during that period, is the emergence of *hypermedia*. By hypermedia, I refer to linked data that is not just textual in nature. In the Shakespeare example, it would be possible to create a hypermedia environment in which, with a

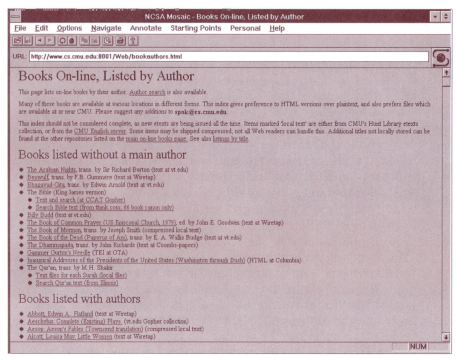

Figure 5.1 A simple hypertext page, with links to various on-line books.

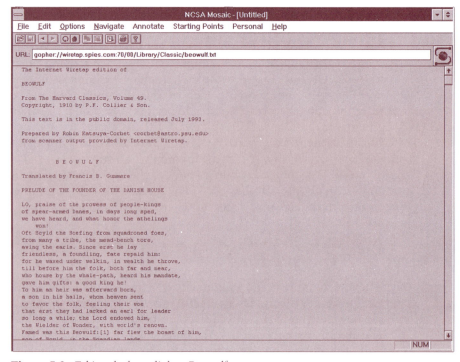

Figure 5.2 Taking the hyperlink to *Beowulf.*

mouse click on the appropriate link, we could take a visual tour of the Venice of Othello's time to help clarify the issues of the play and bring its cultural dimensions into perspective. Perhaps further links could reveal works of Venetian art, while others might lead to snippets of appropriate music.

That this hypermedia model has taken off is confirmed by other events in the computer world. Look at the prevalence of CD-ROM titles, which, in the past year, have begun to live up to the initial sales expectations of their proponents. An application like Microsoft Corporation's Encarta is a multimedia encyclopedia. The multimedia aspect derives from Encarta's ability to display text as well as photographs, moving pictures, sounds, and animation. But the essential navigation tool made available in such an application is hypermedia. An article on Mauritius, for example, provides textual information about the island's history and geography. But a small speaker symbol alerts you to the fact that the story contains audio—you can hear the name "Mauritius" pronounced—while other symbols tell you it's possible to view its flag or listen to its national anthem. All of these actions take place as a result of hypertextual linkages. Click on the relevant symbol and the hypermedia link launches new information.

Mosaic, likewise, is a hypermedia tool. As we saw in Chapter 1, numerous applications, from O'Reilly & Associates *Global Network Navigator* to museum exhibitions like the Library of Congress Vatican Library display, use hypermedia links to make it possible to view information in a new way. The only drawback to hypermedia is that, over a SLIP/PPP link, which most upgrading dial-up users will be using, the downloading of complicated imagery can take time. But we will also learn in Chapter 8 that there are ways of speeding up Mosaic, allowing us the best of both worlds. And, as viewer software and the links between Mosaic and these programs become more sophisticated, the process of acquiring remote data will offer greater rewards.

Browsing Tools with the World Wide Web

Given this powerful hypermedia infrastructure, we need to find effective ways to tap it. We are looking for *client* programs that serve the same function with the **Web** that they do with any other Internet tools. A good client program is one that makes the underlying Internet application easy to use while retaining its power. Client programs that have been developed for the **World Wide Web** are known as *browsers*. Browsers exist for virtually all computer platforms, from X Windows UNIX systems to Amigas, from Macintoshes to the NeXT computer and, of course, the ubiquitous IBM-compatible PC running DOS and Microsoft Windows.

Let's pause for a moment on the word "browser." The term makes sense, because the **Web** allows us to browse through broad libraries of information; an analogy might be to my journeys to used bookstores (a favorite haunt), where I wander up and down the shelves looking for anything that might catch my eye. This process is not, strictly speaking, searching. A search tool is one that allows us to target information and specify exactly what we want; a search finds our goal with pinpoint accuracy. There are client programs on the Internet that do precisely this (or, at least, make some attempt to do so). These are tools like **archie** or **Veronica** and, to a certain extent, **WAIS**. Explain what we need and the software searches.

The Nature of Browsing

The **Web** is not a search tool but a browsing engine. Indeed, one of its frustrations is this very fact. Suppose I am looking for information about a work of Chinese literature called *The Art of War* by Sun Tzu. The book has been widely reprinted and used as a business text by aggressive managers hoping to draw Oriental philosophy into their own business practices. With the **Web** as diverse as it has become recently, it is possible that some information about this work exists, but how would I find it? Until recently, there was no way to start at the top and simply announce to the **Web**: Find *The Art of War*. Instead, I would have to browse, starting, perhaps, at a site like CERN, where a subject catalog can guide me through what is available on the **Web**. I would then progressively refine my choices until I found just what I was looking for, in the process perhaps devoting my entire morning to the job.

And indeed, I would eventually run across the relevant address:

URL: http://biomed.nus.sg/CM/cweb/sunzi/xx/sunzi.xx.html

Having this address, I could then go directly to the site. But the process that uncovered the address was a lengthy one, involving browsing rather than searching.

All this is beginning to change, incidentally, with the appearance of new search mechanisms applicable to the **Web** that we'll discuss in Chapter 9. But it should explain why the early term for **Web** client programs was "browser," and why they are still referred to as such today. Mosaic, perhaps the ultimate **Web** browser, works with information available through the **World Wide Web** infrastructure, repackaging that information to add a remarkable graphic dimension that most other browsers lack.

The www Browser

Figure 5.3, for example, shows us a **Web** page devoted to explaining how the **Web** works. Here we are looking at the site through a browser program called **www**, which is character-based and cannot display graphics. It is optimized to run over a VT-100 terminal-based link, as would be normal with a standard dial-up connection. Notice that every link is displayed with boxed numbers following the text, rather than Mosaic's underlining and color changes. We enter the number, followed by the Return key, to move to that link.

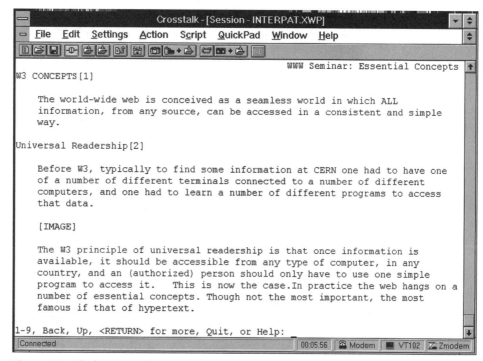

Figure 5.3 The basic **www** browser shows links as numbers that you must enter to move to the site.

Make no mistake about it, **www** is a full-featured browser, one that allows us to access numerous features of the net. But as we can see, it does require that we enter a number of commands to make it work. Usefully, major commands are laid out at the bottom of the screen, while others are provided through the help system. We are a long way from the simplicity of the point-and-shoot, mouse-driven environment with **www**. But the information we are dealing with through the **World Wide Web** remains essentially the same. **www** sits atop the **Web** and exploits its resources.

The lynx Browser

Now let's take a quick look at the **lynx** browser, which is another approach to presenting **World Wide Web** information without embedded graphics or other such niceties. If we examine Figure 5.4, we see the same document that we just looked at through the **www** browser now displayed by **lynx**. The content of the text has not changed. What has changed is the appearance of the text. Although we can't see it in black and white, a color image would reveal that certain areas of the text were highlighted in blue, while the rest of the text is black. The presence of the blue text reveals hypertext links in the document.

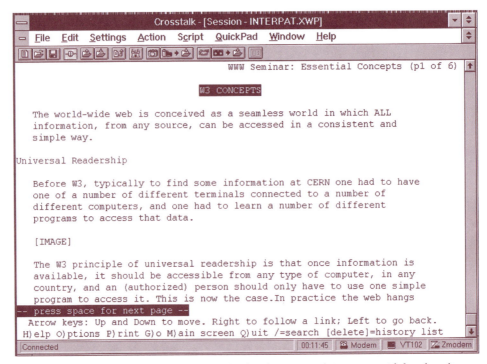

Figure 5.4 **lynx** gives a cleaner on-screen display than **www**, doing away with bracketed numbers to indicate hyperlinks.

Inset images are set off with the bracketed word [IMAGE]. And along the bottom of the screen, as with the **www** browser, we have available a series of the major commands.

If we were to work for long with **lynx**, we would find it a powerful browser for anyone using VT-100 emulation in connecting to the Internet. But as with **www**, we are only seeing part of the story. We miss out on the immediately available graphical niceties, including both images and text formatting, that make using Mosaic such a pleasure. The flip side of this is that both **www** and **lynx** are fast. Moving between pages in either of their environments is a relatively speedy process, because we don't have to wait for the software to process lengthy image or sound files.

The Mosaic Advantage

The contrast between Mosaic and these character-based browsers could not be more apparent. In Figure 5.5, we examine once again the page in question, a seminar about the **World Wide Web** prepared at CERN. Again, we find the same text, because we are accessing the same information source. But this

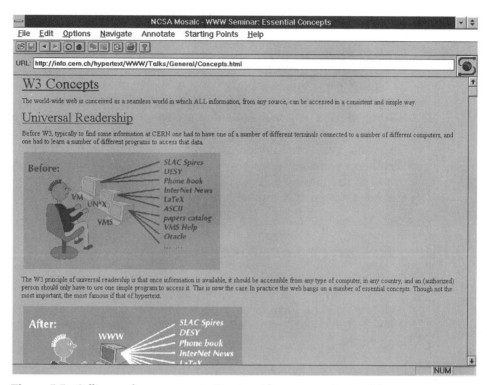

Figure 5.5   Calling up the same page in Mosaic, with accompanying graphics.

time, we note that, with Mosaic's help, we can see much more. The document, in fact, turns out to be an illustrated guide to the **World Wide Web**. Its imagery supports its text in a way that is impossible with either the **www** or **lynx** browsers. But, again because of that imagery, we do note more of a lag time in calling up the page; at least, we do if we are using a SLIP/PPP connection over the telephone lines, rather than a high-speed direct network connection.

Rich as it is, Mosaic is thus revealed as one in a series of browser programs. It would be a mistake to see it as a stand-alone application. Like any network tool, it is a client program that works with other computers to make information resources available in a distributed environment. By distributed, I simply mean that the resources it uses are part of a network that is worldwide in scope; we can use a browser to tap into any of them, no matter how near or far. The people behind other graphical **World Wide Web** browsers wouldn't agree that Mosaic is the Internet interface of the future, pointing out that their tools, like **Cello** or **MacWeb**, possess virtues of their own. But it is clear that out of the entire universe of browsing engines, Mosaic has developed a momentum all its own.

World Wide Web Terminology

Perhaps the most intimidating of the Internet's numerous demands on the newcomer is the need to master its terminology. We computer people tend to speak in acronyms and various forms of shorthand when referring to resources, sometimes forgetting how mystifying these can seem to the novice. Particularly baffling are the long addresses that are used to specify resources in the **World Wide Web** environment. It's time now to explain these, and also to run through terms you'll likely encounter as you prowl through this information system. The **Web** has a series of terms all its own. You needn't become an expert in any of these to use Mosaic, but understanding what they mean will give you a conceptual background that can help in your travels.

Uniform Resource Locators

Our first acronym is URL, or Uniform Resource Locator. A URL can be used to describe the location of a resource anywhere on the network. These lengthy addresses can be forbidding indeed. The document we examined previously through the **www**, **lynx**, and Mosaic browsers, for example, boasts the following address:

```
http://info.cern.ch/hypertext/WWW/Talks/General/Concepts.html
```

That's quite a handful. But if URLs can be lengthy and intimidating, the concept behind them is simplicity itself.

Ponder for a moment what it is that the **World Wide Web** sets out to do. The developers speak in terms of universally available information, accessible to anyone with an Internet connection. But the problem behind that notion is that the Internet is not made up of one single set of computer tools. Anyone who hopes to master it will have to learn how to transfer files with FTP, to work with remote computers using Telnet, to search for information with **WAIS**—in short, the Internet's very range is offset by its complexity. The **World Wide Web**, hoping to connect all of this, must find some way to relate information from one source to information from another. The first need is a universally accepted way of specifying where something is.

That something might exist in any number of formats. After all, a good browser can read USENET newsgroups (Mosaic can do this). It can examine **Gopher**. It can allow you to make a Telnet connection, and retrieve a file. Thus, we want to be able to specify any kind of object on the Internet.

To do this, we set up a URL that tells us right away what kind of resource we are considering. This information is always presented *before* an initial colon; it tells us the access method we must use to reach the resource. The part of the URL *after* the colon indicates more precise information about the location, including the computer address and directory information at the site.

Let's take another look at the previous URL:

```
http://info.cern.ch/hypertext/WWW/Talks/General/Concepts.html
```

http tells us we are dealing with a document in hypertext format (more on the "http" designation in a moment). The information following the colon and two slashes is the machine name. You may recognize this one as the home of the **World Wide Web** in Switzerland: **info.cern.ch**. Following this machine name, we are given directory information. The directory, in typical UNIX fashion, is shown through a series of subdirectories, starting with *hypertext* and branching to another subdirectory called *Talks*, and so on.

The default port for http, incidentally, is 80. In most cases, a URL for an http resource will not contain port information, as this default will be assumed. But if you do see a site with a port listed, be sure to enter that information when you open the URL. Such a site, for example, would look like this:

```
http://www.dickens.com:1234/pub/novels/pickwick.html
```

In the example (a fictitious site, by the way), the numbers following the address tell us that this document is to be found on port 1234 at this site.

So far, so good; hypertext documents are readily spotted through the http designation. But what about a Telnet site, or a **Gopher**? As with any URL, look to the left of the initial colon to find out what kind of resource you are dealing with. Here are common file types as shown through URLs; I illustrate each file type with an example:

Gopher
gopher://world.std.com/
Here, we are specifying a **Gopher** site at a specific address. No further information is needed to reach this **Gopher**, unless the system operates on a nonstandard port, which isn't likely to be the case (almost all **Gopher** servers are found on port 70). But if you do run into a **Gopher** with a number following the address, be sure to specify it when you type in the URL. It will appear in the following format:

gopher://*address:port***/**

Thus, you might find a **Gopher** URL that looked like this:

gopher://cobb.detroit.com:6000/

Just don't forget to add the port number if you do find one.

Files at FTP Sites
file://oak.oakland.edu/pub/msdos/windows3/winzip5b.zip
Again, note the term before the colon. In this case, it is a file available at an anonymous FTP site. The site is specified: **oak.oakland.edu**, as is the complete directory structure you need to know to find the file.

We could also get to an FTP resource by using "ftp" instead of "file" at the beginning of the URL. Consider this URL:

ftp://ftp.interpath.net/pub/

Here, we are given the FTP address, along with directory information, but we are not homing in on a specific file. We wind up in the *pub* directory. We'll see a bit later how Mosaic handles FTP directory displays.

USENET News
news:alt.internet.services
This is a URL pointing at a specific USENET newsgroup. Note that we leave out the two slashes in such URLs. For the Microsoft Windows version of Mosaic, the news server you read from can be specified in the **mosaic.ini** file, as we saw when we set up this file for initial configuration in Chapter 3. The Macintosh version allows you to name this server in your Preferences screen.

Telnet
telnet://locis.loc.gov/
A Telnet site is defined by using the term *telnet* before the colon. In this case, we are looking at the Telnet address of the Library of Congress. If a port specification is necessary, it appears after the address in this format:

telnet://*address:port*/

Now that we've seen the various forms of URLs, it becomes obvious that this methodology is preferable, despite its frequently awkward length, to other forms of pointing strategies. If I were to construct a directory of Internet resources without URLs, I would be forced in each case to adopt a format particular to the access method. Thus I might say "Use anonymous FTP to access **wuarchive.wustl.edu**. The directory is */mirrors/msdos/compression*. The file name is **comp432.zip**." For Telnet, I might say, "Use Telnet to contact **info. cern.ch**." In each case, I am using more verbiage than necessary to describe the resource.

With URLs, I can show the path to any kind of resource in a standardized format. This is useful for cataloguers, and for browsing programs, too. If you know the URL, you can specify it through a variety of means. For example, **www** allows you to enter a URL after the **g** command; this takes you directly to it. With Mosaic, you can enter a URL by pulling down the File menu and typing in the information. And there are a number of other ways you can keep that URL information handy, including adding it to your Mosaic menus as you customize the program for your own use.

But using URLs involves more than addresses. By selecting a hyperlink to a specific URL, you are sending a request to the remote server to open that URL. If, for example, you were to open a URL that specified a GIF file, Mosaic not only would go to that URL, but would also display the picture for you. The same is true of audio files; specify a URL pointing to an audio file and Mosaic plays the file once it makes the necessary network transaction. This effectively means that a good **World Wide Web** browser is a diversified client program, one that can be considered an all-purpose interface. It is a client for FTP, for Telnet, and for the other services we have mentioned. What Mosaic lacks in this regard is an electronic mail function and a USENET newsreader with sufficient capability. Future releases of the program will doubtless add such features.

The Meaning of HTTP

The mysterious HTTP designation stands for hypertext transport protocol, which is the method the **World Wide Web** uses to move information. Specifically, HTTP allows the browser and the remote information server to work together. The process works like this:

- With the help of a browser like Mosaic, the user clicks on a hypermedia link to request information.
- The client uses the address specified in the URL to connect to the **World Wide Web** server it refers to; the client asks the server to send that document.
- The server sends the information and embedded data (including sound, graphics, etc.) to the client.
- It is now up to the client program to reproduce the information on-screen in whatever manner it can. This accounts for the different screen displays between the various kinds of client programs we have examined. It also underlines the importance of a good client program.

Think of the **World Wide Web** as the sum total of these interchanges occurring at every moment. For the **Web** to function, all clients and server computers have to be able to deal with the HTTP protocols to keep this traffic in hypermedia documents going. You will sometimes see **Web** servers referred to as HTTP servers for this reason.

HTML: The Necessary Language

HTML stands for HyperText Markup Language. HTML is the language used in the **World Wide Web** for creating documents. You may also run into something called SGML, or Standard Generalized Markup Language. HTML is closely related to SGML, and both share a basic concept: that content and formatting for any document can be separated. We've already seen a representation of this concept, when we looked at the different **Web** browsers. Each presents the same information, but in differing formats, and to a greater or lesser degree of thoroughness (thus, we see an actual image on the Mosaic screen, but do not when using **www** or **lynx**).

The idea that we can separate formatting and content is powerful when placed in the context of powerful computing resources. It allows a creative designer or page formatter to lay out a document with the same attention to visual detail that would be used in a printshop, or by a desktop publisher using conventional DTP software. What's more, HTML has become a useful tool because it is easy to use. Each HTML file is nothing more than an ASCII file (editable in any text editor), with embedded formatting codes specifying what should be shown on the screen. Not only is formatting laid out in such a document, but the HTML file also specifies the location of the hyperlinks that connect resources across the **Web** to a particular **Web** page.

Let's take a look at an actual HTML file. In Figure 5.6, we're looking at a Mosaic page for The Royal Society of New Zealand, which represents the interests of those involved in scientific research in that country. We can see that there are numerous links to further information, along with icons to click on for more details, and, at the top, an image of the Society's seal.

Now let's examine the same file from the standpoint of the HTML document that exists beneath it. Here is a section of the file:

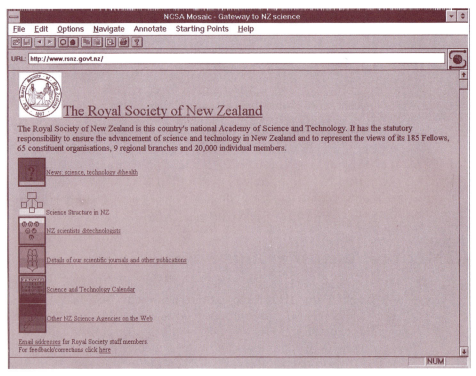

Figure 5.6 An actual HTML file illustrating the home page for the Royal Society of New Zealand.

```
<HTML>

<TITLE>Gateway to NZ science</TITLE>

<H1><IMG align=bottom src="rsnz_trans.gif">

<A HREF="rsnz.html">The Royal Society of New Zealand</A></H1>

<H5>The Royal Society of New Zealand is this country s national Academy of
Science and Technology. It has the statutory responsibility to ensure the
advancement of science and technology in New Zealand and to represent the
views of its 185 Fellows, 65 constituent organisations, 9 regional branches
and 20,000 individual members.</H5>

<A HREF="/cgi-bin/news"><IMG ALIGN=MIDDLE SRC="1.gif"> News: science, tech-
nology &amp health</A><BR>
<!A HREF="/structure/index.html"><IMG ALIGN=MIDDLE SRC="2.gif"> Science
Structure in NZ<!/A><BR>
<A HREF="/membership/index.html"><IMG ALIGN=MIDDLE SRC="3.gif"> NZ scien-
tists &amp technologists</A><BR>
<A HREF="/sir/index.html"><IMG ALIGN=MIDDLE SRC="4.gif"> Details of our sci-
entific journals and other publications</A><BR>
<A HREF="/events/index.html"><IMG ALIGN=MIDDLE SRC="5.gif"> Science and
Technology Calendar</A><BR>
<A HREF="/other/index.html"><IMG ALIGN=MIDDLE SRC="6.gif"> Other NZ Science
Agencies on the Web</A><BR>
<P>

<A HREF="email.html">Email addresses</A> for Royal Society staff
members.<BR>
For feedback/corrections click <A HREF="/membership/database/input_feed-
back.html">here</A>
<HR>

<ADDRESS>
For further information about this server, contact
webmaster@rsnz.govt.nz
</ADDRESS>
</HTML>
```

If we compare the HTML document with the image of the screen shown in Figure 5.6, we realize an essential fact about the **World Wide Web** and, in consequence, about Mosaic: All the graphical niceties of this environment are provided through these ASCII files in HTML format. It is up to the browser at the end of the connection to render HTML into whatever form it can best deliver. The success of Mosaic is largely due to its ability to manage this process to the greatest effect, and with the most user support.

Note the top of the HTML section. Each section of the on-screen document is carefully laid out. Text is specified, and the method of presenting that text. The location and identity of the Society's seal are presented; we see that it is a file called **rsnz_trans.gif**. Each link to further information, which appears either with a color change or with underlining depending upon our monitors, is likewise specified. Any HTML file is given the suffix .html; the one in question is **index.html**. Here is its URL:

```
http://icair.iac.org.nz/news/index.html
```

We could go directly to this document by entering it into Mosaic as a URL. And we know enough about URLs at this point to recognize that the http designation marks this one as a document in hypertext format. Think of the **Web** as being made up of a vast assortment of such documents which point to other documents and various sources of data.

We now begin to see how people build **World Wide Web** sites. In each case, someone has gone to work with an editor to create an HTML file. The files look complicated, but with a little experience, we can master HTML fairly easily (and in a later chapter, we will build a home page using basic HTML to prove this point). It is really only a matter of deciding how we want a page to look and then inserting the proper codes to make the process happen. HTML is a relatively new language, but tools for making the editing task easier have already begun to appear. With conversion software, an editor can take an already created document and translate it into HTML.

The convenience provided will be enormous. Imagine creating a document with Microsoft Word and simply feeding it through a converter to produce workable HTML. Everything will be done except for the hyperlinks, which will have to be added by the document designer (after all, no conversion program can read our minds; these hyperlink choices will continue to be the decisions of an editor sitting in front of a machine). In the works is an advanced form of HTML called HTML+, which will be able to support more complex formats than HTML can currently handle. Interactive forms are one area where we should expect to see much growth, as HTML+ makes it possible for designers to create on-line forms for use in commercial and other organizational settings. HTML+, due to arrive in late 1994, will also make it possible to send e-mail by clicking on an e-mail address from within a document; an e-mail editor will open to allow us to compose our message, and a click will send it.

In addition to converting documents from one format directly into HTML, of course, it is still possible to create HTML documents from scratch using any text editor. Editors designed specifically for HTML are also becoming available; the Sun SPARCstation, for example, has one called HotMetal, while HTML Edit for Macintosh performs the same functions for the Mac, and HTML Assistant is available for Microsoft Windows. HTML editors for the

NeXT computer are perhaps the most advanced of all. It will be fascinating to watch this area of software develop as the demand for **World Wide Web** servers grows; already, commercial interest in creating **Web** sites has generated a demand for consultants who are able to create and maintain HTML documentation.

To learn more about HTML, there are two URLs that may prove of interest. The first leads to a document called *A Beginner's Guide to HTML*, which is available at the following address:

```
http://www.ncsa.uiuc.edu/demoweb/html-primer.html
```

Two other good documents are *How to Write HTML Files* and *Introduction to HTML*. The URLs are, respectively:

```
http://www.ucc.ie/info/net/htmldoc.html
```

and

```
http://melmac.harris-atd.com/about_html.html
```

A look at either or both of these files should provide you with plenty of background. And as you've doubtless come to realize, the best way to keep up with this rapidly growing field is through an active presence on the net.

 Tip: If you find a particularly interesting document and want to know how it was produced through HTML, the quickest way to do so is to pull down the File menu and click on the Document Source . . . menu item. This will pop up a window showing you the HTML code behind the screen. Figure 5.7 shows an example.

Keeping Up with World Wide Web Developments

We can now go back to the original point about the **Web** itself. This tool for connecting computer resources can work with almost any kind of tool available on the Internet. A good browser like Mosaic, then, can become an all-purpose interface, provided we recognize that any browser is going to be stronger in some areas than in others. At present, the **Web** allows us to reach any of the following sources:

- **finger** servers, for locating information about Internet users and retrieving various forms of data.
- **WAIS** databases, for full-text searching capability.
- UNIX manual pages.

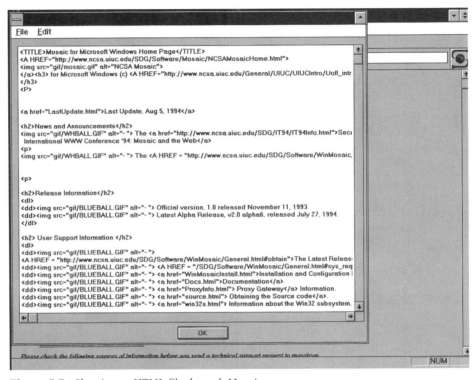

Figure 5.7 Showing an HTML file through Mosaic.

- **HYTELNET**, a browser developed by Peter Scott at the University of Saskatchewan.
- USENET newsgroups.
- **Gopher** servers, the browsing engine created at the University of Minnesota.
- **Veronica**, a search engine for **Gopher**.
- **X.500**, **CSO**, and **WHOIS** services, for locating individuals or organizations.
- **archie**, for finding files.
- FTP, for transferring files between remote computers and your own.
- Telnet, for manipulating remote computers, as in database retrieval and other chores.
- And, of course, anything available in HTML format.

The Mosaic browser opens all these resources up to us in a format that is easy to use and visually pleasing. Future versions of Mosaic, including those being developed commercially by various companies, will firm up existing links to these resources and add others. To keep up with **Web** news about such developments, here are some prime sources.

USENET Information Sources

comp.infosystems.announce	General announcements from the net, often containing **Web** news.
comp.infosystems.www.users	Discussions of client software and how to use it, with numerous new user questions and bug reports.
comp.infosystems.www.providers	Discusses server design, security issues, HTML page layout, and bug reports.
comp.infosystems.www.misc	Discusses any **Web** topics not covered by the above.
alt.hypertext	Devoted to hypertext in all its forms.

Mailing Lists about the Web

You may also want to consider several mailing lists related to the **Web**; these come directly to your mailbox. Here are some good ones, all located at CERN. To subscribe, send e-mail to this address:

listserv@info.cern.ch

In your message, write the following line:

subscribe *list_name your_name*

In other words, to subscribe to the first of the following lists, I would send mail with this message:

subscribe www-announce paul gilster

www.announce	News about software and data sources.
www-html	For technical discussions about HTML.
www-talk	For developers only; it contains technical talk about **Web** software.

Another list you will want to consider is the new MOSAIC-L list. You can subscribe to this list for users and developers by sending mail to this address:

listserv@uicvm.bitnet

or

listserv@uicvm.uic.edu

In the first line of the message (not in the subject) enter the following:

subscribe mosaic-1 *your_name*

HTTP Sites

You can tap CERN again to keep up with **Web** information, this time through a Web document. The URL is:

```
http://info.cern.ch/hypertext/WWW/TheProject.html
```

This is an excellent source for **Web** materials, with numerous links to background information. Using it, you will quickly find a news page:

```
http://info.cern.ch/hypertext/WWW/News/
```

with updates on CERN activity and on **World Wide Web** around the globe.

Chapter Five Notes

1. Othello, III.iii, ll. 177–192. The text is drawn from *The Riverside Shakespeare* (G. Blakemore Evans, textual editor). Boston: Houghton Mifflin Co. 1974.

2. From G. Blakemore Evans's prefatory material to *The Riverside Shakespeare*, an essay titled "Shakespeare's Text" (p. 39).

6

Making Mosaic's Tools Work

At the heart of the Internet are three major applications; ironically, the third of them was an afterthought. It was obvious from the beginning that there had to be some way to transfer files between computers; this was achieved using FTP, or File Transfer Protocol. Just as obvious was that it should be possible for a remote researcher to take the controls of a computer and tap its resources, such as databases or other information manipulation tools, no matter how far apart the two computers were. And that, thought researchers in the early 1970s as they built ARPANET, ought to about do it.

ARPANET was the Internet's precursor, designed as an experimental platform to see whether information could be sent back and forth in the form of data packets. The system would allow for redundancy, because any data packet might take any number of conceivable routes to get to its destination. Defense Department analysts liked that; it implied that in the event of a catastrophe like nuclear war, the nation's computers would still be able to talk to each other even if a sizable chunk of their communications infrastructure were destroyed. Later, we came to see this redundancy as a superb means of moving data safely. If one link goes down, who cares? The data travels by another.

The third Internet protocol was electronic mail, and it was something of a surprise to early designers. It had never occurred to them that people might want to start sending messages back and forth across this network. But the steady growth of messaging soon made it clear that e-mail would be a prime mover for researchers, who found all the benefits of e-mail that we take for granted today—it's quick, it's asynchronous (the person doesn't have to be on the other end to receive your message, which is kept in a mailbox until it can be read), and it's easy to fit into a work schedule that already includes plenty of computer time.

Mosaic is good at handling two out of the three protocols. It is electronic mail that is the trouble spot. A primitive e-mail feature already exists inside Mosaic, and it is used to return comments to developers at NCSA so they can keep records of bug reports and attempt to fix them. We can assume that future versions of Mosaic will come with vastly expanded mail capabilities, and certainly this is one area that commercial Mosaics, licensed from NCSA, will take as their point of departure. For now, as you will see, Mosaic presents little to charm the heavy e-mail user. But wait until you see what it can do with FTP and Telnet!

File Transfer Protocol through Mosaic

While e-mail is generally how we begin to use the Internet (it's relatively simple, and provides dramatic proof of our new-found connectivity), FTP is what takes us on our first journeys. The thrill of FTP is that it lets us log on to remote computers to retrieve files. Millions of computers throughout the world contain information, and a certain subset of these, thousands of them, make all or part of their information available to the general public. We can log on to such machines using any FTP client program and examine the holdings there. When we want to retrieve something, we only have to specify what it is, and we are soon receiving the file. It could be a document, a program, an image, or even a sound or movie file.

Anonymous FTP Illustrated

When a system administrator places computer resources into a public area on a server computer, the materials made available can be reached by following a certain convention. We want to log on to the server with the user name **anonymous**. Entering this as our user name tells the server computer that we are trying to access the publicly available areas of the server's holdings. We are then asked for a password. The password we enter should simply be our e-mail address. Using a UNIX shell account, the procedure is relatively familiar. It looks like the following:

```
% ftp oak.oakland.edu
Connected to oak.oakland.edu.
220 oak.oakland.edu FTP server (Version wu-2.4(1) Fri Jul 8 19:16:51 EDT 1994)
ready.
Name (oak.oakland.edu:gilster): anonymous
331 Guest login ok, send your complete e-mail address as password.
Password:
230-
230-                              Welcome to
230-                    THE OAK SOFTWARE REPOSITORY
230-          A service of Oakland University, Rochester Michigan
230-
```

```
230-  If you have trouble using OAK with your ftp client, please try using
230-  a dash (-) as the first character of your password this will turn
230-  off the continuation messages that may be confusing your ftp client.
230-  OAK is a Unix machine, and filenames are case sensitive.
230-
230-  Access is allowed at any time. If you have any unusual problems,
230-  please report them via electronic mail to admin@Vela.ACS.Oakland.Edu
230-
230-  You are user #98 out of 400 maximum users.
230-  The current local time is Mon Aug 8 08:20:03 1994.
230-
230-  Hint: You can log into OAK using the name "ftp" instead of "anonymous"
230-        to reduce typographical errors while logging in.
230-
230-Please read the file README
230-  it was last modified on Tue Apr 26 10:56:15 1994 - 104 days ago
230 Guest login ok, access restrictions apply.
ftp> cd pub
250 CWD command successful.
ftp>
```

Notice that, as with any shell account, we are forced to do the hard work ourselves; that is, we must enter command information to tell the system what to do. You can see that I have entered **anonymous** as my user name; the password doesn't show up (for security reasons), but I have typed in my e-mail address, followed by a Return. I have then been given a screen full of information about the server I have contacted (this is one of the major software repositories available on the Internet). I have given the **cd pub** command to be sent to the *pub* directory. There, I am sitting at a prompt while the system waits for me to act.

Now let's look at the same session as run through Mosaic. The difference, as we'll see, is striking. Perhaps most obvious is that, when we want to go to a particular destination, we need to enter the appropriate URL (Uniform Resource Locator). To do so, we need to open the File menu, as shown in Figure 6.1.

We will want to click on the top item, Open URL . . . , which will pop up a dialog box as shown in Figure 6.2. The information in the dialog box is straightforward. The URL: field tells us the current URL; remember, this means the location of the document we are currently looking at on-screen. The Current Hotlist: field tells us that if we add a URL to our hotlist (more about how to do this in the next chapter), that document will be added to the Starting Points menu at the top of Mosaic. We can see the Starting Points document shown in the field to the immediate right of the URL: field. If we were to click on the down arrow in the dialog box here, it would result in a list of the other URLs in the Starting Points menu, and we could choose any of them as the URL to which we wanted to go.

For now, though, we are concerned with the URL: box. Putting the cursor into that field and clicking will cause the current URL to be highlighted in blue.

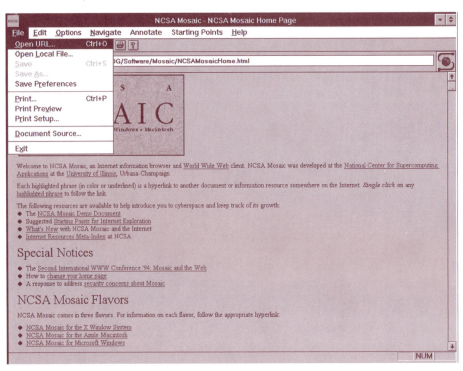

Figure 6.1 Pulling down Mosaic's File menu.

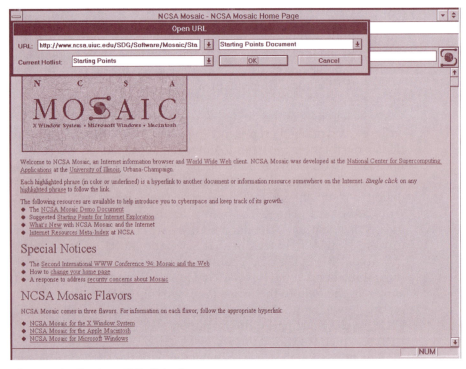

Figure 6.2 The Open URL dialog box.

Anything we then type will supersede the URL that is already there. To move to an FTP site, the syntax is simple. We use a URL set up in the following way:

ftp://*site_address*/*directory*/

So, for example, if we want to go to the FTP site at **oak.oakland.edu**, we would simply enter this URL into the URL box:

```
ftp://oak.oakland.edu/
```

If we wanted to proceed directly to the *pub* directory, we could give this URL:

```
ftp://oak.oakland.edu/pub/
```

In Figure 6.3, you can see the result of opening the first of these URLs, which places us in the FTP server's root menu. Take a close look at this figure now.

The immediate difference between using Mosaic as our FTP client and going through a shell account to perform the same operations is the graphical ease of using Mosaic. We have at our disposal the directory structure at the site, laid out using graphical symbols that make it easy to visualize where we are (getting lost when using FTP through a shell account is a common phe-

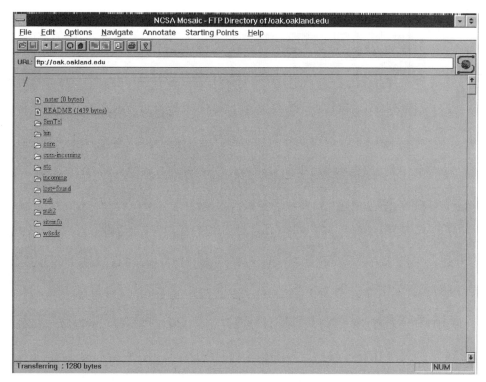

Figure 6.3 An FTP directory as seen through Mosaic.

nomenon). Notice also that we have different symbols depending on the resource we are examining at the time. Text documents like **README**, for example, are shown as miniature pages with the corner of the leaf turned down. The rest of the items are shown as tiny folders; these indicate directories. All of these items are underlined. We know now that the underlining indicates the presence of a hyperlink; there is, therefore, more information behind each of the symbols, available through a click of the mouse.

And did you notice how easy it was to get in? Rather than being forced to type in the word **anonymous** and then our password, we find that we move automatically to the directory we have specified. Mosaic has handled the login process for us.

Changing Directories with Mosaic

So far, so good. Mosaic lets us read information on-screen. But let's now choose a directory. I will move the cursor to the *pub* directory (the cursor turns into a small hand symbol, revealing the hyperlink). Clicking on this directory item causes the screen to change as we move to the directory. The change is shown in Figure 6.4.

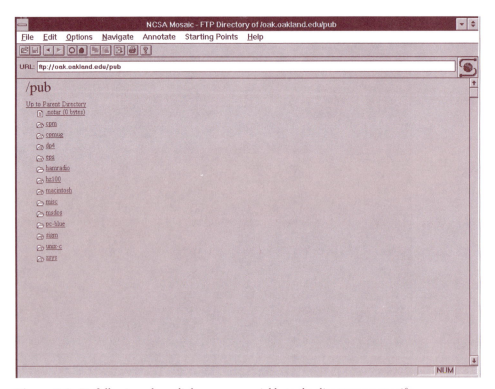

Figure 6.4 By following a hyperlink, we move quickly to the directory we specify.

Once again, we have the directory tree, this time starting with the */pub* directory, which is shown at the top of the screen, and illustrating the various subdirectories beneath it. Directly under the */pub* statement is a useful item: Up to Parent Directory. The underlining tells us that this is a hyperlink. If we were to click on it, we would move back to the directory immediately preceding the current one. To do this with a shell account would require a command such as **cd ..** to achieve the same result. And, of course, we would have to manually enter this command.

Reading Files at the Site

It is possible, no matter how we access an FTP site, to read a document on-screen or to retrieve it. Let's pause for a moment to read the **README** file on-screen. To do this with a shell account would require a complex command (something on the order of **get** *file_name* "**|more**"—one mistake in syntax would force you to type the entire sequence again, but if you did it right, the document would be placed into the **more** viewer, a UNIX program, and you could read it page by page on-line). With Mosaic, the procedure is simpler. We simply click on the file in question. The result is shown in Figure 6.5.

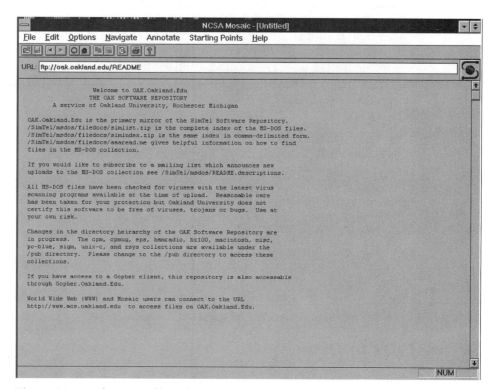

Figure 6.5 Reading a text file on-line.

The ASCII file soon pops up on the screen. Notice that, if it were a multi-page document, we could move around in it by using the scroll bar to the right of the screen. And once we have finished reading it, we can look to the icon bar at the top of the screen, where we see two buttons, one with a left-pointing triangle, one with a triangle pointing to the right (we'll examine the rest of the Mosaic toolbar in Chapter 7). Choosing the one pointing to the left and clicking on it takes us back to the previous screen, which in this case is the root directory at **oak.oakland.edu**. Click on this item now.

Mosaic and File Compression

We have just seen how Mosaic can display a text file on-screen. But this program can do more. The beauty of this browser is that it understands how to interpret the different types of files it encounters. Numerous text files on the Internet are compressed to save disk space, usually employing the UNIX **compress** command, as well as the **gzip** commands from the Free Software Foundation. If we were to click on such an item, Mosaic would decode the compression and display the file on-screen for us to read it.

But note this: The program doesn't do well with files that contain two or more extensions. In particular, files with listings like **info.tar.Z** cannot be read in this way; such a file is set up as a file archive (thus the **tar** suffix) and has been compressed (as shown by the final **Z**. We can retrieve this type of file, but rather than reading it on-screen, we would have to load it to our own hard disk and then unpack it. More about this procedure in a moment.

In Figure 6.6 we have located a binary file that has been compressed, in this case using PKWARE's PKZIP program (we know this because the file extension is **.zip**). The file's URL is:

```
file://oak.oakland.edu/pub/msdos/windows3/abcwin31.zip
```

It's the sixth file down from the top in this directory listing. Notice here that, once again, we are using icons to help us do our job. The few text files available in this directory are shown without an icon, whereas all the others are shown with an icon that tells us we are dealing with a binary file.

Although Mosaic can display some formats of compressed text files, it can do nothing to display a compressed binary file. And, in any case, although it can display text files that have been compressed with the UNIX **compress** program and the **gzip** program from the Free Software Foundation, it cannot understand other forms of compression, like PKZIP. For these, we have to explore the various options for loading files to our own hard disks. We examine these next.

Saving Files to Disk

Suppose we want to save a text file for later use. To do so, we can pop down the File menu, and look for menu items marked Save and Save As. . . . Choosing

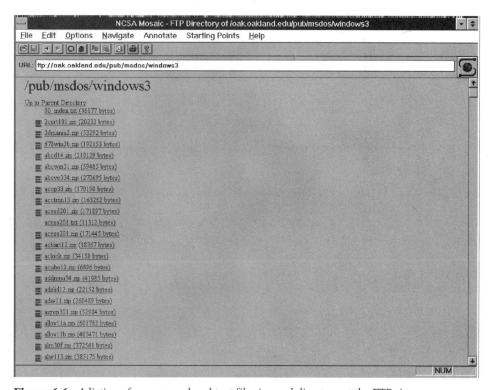

Figure 6.6   A listing of compressed and text files in a subdirectory at the FTP site.

the first saves the file under the name it already contains. But since we are using a Windows system and may well be looking at a text file with a UNIX style name (hence, it may contain more characters than are permissible in a DOS file name, or multiple extensions, or other problems DOS can't handle), we would probably choose to change its name. We can do this through the Save As . . . command. This pops up a dialog box showing the file as currently named, and allows you to change the name and set up the directory in which it will be stored.

All of this comes with a strong proviso, however. If you are using the Macintosh version of Mosaic, the process is seamless. You will choose the Save As . . . option from the File menu, and will be given a dialog box that gives you the opportunity to save the file as straight text or in HTML format. Unfortunately, the Windows version does not yet, at the time of this writing, support this feature. It will though, and by the time you read this, the feature may already be included. But if it is not, here is what you can do:

1. Pull down the Options menu, as shown in Figure 6.7.
2. Select the first item, Load to Disk, and click on it. Verify that a check mark now appears alongside this item when you pull the menu down

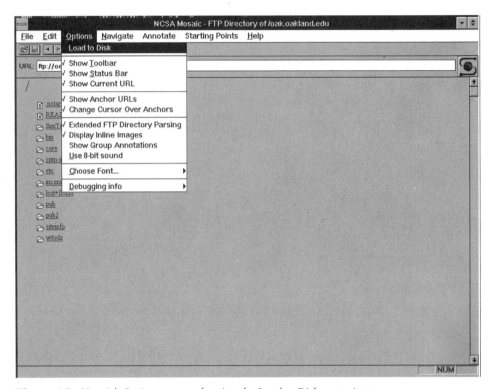

Figure 6.7   Mosaic's Options menu, showing the Load to Disk menu item.

again. This is a toggle switch; in other words, once you have clicked on the item, the check mark stays there to show you the option is still active. You will have to click it again later to turn this option off.

3. Move to the file you want to read and click on it. The file will not appear on-screen. Instead, you will receive a dialog box, as shown in Figure 6.8.

4. You can now rename the file as necessary and put it in whichever directory you choose. The file will be available for printing or editing.

5. Pull the Options menu back down and click once again on the Load to Disk option. This turns off the option. If you fail to do so, Mosaic will attempt to load any future item you click on to your disk.

There is a handy keyboard shortcut that users of Mosaic for Microsoft Windows can use to avoid the problem in step 5. If you point to the file you want to retrieve and use a Shift-click combination (that is, hold down the Shift key and click with your mouse on the file in question), it will be transferred to your disk. Better still, the transfer will occur only for that file. The next hyperlink you access will display normally. This saves you from multiple menu

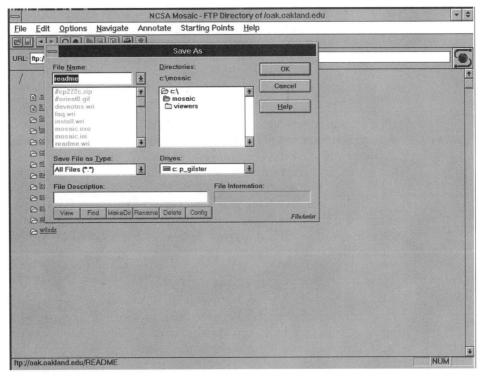

Figure 6.8   This dialog box allows you to enter information about the file name and directory of the file you are downloading.

accesses to turn the toggle switch on and off. Macintosh users need only click on the file they want to retrieve, which will cause the Save File dialog box to appear.

You will notice one difference between Mosaic and other methods of FTP retrieval. Mosaic makes no provision for multiple file downloads. With a shell account, I could use the **mget** command followed by file names to retrieve the files I needed. With Mosaic, I must go one file at a time.

Mosaic and Other File Types

Mosaic's ability to work with a variety of file types makes using it with FTP a snap. All you have to do is point to the item we want and click on it. You have already seen that if this item is a text file, the file will be displayed on-screen. You also know that there are ways of working with compressed text files (at least in some formats).

But there is more. Suppose you encounter a GIF file on-screen at an FTP site. If you want to see this file, all you have to do is to click on the file name. The file will be transferred and will then appear on your screen, run through the appropriate viewer. The same is true of audio files. Again, the **mosaic.ini** file comes to your rescue by providing the pointers to the appropriate viewers. Note how useful this capability is. By allowing you to link to external viewers, Mosaic frees you to set up file types and view them without regard to the resources actually built into the Mosaic program. This ability to juggle other software adds considerably to Mosaic's flexibility.

Again, however, the question arises as to how to save files like these. Mosaic normally doesn't save audio and video to disk; it displays or plays them for you. You have to tell the software if you want to save a particular file. To do so, you again must use the Options menu and once again click on the Load to Disk command (or else use the Shift-click shortcut); the Macintosh version also requires you to use the Load to Disk command. Doing so pops up the same dialog box you have just seen (or its Mac equivalent), allowing you to rename the file if necessary and set up the directory in which you'd like to locate it. Mosaic will not display the file in question, but it will save it so that you can play it later on your own.

Needless to say, this can be a time-consuming process, whether you intend only to display or also to download and save a file. Fortunately, the Windows version of Mosaic provides you with the information you need about file size in parentheses after each file name. This makes planning ahead possible; you don't get stuck in a half-hour download of a file you were only mildly curious about. But always be sure to check those file sizes for precisely this problem.

Using Mosaic with Telnet

Telnet is the second of the Internet's big three protocols, and the one we will use in manipulating the resources on remote computers, such as databases. The range of information available through Telnet is nothing short of remarkable, and growing all the time. With Mosaic, we can use whichever client program we choose for Telnet. Mosaic will call upon this client to run the Telnet session. When we are through, it's a simple matter to return to Mosaic.

Opening a Telnet URL

Recall that in Chapter 3 we edited the **mosaic.ini** file to set up a Telnet viewer. Since I am using NetManage Inc.'s Chameleon software, for example, my **mosaic.ini** file contains this line:

```
telnet="c:\netmanag\telnet.exe"
```

The information appears in the [Viewers] section of the **mosaic.ini** file. At this point, you should make sure your own **mosaic.ini** file contains the necessary pointer, or your attempted Telnet sessions will fail.

To open a Telnet session with a given site, pull down the File menu and select the Open URL . . . option. Type in the uniform resource locator of the document you are after. The syntax for Telnet is as follows:

telnet://*site address:port/*

The port address is optional; you only use it if the Telnet server you are trying to reach uses a nonstandard port. If it does, you will know this because the address will have a string of numbers after it, as in this address:

```
culine.colorado.edu 859
```

Such an address would have the following URL:

```
telnet://culine.colorado.edu:859/
```

A straight Telnet address using standard ports has no numbers after the address. Thus, the address **michael.ai.mit.edu** appears in URL form this way:

```
telnet://michael.ai.mit.edu/
```

A Sample Telnet Session

Let's open a sample Telnet session with the address just given. To do so, we pull down the File menu, choose the Open URL . . . option, type in the address, then click Ok (or else press the Return key) when we are finished. The Telnet screen should then appear as shown in Figure 6.9.

Notice what has happened here. The Telnet application has appeared in a window of its own, called up by Mosaic when we typed in the correct URL. The Telnet session itself is now running in that window; as you can see, we have connected to MuseNet, the Multi-User Science Education Network, with access to various interactive computer environments. The interface is straight VT-100; we are running a Windows session using a Telnet program through the help of Mosaic, but we do not receive the graphical support we have grown accustomed to with other Mosaic tools. Nonetheless, the Telnet capability is here; we can use Mosaic to launch the Telnet session as readily as launching the Telnet program separately, with the benefit that we don't have to leave the Mosaic program to do it.

Figure 6.10 shows another Telnet session in progress. I have opened the following URL:

```
telnet://libserv.msstate.edu/
```

The figure shows the initial screen at Mississippi State University's library.

You may be wondering how you would know which user name or password to use at a particular Telnet site. This is indeed a problem, since each site

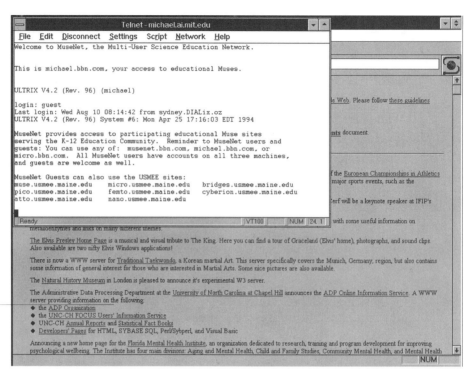

Figure 6.9 The Telnet screen, appearing as a window within Mosaic.

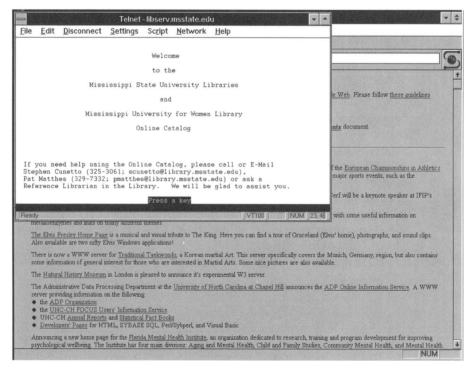

Figure 6.10 A Telnet session with the Mississippi State University Library.

may have its own login procedure, and many sites are restricted to authorized users, such as those at heavily used academic collections. The best thing to do is to examine lists like Scott Yanoff's *Internet Services List* (also known as *Special Internet Connections*), which appears regularly and collects information from all over the network about sites to examine. To see the Yanoff list, you can use Mosaic to travel to the following address:

```
http://slacvx.slac.stanford.edu:80/misc/internet-services.html
```

Long-time Internet users will recognize this list, but perhaps may not realize that it is available through the **World Wide Web**. The benefit of connecting through Mosaic is that the *Internet Services List* is provided with accompanying hyperlinks, so that when you find a resource you are interested in, you need only click on it to activate the link. This makes the printed version seem archaic!

Figure 6.11 shows the *Internet Services List* as called up in Mosaic. Note that at the top of the page, under Agricultural Information, Family Issues, Food and Nutrition, are listed a number of Telnet sites. Each is underlined, revealing the presence of the hyperlink. A click on any one of these calls up your Telnet program, and you are off. The Yanoff list, incidentally, is already set up on the Starting Points menu. Click on the top choice, Starting Points Document, to move to a useful array of Internet resources, among which is the Yanoff list. Mac users can look at the bottom of the Navigate menu, where Network Starting Points provides a submenu of hyperlinks to the same popular Internet resources.

Gopher and Mosaic

Mosaic is likewise a useful **Gopher** mechanism. This is handy because **Gophers** are proliferating, largely spurred by their ease of use. All you have to know to get **Gopher** up and running is that it is necessary to move an on-screen pointer to the item desired, and then press the Return key to activate it. Legions of novice Internet users have accessed resources for the first time through **Gopher**.

Mosaic keeps **Gopher** easy to use and, by providing it through the same interface by which you can use Telnet and FTP resources, Mosaic emphasizes the "one size fits all" approach to the Internet interface. Let's take a look at how Mosaic handles **Gopher** now. Figure 6.12 shows the **Gopher** at CICNet, as seen from its top menu.

As with FTP, there are icons next to the various menu items. Mosaic is not particularly ingenious in how it displays **Gopher**; any good **Gopher** client can do the same things and more. But I think you will agree that the interface provided is a touch more pleasing than the straight VT-100 interface accessible through a shell account.

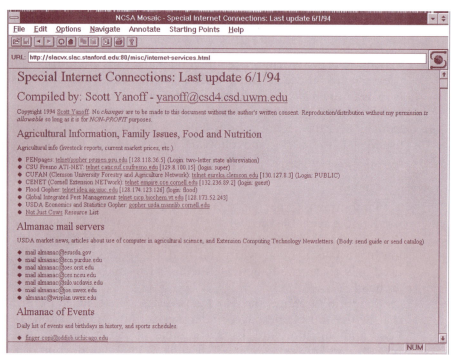

Figure 6.11 The Internet Services List as viewed through Mosaic. This is a key Internet resource, no matter how you access it.

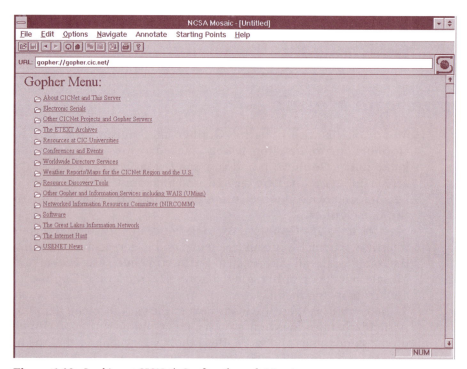

Figure 6.12 Looking at CICNet's **Gopher** through Mosaic.

To open a **Gopher** session, pull down the File menu, choose Open URL . . . , and enter the address in the following form:

   gopher://*site_address:port/*

As with our Telnet sessions, port information is included only if specified. Normally, **Gopher** defaults to a particular port and no port information is required. The URL of the CICNet **Gopher** shown in Figure 6.12 is:

```
gopher://gopher.cic.net/
```

We can see the URL in the URL field on the Mosaic screen. And as we have seen, we can also move to a **Gopher** server through a hyperlink; the Yanoff list contains numerous **Gopher** connections.

To move between the various menu items in a **Gopher**, we simply put the cursor on the item we want to see and click on it. The material is quickly transferred to our screen. In Figure 6.13, I have clicked on the Electronic Serials menu item from the top menu and have moved deeper into the menu structure until I came to a publication called *Radio World*. The full text of the document is now available, and can be read progressively by using the scroll bar at the side of the screen.

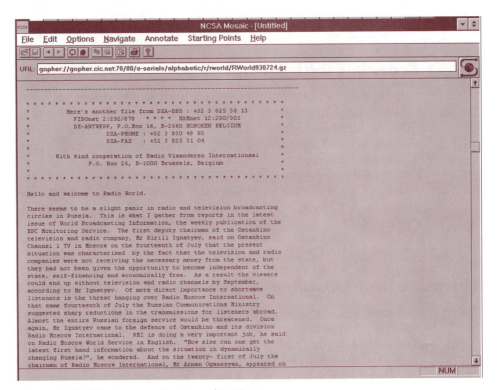

Figure 6.13   Viewing an on-line journal in Mosaic.

To move around in **Gopher**, I can use the icon bar in Mosaic. The left-pointing triangle icon takes me up one level. The right-pointing triangle will go deeper into the menu structure, but only if I have already gone there. In other words, the left-pointing icon only becomes available once I have moved to a menu level, withdrawn from it, and then want to go back to it; otherwise it is dimmed.

You can accomplish the same movements using the menus, of course. The Navigate menu provides you with Forward and Back commands which actually illustrate what is happening better than the icon bar. When you move backward and forward through **Gopher**, you are actually moving backward and forward in terms of what Mosaic remembers of your activities. If, for example, you visited a **Gopher** page, then went back one level, then forward again, Mosaic would have a record of those movements and would be able to progressively go back through them. It would not, however, understand each of your commands in terms of the **Gopher** you were using. Thus, you might wind up visiting the same menu level twice even though you were repeatedly using the Back command.

Searching WAIS and Other Indices

Mosaic can be used to search various kinds of indices. The underlying application isn't terribly important in terms of what you see on the screen, because the same interface is employed no matter what manner of search you are running.

finger Searches with Mosaic

In Figure 6.14, for example, you are looking at a **finger** search screen. I have launched the basic search screen and have entered my own address to retrieve **finger** information (to do this, I simply moved the cursor into the search field and then typed the query.) Having entered this information, I pressed a Return to activate the search.

The **finger** server at this gateway is interesting; it provides bitmapped pictures of faces (where available) along with textual data. If you want to see some sample **finger** information along with the faces behind it, use the following URL:

```
http://cs.indiana.edu/finger/gateway/
```

Veronica and Mosaic

Of course, a searchable index can be made available from numerous different sources. **Veronica** provides just such a reference; I can search **Veronica** much the same way that I ran the previous **finger** search—by keying in the information I wish to search for. Figure 6.15 shows the search screen. Notice that it is in exactly the same format. I move the cursor to the search field, click once, and then enter my information.

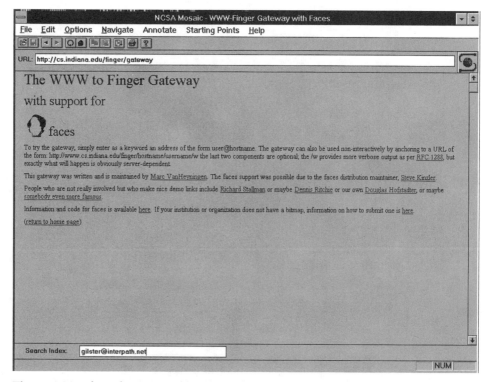

Figure 6.14   Through a gateway like this one, you can set up a **finger** search with Mosaic.

I set up a search by typing in the keyword **html**. The results are returned in the form of a **Gopher** menu, as shown in Figure 6.16. I would click on any of these items to move directly to it.

Veronica is a wonderful search tool; it allows you to search through the universe of **Gopher** menu titles to find any that meet your search criteria. A full explanation of all the **Veronica** search options is outside the scope of this book, but you can read a great deal more about both **Gopher** and **Veronica** in my book *Finding It on the Internet* (John Wiley & Sons, Inc., 1994). Remember one key fact: **Veronica** does not run full text searches of the items at a particular **Gopher**. All it can look for are the menu titles it finds in Gopherspace.

Other Kinds of Indexed Searching

Other kinds of index searches are also possible with Mosaic. Figure 6.17, for example, shows you what a search in a **WHOIS** database looks like. Mosaic, as you can see, makes the search process easy by offering the same interface each time. It's even possible to set up an **archie** search. Consider the form Mosaic presents in Figure 6.18.

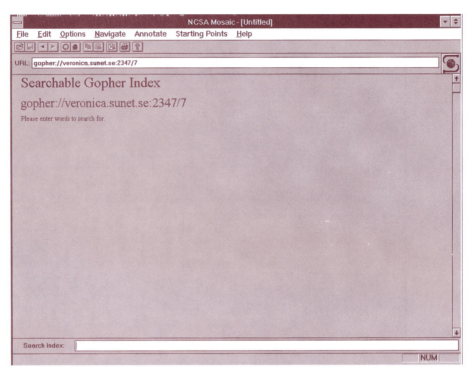

Figure 6.15 Using **Veronica** to search for HTML information.

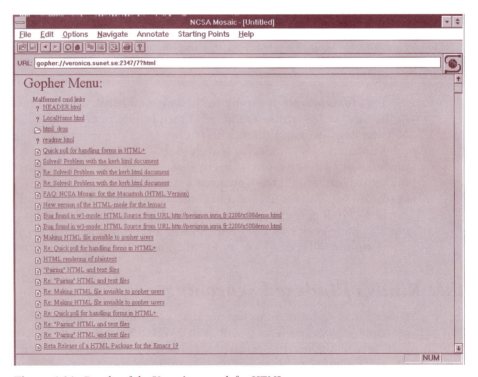

Figure 6.16 Results of the **Veronica** search for HTML.

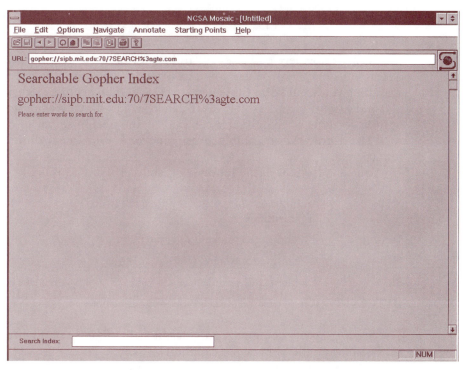

Figure 6.17 A basic search screen for **WHOIS**, as seen through Mosaic.

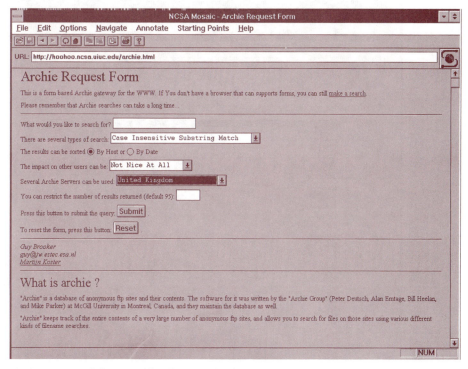

Figure 6.18 A full-powered **archie** search screen.

Perhaps nowhere else does the full power of Mosaic as a browser come so clearly into play than when you can compare it to the line-oriented kind of searching you would otherwise have to cope with in **archie**. Here, your options are laid out in clear fashion. You can use pull-down menus to set **archie** options for type of search, and can choose the **archie** server to use the same way. The degree of control this gives you over a notoriously difficult system is remarkable.

You can also search the following resources using Mosaic:

X.500   An Internet white pages services, allowing you to search for people and organizations.

TechInfo   A menu-based information system.

Hyper-G   A hypermedia system.

Ph   A white pages service.

HYTELNET   A hypertext resource guide to the Internet.

The *Starting Points* document provides links to all of these. Figure 6.19 shows off Ph, an example of Mosaic's capability.

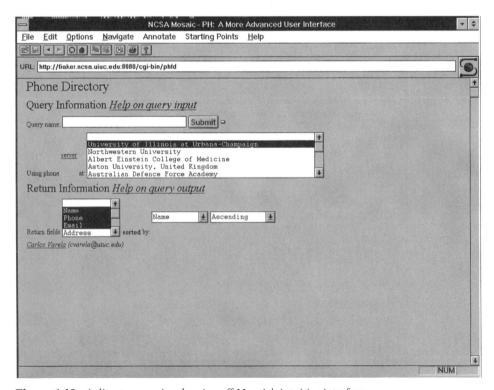

Figure 6.19   A directory service showing off Mosaic's intuitive interface.

The Problem with WAIS

Of course, when we think about searchable indices, we generally think in terms of **WAIS**, or **Wide Area Information Servers**. **WAIS** allows us to search for specified text; it has made possible the establishment of numerous databases of various kinds of information on the Internet, searchable through a common interface. Searching **WAIS** databases with a VT-100 interface, usually with the **swais** program, is difficult indeed, but using Mosaic could make the task much simpler, even if it does not offer quite as much power (relevance feedback, for example, is not available through Mosaic).

Unfortunately, while the UNIX version of Mosaic does support **WAIS** searching, the Macintosh and Windows versions do not. This means that Macintosh and Windows users cannot use Mosaic as an actual **WAIS** client. Instead, the way to reach a **WAIS** resource through Mosaic is, unfortunately, to open a Telnet connection to the **WAIS** site. I say "unfortunately" because this involves going through the same set of difficult commands using the **swais** client program that you would use if you were limited to a VT-100 session anyway. The Mosaic advantage here is simply that you can continue to use Mosaic as your primary program, launching Telnet from within it. Otherwise, the situation is limited and awaits the development of better **WWW-WAIS** connections.

The nature of this limitation tells us something about Mosaic itself. The program, remember, is best considered as a browser for the **World Wide Web**. As a client, it offers the ability to tap Internet data and present it in a particularly useful format. Other client programs can do the same thing with various services, such as **Gopher** or **WAIS**. When Mosaic runs into something that it can't handle internally as a client program, it must invoke an external program to do the same thing, which is why we had to set up a separate Telnet program in our **mosaic.ini** file. Mosaic doesn't have the internal workings to handle Telnet itself.

To get around the problem with **WAIS**, NCSA has set up a gateway located at this address:

```
www.ncsa.uiuc.edu:8001
```

The gateway simply makes the necessary translation to allow Mosaic to function with a **WAIS** database. Several private gateways exist to **WAIS** servers, but at the time of this writing, the NCSA gateway we would like to use was not working. You may want to keep an eye on the above site, however, for further developments. You can also track developments by following changes to the *Starting Points* document. At present, the URL for this document is:

```
http://www.ncsa.uiuc.edu/SDG/Software/Mosaic/StartingPoints/NetworkStarting Points.html
```

This document contains generous information about Mosaic's treatment of the various data types.

Table 6.1   A List of **WAIS** Sites Available by Telnet

URL	Site	Login
telnet://swais.cwis.uci.edu/	University of California at Irvine	swais
telnet://nnsc.nsf.net/	NSF Network Service Center, Massachusetts	wais
telnet://quake.think.com/	Thinking Machines Corp., Massachusetts	wais
telnet://sunsite.unc.edu/	University of North Carolina at Chapel Hill	swais
telnet://kudzu.cnidr.org/	Clearinghouse for Networked Information Discovery and Retrieval, North Carolina	wais

For now, however, you should also be aware of the various Telnet-accessible **WAIS** sites. Table 6.1 shows the current list. Reach any of these addresses by opening the relevant URL and logging on as specified.

InfoSeek: The Shape of Things to Come?

Searchable indices are something we need more of; they allow us to go straight to what we need, often finding resources we hadn't realized existed. It is likely that as the Internet matures, and especially as new commercial applications become available, we will see a great many new indices appear. InfoSeek is a case in point. Its founder, InfoSeek Corporation, has set about developing an Internet search facility that makes retrieval of information both easy and accurate. The service uses full-text search capability that works with existing Internet tools. The result for Mosaic users is a point-and-shoot interface with the ability to retrieve, browse, and search for data.

Figure 6.20 shows you how InfoSeek looks on-screen. I have just entered a query by putting the cursor in the query field and typing my search terms. As you can see, my query is expressed in plain English (the system uses so-called *natural language* tools that make this possible). I am asking for information about the manufacturers of satellite dishes. The query is fed into a trial version of Ziff Communications Computer Select database, containing more than 140 computer publications. At the time of this writing, the service was in its experimental phase. The developers plan to make their search software accessible to others who want to make information available over the Internet. It will be interesting to see how the InfoSeek search engine fares in the Internet community in comparison to other textual searching mechanisms like **WAIS**.

For more information, you can use the following URL:

```
http://www.infoseek.com/
```

Here, you can learn how to open an account. Accounts require a user name and password; full information is available at the site.

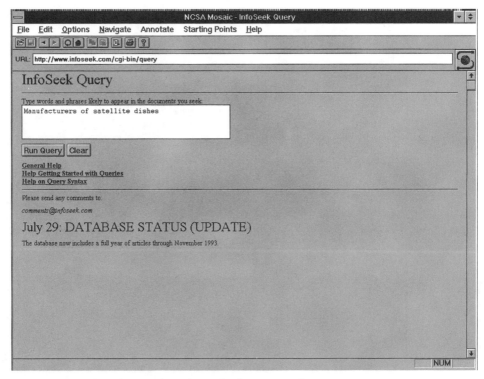

Figure 6.20   InfoSeek is another take on database retrieval.

Reading the News

Mosaic as USENET newsreader? It can be done, although without the bells and whistles of fancier newsreaders. Remember that in Chapter 3 we set up the **mosaic.ini** file to reflect our own news server. Now we can use Mosaic to look at newsgroups on-screen. The format for opening a URL to a newsgroup looks like this (note the absence of slashes after the colon):

news:*newsgroup_name*

All we need to do is to specify which group we want to read. Thus, suppose we would like to look at the popular **alt.internet.services** newsgroup. We would set up the URL this way:

```
news:alt.internet.services
```

The result is shown in Figure 6.21.

Each message is established with a hyperlink, as shown by the underlining and color change. Clicking on any of the messages calls that message to the screen. One intriguing feature about using Mosaic as a newsreader is that hyperlinks are provided to referenced documents. We might, for example, see

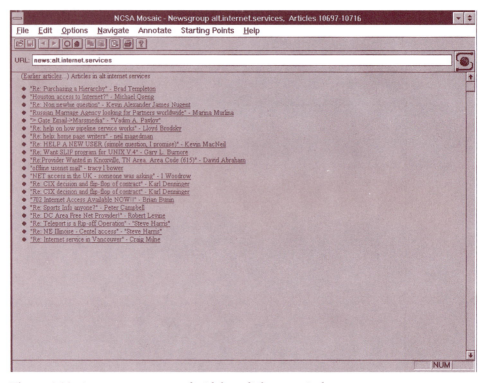

Figure 6.21   A newsgroup presented with hyperlinks to particular messages.

a link to the document someone was replying to; we could then read that document to place the ensuing one in the appropriate context.

That said, it is nonetheless true that Mosaic is not the ideal newsreader. We can't, for example, reply to documents using it; we're limited to reading them. Nor can we post articles of our own. And because Mosaic wasn't set up to track our USENET exploits, it does not allow us to subscribe to particular newsgroups. A good USENET reader like Trumpet for Windows or Nuntius (for the Mac) allows us to specify newsgroups to which we want to subscribe, so that when we log on the next time, our newsreader knows what we have already read and what we haven't. With Mosaic, we are limited to telling it each time what we want to see, and accepting whatever it happens to find.

Mosaic and Electronic Mail

If Mosaic doesn't excel as a newsreader, its capabilities as a mail program are even more truncated. There is one form of mail available to you—you can send a message to the developers of Mosaic. To do so, pull down the Help menu and click on the Mail to Developers . . . option (Macintosh users will find a Mail

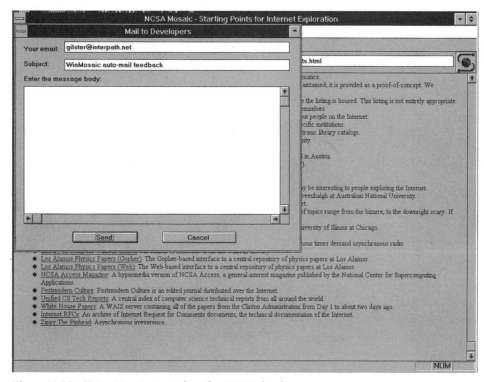

Figure 6.22 Using Mosaic to send mail to NCSA developers.

Developers option on the File menu). The screen you see should look like the one in Figure 6.22.

Now you can see why it is important to insert your own e-mail address when modifying the **mosaic.ini** file as we did in Chapter 3. This return address is inserted into the mail you are sending to the developers. And remember: Your mail to this site is going to a busy bunch of people, so think thrice before sending. Also be aware that the Software Development Group at NCSA values bug reports; after all, users are engaged in a massive testing project for Mosaic as it develops. The key to making a good bug report is to tell NCSA everything it needs to know to duplicate the problem. This means passing along any messages produced by Mosaic itself, along with a URL so the problem can be duplicated at NCSA.

Information about previously reported bugs is provided on the NCSA home page, and you are asked to check there first before sending reports, comments, or suggestions.

7

Exploring Mosaic's Menus

Although Mosaic makes network navigation simple by offering hyperlinks to data, the program contains numerous features that aren't immediately obvious. Some of these are tools you will find extremely useful. The ability to create annotations, for example, is frequently untapped; in this chapter, I will explain how that feature works, and show you how Mosaic can customize your Internet travels in ways you would not have imagined. Think of a digital, networked rolodex with notes only you can see, wherever you want to put them. Imagine all this built into your network browser instead of handled through external programs.

Then there is your ability to set up a hotlist, containing places you want to go to repeatedly on the **Web**. You know that URLs specify the location of specific resources; you've also seen that they are unwieldy. Make a single mistake typing in a URL and you will receive nothing but an error message. Fortunately, Mosaic makes it easy to add the current document URL to your hotlist so you can return there quickly. The program also allows you to tinker with its menu structure to create an individualized navigation tool. Find that you don't visit many of the sites set up for you when you first run Mosaic? This chapter will show you how to change them and build feature-laden menus of your own.

We will consider the menu structure of Mosaic with care. Some functions are more obvious than others, but for the sake of clarity, we'll take a look at each of the pull-down menus the program offers to consider how they function. The emphasis is on the Microsoft Windows version of Mosaic, but the Macintosh version is very similar (and I'll note areas where some differences do occur). Once we master Mosaic's menus, we're ready to customize the program further by tinkering with some of the more arcane functions of the **mosaic.ini** file, as explained in Chapter 8.

Mosaic Annotations

I was once a hapless graduate student working on a project that threatened to consume every spare moment of my time for years to come. Specifically, I needed to make note cards. The idea was to create one note card for every single line of Anglo-Saxon poetry that was extant. Ending in 1066, the Anglo-Saxon period in Britain was not hugely prolific in poetry, but some 30,000 lines of verse do remain, all of them in challenging, alliterative meter. My job was to catalog them, one by one, to figure out how the meter worked. Stop for a moment, and visualize 30,000 notecards. Is it any wonder I wound up writing about computers instead?

One of the things we should be able to turn our computing power toward is the simplification of such processes. Software programs like InfoSelect (from Micro Logic Corp.) make this possible on stand-alone machines by creating electronic notecards that can be readily cross-referenced. You can enter a search term that might appear anywhere on a given card and the software will take you directly to the card. We now need to extend such capabilities into the environment of networked information. Obviously, the **Web** is the place to do this, because it is built up of information that is already hyperlinked.

Along comes Mosaic, with one of the Internet's best ideas—a way of referencing networked documents by adding private notes to them. Anyone can see the document our note discusses, but only we can see the note. Thus, we create a bridge between the universe of public networking and the individual desktop. We make it possible to think in terms of a personalized Internet environment, one that we can modify through our annotations and further customize by our choice of frequently visited sites. The ramifications for business are obvious, for a customized Internet takes on whatever shape the network traveler decides to give it.

The Nature of Notes

Mosaic's notetaking capability is not difficult to understand. When you create a note, or annotation, it is stored on your own computer. When you go back to the document about which you made the note, you will find a reminder that there is a note available at the end of the document. (Macintosh users will see it in the form of a hypertext link. Microsoft Windows users will see a reminder that an annotation is there; they then need to click on the Annotate menu, followed by the Annotate submenu item, to see it.) In either case, you can add personal information to whichever document you are looking at.

How would you use such information? Think for a moment about the vast size of the Internet, and the fact that your biggest challenge in using it is to find the information you need. Your annotations can remind you what is available at a particular site without having to go through its various hyperlinks again. You might, perhaps, want to jot down the e-mail address of a contact at the site, without having to dig deep into the menu structure to find it each time.

You might want to refer to other documents that have similar types of information, or perhaps just add a whimsical comment or two about the nature of what you've found.

In Chapter 8, you'll see that customization can go still further by letting you create home pages of your own, with individualized hyperlinks. Combine notes and personal home pages and you have created a powerful information tool, provided you learn how to use it.

Creating Annotations

Let's now use Mosaic to travel to a site and create our first annotation. The site I'll choose is an intriguing one; the home page is titled Telecom Paris, and we will find links here to a wide range of resources, both related to France and to the Internet at large. The URL is:

```
http://mistral.enst.fr/
```

Its home page is shown in Figure 7.1.

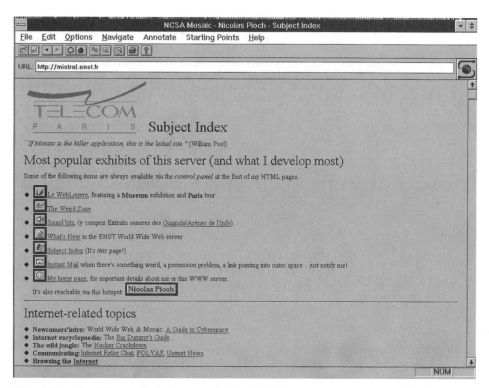

Figure 7.1 The Telecom Paris home page. Note the links to intriguing resources like the Louvre.

We are going to examine a wonderful on-line exhibit made available by the Louvre. Several exhibitions were on-line at the time of this writing, perhaps the best of them being Les Tres Riches Heures du Duc de Berry. This volume is a classic example of a medieval book of hours. Such books were assembled to provide text for each hour of the liturgical day, and often included calendars and supplementary prayers, along with beautiful artwork. Painted between 1412 and 1416, the illustrations in Les Tres Riches Heures are some of the finest examples of manuscript illumination that have survived the medieval era.

Jean de Berry was a nobleman and patron of the arts who died shortly after the Battle of Agincourt in 1415. If we delve into the Louvre exhibition by following the hyperlinks from its home page, we find ourselves on a page showing the first of a series of images from Les Tres Riches Heures, as shown in Figure 7.2.

Note the format here, which is fairly typical for pages on the **Web**, at least where exhibitions of photographs and artwork are concerned. We have several in-line images, small enough to be viewed from within Mosaic itself. Along with them is text explaining a little about each picture. If we move the cursor to any one of these images, it turns into a small hand, indicating we can click again to see the full image.

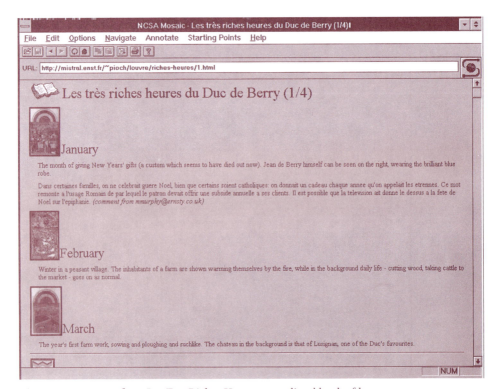

Figure 7.2   Images from Les Tres Riches Heures, a medieval book of hours.

Of course, calling up the full image can take time, particularly over a SLIP connection. We may find, after looking at all the images, that one or two in particular stand out; we might want to see them again, while choosing not to view the others at full size. Figure 7.3, for example, shows a particularly striking illustration of winter in a medieval village. We'd like to see it again.

Figure 7.3 One of the loveliest illustrations from Les Tres Riches Heures, called to full size by clicking on the smaller image.

This is a perfect place for an annotation. Here is how to proceed:

1. Drop down the Annotate menu.
2. Write your note in the annotation field.
3. Save the note by clicking on the Commit button.

Figure 7.4 shows the annotation being made. I have clicked on Annotate and have been presented with a field within which I can enter my note. The note is shown, along with the various options now available to me.

Annotation Options

By choosing Commit, we have created a permanent annotation. It will be there the next time we return to this page. We will be clued in to its presence by a note at the bottom of the document, as shown in Figure 7.5. Note that the statement Personal Annotations appears at the bottom edge of the document; it might not, therefore, be visible when we first examine the page until we scroll down to it. It would be helpful if we could place the notice of the annotation elsewhere, but this is not possible.

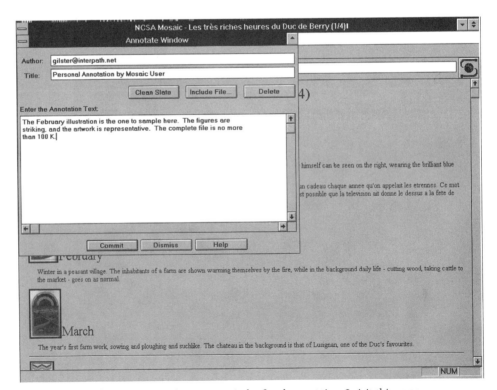

Figure 7.4 Making an annotation as a reminder for the next time I visit this page.

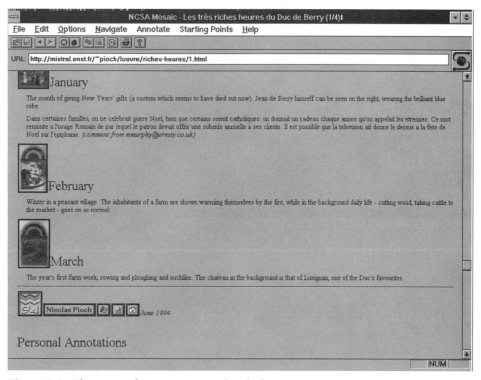

Figure 7.5 The page with annotation noted at the bottom.

When you see the Personal Annotations statement, choosing the Annotation menu and clicking on Annotation will open and display it. But there are other possibilities:

- If you had chosen Dismiss rather than Commit from the Annotate window, you would have been able to discard the annotation. Once an annotation has been recorded, the Dismiss button is simply used to close the Annotate window.

- The Help button provides help (or, at least, it will when this feature is implemented).

- Both the Author: and the Title: fields can be edited. The default entry in the Author: field is the e-mail address you specified when you edited the **mosaic.ini** file. You can change the title to whatever you like.

- The Clean Slate button erases the contents of the Annotation text field.

- The Include File . . . button allows you to include the file of your choice in the annotation. (This option has not yet been implemented in the Microsoft Windows version of Mosaic.)

- The Delete button deletes highlighted text, and is likewise not yet implemented.

And, when an annotation is present, the Annotate menu itself allows two further choices:

- The Edit this annotation button allows you to change what you have written.
- The Delete this annotation button allows you to remove it entirely.

Thus far we have concentrated on personal annotations, but Mosaic can also handle group annotations that are maintained on a group server. To switch between the two, it is necessary to make changes to the **mosaic.ini** file. We will discuss these and other changes to **mosaic.ini** in Chapter 8.

Annotations on the Macintosh

Macintosh users will find annotation just as valuable a tool as Microsoft Windows users. They can create notes by selecting the Text . . . option from the Annotate menu, which will cause an annotation window to appear. The note can then be written and saved by clicking on the Ok button. Clicking on the link thus created will cause the annotation to appear. The presence of an individual hyperlink for each annotation places the Macintosh version, as of now, ahead of the Windows version in terms of flexibility. (As this book goes to press, the Microsoft Windows version has added this feature.)

Using a Hotlist

The simplest of Mosaic's tools, and by far the best, is its ability to maintain a hotlist of frequently visited sites. The more you navigate the Internet with Mosaic, the more you'll come to appreciate this feature. Thus far, we have looked at different sites by pulling down the File menu and choosing the Open URL . . . option. This allows us to type in a URL and choose it as our destination, and indeed, we've found that we could move to any site necessary using this method. We've also examined sites by pulling down menus and clicking on them; the Starting Points menu is an example.

Not all URLs are a problem; it's comparatively simple, for example, to type in **telnet://info.umd.edu/** to open a connection to the University of Maryland's library. But some URLs can be unwieldy, as you've already noticed. Here, for example, is the kind of URL you'll more commonly encounter:

```
http://edb518ea.edb.utexas.edu/html/LatinAmerica.html
```

No matter how good a typist you are, it requires certain memory skills and a sure hand at the keyboard to get all of this right; if you don't, you'll receive a message like the one shown in Figure 7.6.

We could, of course, find the site we want to visit by following hyperlinks, but this can be a time-consuming process that takes us through a lot of unnec-

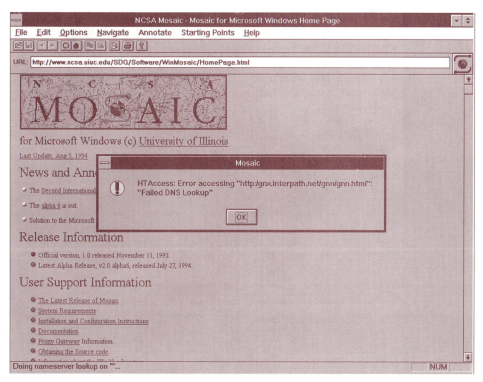

Figure 7.6   An error message results when you mistype a URL.

essary terrain. What we would like is the ability to use Mosaic's menus to go instantly to the site in question, and this is exactly what a hotlist makes available. With it, we can begin the menu customization process.

Let's take a look at the built-in options that already come with the program. Figure 7.7 shows the Starting Points menu, some items of which contain submenus of their own. All these sites represent places the Mosaic team decided to include with the program; they're destinations that can help maximize your performance with Mosaic and keep you up with the latest news about the program and about the **World Wide Web** in general. A variety of general information sources is also provided, showing you links to **Gophers**, **finger** sites, and so on. Choosing a menu item takes away the typing drudgery and, of course, eliminates the chances of making keyboard mistakes. Of course, the links set into the menu must be up to date or you may still get an error message.

If you take a look at the **mosaic.ini** file, you will see a section called [HotList]. Here is what it looks like:

```
[HotList]
URL0=*Local C: Drive,file:///c|/
```

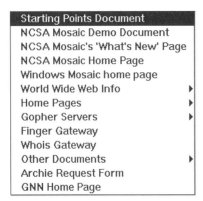

Figure 7.7 The Starting Points menu. Note the pointers to submenus, shown by the small pointers at the right of the menu.

```
URL1=*Mosaic Home Page,http://www.ncsa.uiuc.edu/SDG/Software/Mosaic/NCSAMosaicHome.html
URL2=*Mosaic Demo Page,http://www.ncsa.uiuc.edu/demoweb/demo.html
URL3=http://cs.indiana.edu/cstr/search
URL4=*CICA Windows Archive,file://ftp.cica.indiana.edu/pub/pc/win3
URL5=*WUArchive,file://wuarchive.wustl.edu/
URL6=*Expo Map,http://sunsite.unc.edu/expo/expo/expo_map.html
URL7=http://rs560.cl.msu.edu/weather
URL8=http://www.ncsa.uiuc.edu/SDG/Software/Mosaic/Docs/whats-new.html
URL9=http://neuromancer.lib.uchicago.edu/david/drfun.html
URL10=http://www.ncsa.uiuc.edu/SDG/Experimental/vatican.exhibit/exhibit/e-
music/Music_room1.html
URL11=*Fill-Out Form Example #1,http://www.ncsa.uiuc.edu/SDG/Software/Mosaic/Docs/fill-
out-forms/example-1.html
```

DO NOT EDIT THIS PORTION OF THE **MOSAIC.INI** FILE. I am showing it to you for purposes of illustration only; trying to edit it can cause difficulties with Mosaic's display of your menus. As you're about to see, there is a much simpler way to edit this section using Mosaic's menus from within the program. For now, simply realize that the **mosaic.ini** file maintains information about which sites will be made accessible through these menus.

Accessing Mosaic's Hotlists

Any list of resources can be considered a hotlist, from the Starting Points items to any of the submenus preconfigured in your **mosaic.ini** file. The QUICK-LIST is also a hotlist, but it is different; it is the only hotlist that does not show up as a menu. More about the peculiarities of the QUICKLIST shortly. For now, the key to hotlist use is that you can create hotlists of your own.

You can reach your hotlists by opening the File menu and taking the Open URL . . . option. Look at the field created when I do this, as shown in Figure 7.8. As you can see, a field called Current Hotlist exists, and contains a pull-down menu. The current hotlist is shown in the Current Hotlist field; at the

Figure 7.8 The Current Hotlist box, which provides quick access to the various hotlists.

moment, the hotlist is Starting Points. You can click on the down arrow to drop the menu. It contains a list of hotlists currently available. You can choose another by moving the cursor to the desired hotlist. At that point, the documents in the hotlist will be available from the dialog box. Figure 7.9 shows the hotlist menu after it has been dropped down.

To see the documents available in the current hotlist (they appear as menu items), simply drop down the menu to the right of the URL: field. Figure 7.10, for example, shows the items available in the Gopher Servers hotlist.

Each of the hotlist documents is shown with the document's URL. Thus, the URL for Gopherspace Overview is:

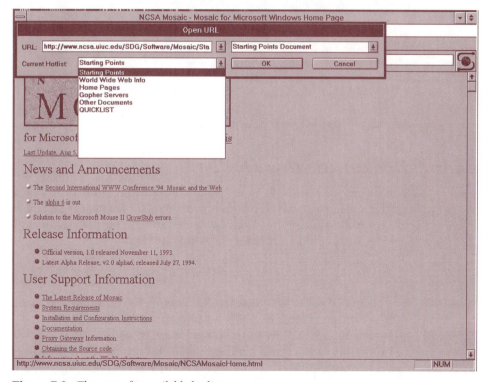

Figure 7.9 The menu for available hotlists.

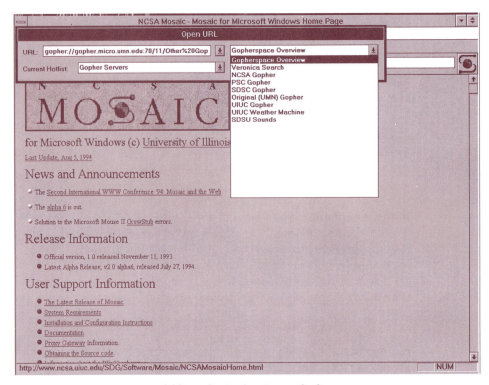

Figure 7.10   Menu items available on the Gopher Servers hotlist.

```
gopher://gopher.micro.umn.edu:70/11/Other%20Gopher%20and%Information%20Servers
```

Not all of this URL can be seen in the field because of its length.

Adding Documents to a Hotlist

The beauty of Mosaic is that any document that is currently being displayed can be added to whichever hotlist you choose. This gives you considerable control over Mosaic's menus. Let's say, for example, that I would like to add the following document to my Starting Points hotlist:

```
http://gnn.interpath.net/gnn/gnn.html
```

All I need to do is to display the document, and then choose the Navigate menu. From it, I click on the Add Current to Hotlist submenu. The process is shown in Figure 7.11, with the page I want to add in the background.

Examine Figure 7.12, and you will see that the item, listed as GNN Home Page, is now available at the bottom of my Starting Points menu. To reach it now, all I have to do is pull down the menu and click on the item. You can see

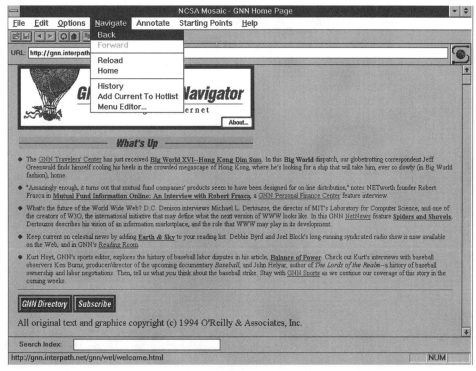

Figure 7.11   The Navigate menu. Note the Add Current to Hotlist item, which we will use to add the current page to the hotlist.

that, by giving us the ability to choose which menu or hotlist to place this information on, Mosaic has made it possible to order sites in whichever way is the most productive.

Using the Mosaic QUICKLIST

If you are an observant reader, you probably noticed in Figure 7.9 that among the hotlists available is one called QUICKLIST. Unlike the other hotlists, the QUICKLIST is a list of URLs that does *not* appear as a pull-down menu at the top of the Mosaic screen. Instead, you select it by choosing the File menu, taking the Open URL . . . option, and selecting the QUICKLIST item. At that point, the URLs available on the QUICKLIST can be displayed by pulling down the URL window to the right, as shown in Figure 7.13. Choosing any one of these items and clicking the Ok button will take you directly to the site.

Why use the QUICKLIST in the first place? Because there are bound to be sites that you are interested in and would like to return to, but which you may not want to install on your menus. The QUICKLIST allows you to go to them but keeps them off the regular Mosaic menu structure. You add items to the

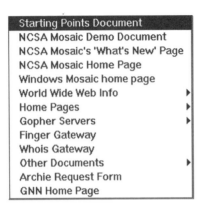

Figure 7.12 The new item has been added to the Starting Points menu.

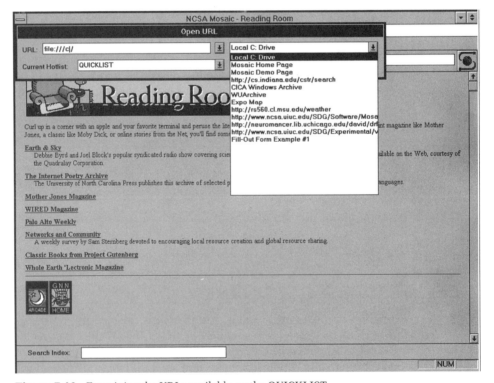

Figure 7.13 Examining the URLs available on the QUICKLIST.

QUICKLIST in the same way you add items to any hotlist; go to the document in question, pull down the Navigate menu and click on Add Current to Hotlist. Just remember that QUICKLIST must be selected as your current hotlist. Another advantage of using the QUICKLIST is that there is no size restriction on the list. All other hotlists are limited to forty entries.

Let's pause for a moment on that point. Mosaic accommodates up to twenty user-configurable menus, along with the QUICKLIST, so you have no shortage of available menu space for customizing your environment. Top-level menus, as you would expect, show up on the main menu bar at the top of the screen; other menus will be listed as pop-out menus from one of these top-level items. Forty entries is the maximum number that any of the menus can have. And, if you include a menu within a menu, that item is considered one of the forty available.

Examples of Hotlists

A variety of options are available if you choose to set up hotlists to customize Mosaic. There is no one right way to do it; each user will want to create a hotlist fitting his or her work or leisure profile. A biologist, for example, could easily set up a hotlist specifically devoted to biological issues, with links to Telnet sites, FTP archival collections, **Gopher** servers and any other information related to his or her field. A librarian could establish a hotlist consisting solely of libraries with Internet-accessible catalogs, thus providing useful examples of how various libraries are implementing their on-line catalogs. An artist could set up a unique hotlist pointing to all the museum exhibits available on the network.

Now that we know how to move around with a hotlist and how to choose which hotlist is current so we can add items to it, we need to complete another part of the puzzle. After all, if Mosaic allows us to have twenty configurable menus, and NCSA distributes it with just one of these, the Starting Points menu, we need to set about organizing our own lists, arranging them to suit our needs. The Menu Editor is the primary tool for doing this.

Mosaic's Menu Editor

Our goal isn't just to learn how to create hotlists. We also want to know how to edit them, so we can remove items when we choose or sort items alphabetically. The hotlists, after all, are going to be the most visible way that we customize this program.

The Menu Editor Screen

To reach the Menu Editor, we pull down the Navigate menu and take the Menu Editor option. What we see should resemble Figure 7.14. The left side of the Menu Editor window contains the user-configurable menus; notice that it also contains the QUICKLIST, which, as we have seen, is the only hotlist that does not appear as a menu at the top of the main Mosaic screen.

Now let's assume we have been navigating the **Web** and discover a document that we would like to return to frequently. The URL is as follows:

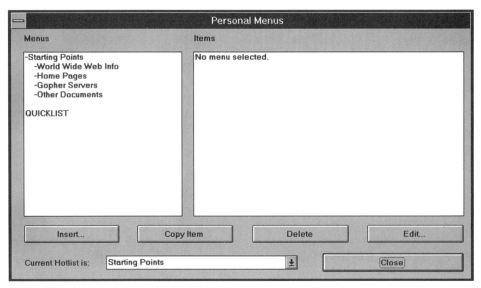

Figure 7.14   Moving into the Menu Editor.

```
http://physics7.berkeley.edu/home.html
```

This is a site managed by the Center for Particle Astrophysics, which is maintained by the National Science Foundation's Science & Technology Center; its home page is shown in Figure 7.15.

Perhaps we'd like to include the server here in our Home Pages submenu for future reference. To do so, we call up the Menu Editor and select the menu we would like to edit. Clicking on that menu calls up the list of items currently in it. Figure 7.16 shows the Menu Editor with the Home Pages menu selected, and the items on that menu shown in the Items window to the right of the image.

If we were to simply click the Insert . . . button at this point, the home page at the Center for Particle Astrophysics would be added to the menu. If we specified no location in the list, it would be added to the end of the list. So let's pick the place we would like to insert the new document and proceed. Although the **mosaic.ini** file in its default format, as provided by NCSA, does not appear with its menu items sorted alphabetically, it will probably make sense to sort new items that way so they are easy to find. (Consider using this approach with any new menus you create.)

To add the item, we place the highlight wherever we would like the new menu item to go. The document we are adding will appear immediately *before* the highlighted item. Remember this principle: When you highlight a location, your document will always be inserted *before* the highlighted item.

When we click on the Insert . . . button, a second, smaller window pops up, as shown in Figure 7.17. This is an interesting window. Mosaic is simply con-

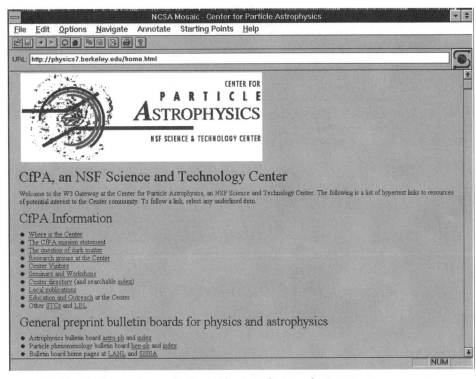

Figure 7.15   The home page at the Center for Particle Astrophysics.

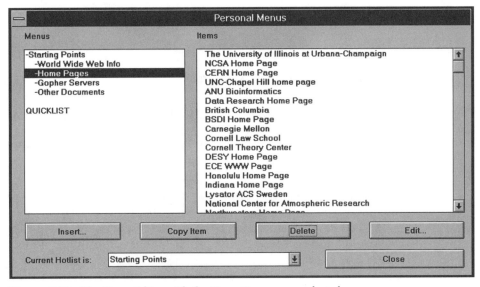

Figure 7.16   The Menu Editor with the Home Pages menu selected.

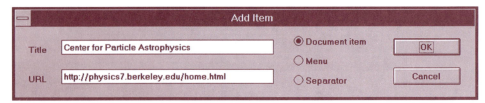

Figure 7.17 The Add Item dialog box. You can choose between adding documents, menus, or separator marks.

firming what we are doing. Note that the program is suggesting the title that will appear in our menu—in this case, it is *Center for Particle Astrophysics*. We could edit that title if we chose. We also see the URL. And to the right of this information are three buttons. The one marked Document should be chosen, to indicate that we are adding a document to an existing menu.

Clicking on Ok inserts the document. Choosing the Close button exits us from the Menu Editor. We can now confirm the insertion by going to the Starting Points menu and choosing the Home Pages submenu, where we will find the new item. And we can see that by using the Menu Editor, it is possible to set up Mosaic with particularly useful items always available and sorted alphabetically, or in any other order we choose.

Inserting Menus and Separators

A variety of options are available through the Menu Editor. We are not limited to adding single documents to preexisting menus; in fact, we can tailor the entire menu structure of Mosaic to fit our own needs. Let's now examine how to use the Menu Editor to its full extent by looking at how to insert other menus.

Inserting Top-Level Menus

Suppose you would like to add a top-level menu to Mosaic. Let's say you'd like one called Personal, which contains various URLs you find interesting in your hobbies. To do this, pull down the Navigate menu and again choose the Menu Editor option. When the Menu Editor window pops up, click on the blank line above QUICKLIST. Now click on Insert . . . , which will cause the Add Item window to appear with the Title field available and the Menu control button active. You can type the new menu title into the field and click on Ok to create the menu. The new menu will appear at the top of the Mosaic page.

Of course, at the moment, this menu is empty; were you to click on it, nothing would happen. You can now use the menu editor to add items to fill up this menu. The procedure used is the same as the preceding, when we added the Center for Particle Astrophysics page to the Home Pages menu. You can add as many items to this menu as you choose until you reach the limit of forty.

Adding Submenus

You can also add submenus to existing menus. To do so, pull down the Navigate menu and choose the Menu Editor option. Highlight the menu to which you would like to add the submenu. Click on Insert . . . , which will cause the Add Item window to appear. Choose the Menu button and click on Ok. The submenu will now appear beneath the top menu item.

Inserting Separators

A separator appears as a straight line that divides a menu into sections. You can use it if you keep different categories of menu items available on the same menu and want to distinguish them. To add a separator, simply highlight the menu to which you want to add it (and then the place on that menu where you want it to appear) and click the Insert . . . button. Click the Separator control button, then Ok. The separator will now appear on the menu.

Other Menu Editor Options

Here are the other options offered by the Menu Editor. Mastering them will give you full control over your Mosaic environment.

Copy Item Adds the title and URL of the selected document to a buffer. This item will be the next document to appear in the Add Item window. Copy Item can thus be useful as a way of reorganizing your menus. Suppose, for example, that you would like to rearrange your menus into alphabetical sequence. You can choose an item, place it into the buffer, and insert it to the place you think it should appear. You can then use the Delete button to remove the other instance of the same item. In the absence of a sort feature, Mosaic's menus must be hand-edited to achieve this result.

Delete Removes the current item or menu. You will be queried as to whether you really intend to perform this action. Both menu items and menus themselves can be deleted in this way. The QUICKLIST cannot be deleted but, of course, items on the QUICKLIST can be.

Edit Opens the Edit Item window, which lets you edit the highlighted menu name. If a document is highlighted, this window allows you to edit either the name or the URL.

 Note: As you've seen, it is possible to add items to menus using either the Add Current to Hotlist choice on the Navigate menu or else by using the Menu Editor itself. The advantage of using the hotlist approach is that you only need to click on the hotlist item to insert the current page in whatever hotlist is available. The disadvantage is that the item is always added to the end of the current hotlist. If you want to have control over where you place the item on a menu, it makes more sense to familiarize yourself with the Menu Editor and simply use it when you want to add to a menu.

Using Mosaic's History Feature

As if Mosaic didn't provide enough ways to navigate the Internet, the program also provides a history feature, which is a list that records every document you have decided to display in the current session. Let's take a look at the History window. Open it by pulling down the Navigate menu and choosing the History option. You will see something like Figure 7.18, although your own history of sites will doubtless differ from mine.

The History window shows you the current history; that is, the history of your travels during the current network session. The URL of the current document is highlighted. You can move around in the list in two ways. Either choose an item and click on Load, or else simply double-click on the item, which will take you directly to the document.

Advantages of the History List

There are several advantages provided by the history list. Like the QUICKLIST, it establishes a series of destinations which do not need to appear on your main menu structure. You can move through the list to go back immediately to an item you had noticed earlier in your session without having to key in a lengthy URL. This is especially valuable when you are simply exploring sites, trying to determine which is best for your purposes, and find that you are frequently going down the wrong path. Retracing your steps is easy.

History List Commands

I've just shown you that the easiest way to use the History list is to pull down the Navigate menu and choose the History item. There, you can click on Load

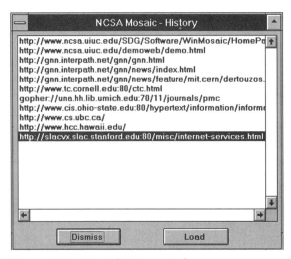

Figure 7.18   Mosaic's History window.

to go directly to a site or else Dismiss to make the History list disappear. But once you've used the list for awhile, you will probably want to take advantage of some of Mosaic's shortcuts. There are two ways to do this.

1. Use the Navigate menu again. You can choose either the Back or Forward menu item to go in either direction. This is handy if you are simply trying to move back up to the immediately preceding site.

2. Use the toolbar. Mosaic provides a variety of toolbar options, as shown in Figure 7.19.

Each of these is helpful insofar as it allows you to accomplish an action with a quick mouse click, rather than calling down a menu to do it. Read on to learn how to use this toolbar not only in your work with the History list but also with other Mosaic functions.

The Mosaic Toolbar

A toolbar is either a blessing or a curse, depending on two things: how well it is designed, and how graphical your nature happens to be. I have seen toolbars with icons so inscrutable that figuring out what they were for was more trouble than using menus to do the same job. On the other hand, once you master a toolbar, it is easy to move to it and click on its icons for fast operations. Here are the definitions of the options on the Mosaic toolbar shown in Figure 7.19.

Opens the Open URL box. This allows you to type in the URL of your choice and provides access to the Hotlists.

Saves the current document to disk. In the Microsoft Windows version of Mosaic, this option has not yet been implemented.

Takes you to the document immediately preceding the current one in your History list.

Takes you to the document immediately following the current one in the History list. If you are at the end of the History list, the left arrow button will not be available.

Reloads the current document. This can be helpful if a document loads improperly, presenting you with only a partial screen image.

Returns to the home page defined in the **mosaic.ini** file. Remember that it is good practice to change your default home page so that the NCSA server does not become overloaded. One way to do this was explained in Chapter 3; in Chapter 8, you will learn how to set up a home page of your own by designing a set of customized sites and an actual HTML document.

Figure 7.19 The Mosaic toolbar.

Copies the current selection to the clipboard. This capability is not yet implemented in the Microsoft Windows version of Mosaic.

 Pastes the clipboard contents into the active window. Again, this is not yet implemented in the Microsoft Windows version.

 Opens the Find box so that you can search for a particular keyword in the current document.

 Opens the Print box, allowing you to print the current document.

 Opens the About NCSA Mosaic for Microsoft Windows panel.

 Note: If you dislike toolbars or would simply prefer not to have the toolbar on-screen, you can hide it by choosing the Options menu and choosing the Show Toolbar item. This is a toggle: Clicking on it will turn off the display; clicking again will reactivate the toolbar (the check mark reappears).

Mapping Mosaic's Menus

We have already covered the major Mosaic menu items. Let's now run through the menus one by one to obtain an overview and to note any details we haven't yet discussed.

The File Menu

Figure 7.20 shows the File menu. The following list gives a brief description about each menu item.

Open URL . . .   Opens a dialog box in which you can enter a URL for a document. Clicking on Ok takes you to that document. Also provides the current hotlist and allows you to change it.

Open URL...	Ctrl+O
Open Local File...	
Save	Ctrl+S
Save As...	
Save Preferences	
Print...	Ctrl+P
Print Preview	
Print Setup...	
Document Source...	
Exit	

Figure 7.20   The Mosaic File menu.

Open Local File . . .   Allows you to open a file on your computer. A dialog box opens that allows you to select the file. Click Ok to call it up in the document view window.

Save   Saves the current document on your computer. The Microsoft Windows version of Mosaic implemented this feature with version Alpha 7 as this book went to press (it was not available in Alpha 6).

Save As . . .   Saves the document with your choice of formats, from ASCII to HTML. The Macintosh version of Mosaic now makes this feature available; it is not yet available on Windows version Alpha 6, but is now available through version Alpha 7.

Save Preferences   Saves the options listed on the Options menu. Also saves the current location of the document view window.

Print . . .   Allows you to print the current document.

Print preview   Previews the document about to be printed.

Print Setup . . .   Controls your printing options.

Document Source . . .   Displays the source file for the document displayed. Use this option to view the HTML source code for a given document. From within the window thus created, you have the choice of saving the file to disk or copying highlighted text to the clipboard.

Exit   Closes the window and exits Mosaic.

The Edit Menu

The Edit menu is a simple one, containing just two items.

Copy   Allows you to copy the selected text to the clipboard. Note that there are only certain places from which you can select text. Text can be selected in the Document Title and Document URL fields, as well as the document source window and the text-entry fields in the dialog boxes. You cannot select text in the document display area.

Find   Calls up a dialog box in which you can enter characters, words, or phrases in the Find What: field. You have the option of setting up a case-sensitive search by clicking on the Match Case box. The Find Next button allows you to search for the selection. The search capability is limited to the current document.

The Options Menu

Shown in Figure 7.21, the Options menu is the most complex of the Mosaic menus. We've already examined the meaning of some of its choices. Here's is a quick tour of the whole thing.

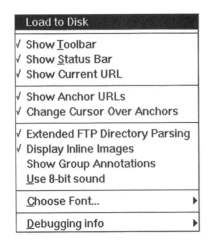

Figure 7.21 The Options menu, the most complex menu in Mosaic.

Load to Disk   Allows you to save a file to your hard disk. When you click on this item, a check mark will appear next to it. This indicates the option is active. The next time you move to a URL, you will be given a dialog box that allows you to save the document or file on your disk (the file will not appear on the screen). We discussed the file saving process in detail in Chapter 6.

Note: All files are saved in binary mode and in the original file format. This means you can ignore the Save File as Type: field when you are saving material to disk. Remember, at this point we are dealing with alpha software; various features that may appear surprising or redundant will doubtless be smoothed out in later versions. This accounts for some of Mosaic's peculiarities.

We must pause momentarily to discuss file formats. Windows, like the MS-DOS operating system that runs beneath it, requires that file names be no longer than eight characters long, with an optional three-letter extension separated from the first part of the name with a period. Because files available over the **World Wide Web** often use names that are longer than this, you must do one of two things when you save them to disk:

1. Change the file name to fit the **DOS** parameters when you call up the Load to Disk box. You will be given the option to choose directory and file name when this box appears.

2. Proceed without changing the name. In this case, Mosaic will make the changes for you. If the first part of the name is longer than eight characters, Mosaic will truncate it to eight. If more than three characters appear after the period, Mosaic will use only the first three of these. Multiple periods in a single file name will cause everything between the periods to be dropped.

Changing the file names yourself is the best course of action. Although Mosaic can do it for you, the resulting file names may not be clear to you. Always name your files to ensure maximum recognizability.

Show Toolbar

Controls display of the toolbar. You can toggle this switch on or off by clicking on it. If a check mark appears here, the toolbar will be active.

Show Status Bar

Displays the status bar at the bottom of the screen.

Show Current URL

Displays the current URL in a window at the top of the screen.

Show Anchor URLs

Displays the URL for any document with hyperlinks. This is a handy switch to keep active, because when you move the cursor to a hyperlink, even when you don't click on it, you will be shown the URL associated with it. The URL will appear in the status bar at the bottom of the document view window.

Change Cursor Over Anchors

Allows the cursor to change shape to indicate when it is pointing to a hyperlink. In the Windows version of Mosaic, it will turn from an arrow to a small, pointing hand. When no check mark appears next to this item, the cursor will not change in this context.

Extended FTP Directory Parsing

Displays file sizes and icons, along with file and directory names, during an FTP session. When this option is turned off, only the file and directory names are displayed.

Display Inline Images

Causes inline images to be loaded when a URL is accessed. When this option is turned off, a small icon is loaded instead. You can then click on the icon with the right mouse button to load the inline image. We will consider why you would want to turn this option off in Chapter 8 as we discuss customizing Mosaic.

Show Group Annotations

Displays all group annotations within a given document. Group annotations, as opposed to personal annotations, are maintained on a group server and are accessible by any of those using that server.

Use 8-bit Sound

Causes sound files to be sent to 8-bit system software.

Choose Font . . .

Allows you to customize the screen display of HTML documents viewed through Mosaic on your computer. The following options are available through this menu item (a submenu will appear, listing them).

Normal	The style used for paragraphs.
Header 1 through Header 7	The style used for section header levels.
Menu	The style used for menu entries.
Directory	The style used for directory and file names.
Address	The style used for addresses.
Block Quote	The style used for quotations that appear set off from the surrounding text.
Example	The style used for code samples.
Preformatted	Helpful in situations where the document's author specifies the format of the text.
Listing	The style used for longer code samples.

To use the Choose Font . . . options, drag the cursor to the paragraph style you would like to change. When you select one, a font selection window appears, as shown in Figure 7.22. You can then choose a new font, style and point size.

The Navigate Menu

Here is a summary of options available on the Navigate menu. We have already discussed the use of most of these.

Back	Moves back to the previous document in your History list.
Forward	Moves forward one document in your History list. If the current document is the last in the History list, this option will be disabled.

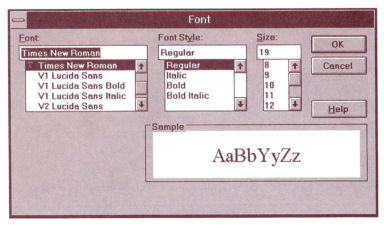

Figure 7.22   The Font selection window gives you control over the appearance of HTML documents.

Reload	Reloads the current document.
Home	Moves to the home page specified in the **mosaic.ini** file.
History . . .	Opens the History window, in which a list of URLs of documents displayed during the current session is available. You can use this window to navigate by double-clicking on any entry on the list, or by choosing an item and clicking the Load button.
Add Current to Hotlist	Adds the URL of the current document to the hotlist.
Menu Editor . . .	Opens a window allowing you to edit user-configurable menus.

The Annotate Menu

We have already discussed using annotations in detail earlier in this chapter. Here is a summary of the options available on the Annotate menu.

Annotate	Calls up the Annotate window, where you can enter an annotation for the current document. You can also view annotations you have previously made to this document.
Edit This Annotation	Calls up the Annotate window so that you can edit its contents or delete the annotation. This menu entry is only active when you are viewing an annotation.
Delete This Annotation	Deletes the current annotation. This menu entry is only active while you are viewing an annotation.

The Starting Points Menu

Starting Points is a helpful menu for the novice; it contains sites chosen by the NCSA that are already set up for you. All that is necessary is to click on one of these sites and Mosaic will take you to it. As you have seen, the Starting Points menu can be edited. As your experience with Mosaic grows, you will doubtless

Figure 7.23 Mosaic's Starting Points menu, as configured by NCSA.

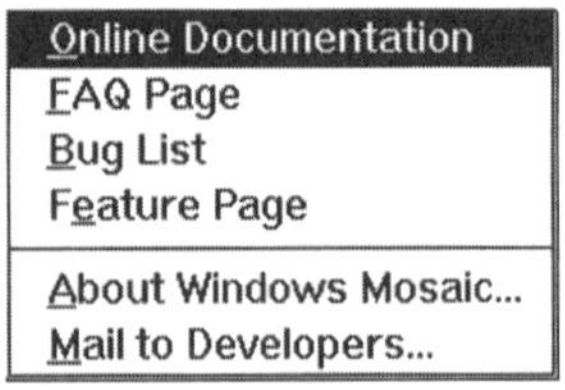

```
┌─────────────────────────────────┐
│ Online Documentation            │
│ FAQ Page                        │
│ Bug List                        │
│ Feature Page                    │
├─────────────────────────────────┤
│ About Windows Mosaic...         │
│ Mail to Developers...           │
└─────────────────────────────────┘
```

Figure 7.24   The Help menu.

want to delete some items currently on it and add others of your own choosing. The Starting Points menu is shown in Figure 7.23.

The Mosaic sites on this menu provide a useful way to keep up with happenings at NCSA and the continuing development of the program. In addition, there are submenus, each shown by a small, right-pointing triangle. Here you can access **World Wide Web** materials, a variety of home pages, and numerous other documents. You also have access to FTP sites and **Gopher** servers, as well as **archie**, **WHOIS**, and **finger**.

All in all, the Starting Points menu is a good guide; it shows you the range of capabilities possessed by Mosaic. Just don't be afraid to modify it as necessary. A key benefit of Mosaic, as you'll see again in the following chapter, is its ability to be customized.

The Help Menu

The Microsoft Windows version of Mosaic does not yet include a help file. However, the items on this menu will soon be implemented. The Help menu appears in Figure 7.24. Here is a summary of its features:

Online Documentation   Connects to NCSA Mosaic for Microsoft Windows User's Guide online.

FAQ Page   Connects to NCSAs Frequently Asked Questions page.

Bug List   Connects to an NCSA page listing known bugs in Mosaic.

Feature Page   Connects to a page listing features in the various versions of Mosaic.

About Windows Mosaic   Contains the version number, names of developers, and e-mail addresses for bug reports.

Mail to Developers   Allows you to send a question or report to the developers. Remember, always attempt to solve any problems on your own, because the developers are extremely busy.

We have now completed a tour of Mosaic's menus. It's time to consider various customization options not already covered. We'll also see, in the next chapter, how to set up a unique home page, not only to take the strain off the overloaded NCSA server, but also to provide you with a personal gateway to the **World Wide Web**.

8

Customizing Mosaic

Mosaic presents us with numerous opportunities for customizing our Internet environment. We have already considered some of these. For example, the program's Menu Editor allows us to open a Personal Menus window. There, we can change the contents of various menus or create entirely new ones. And because Mosaic can cope with as many as twenty user-configurable menus, we have plenty of room to set up whatever information structure we choose.

Users coming to Mosaic after experience with UNIX-driven shell accounts have to get used to this new way of thinking. The UNIX tools we use when dialing in to a service provider's computer offer abundant command switches, making it possible to perform a huge range of Internet tasks. This means we can enter a command followed by optional settings that cause the UNIX program to perform specific actions. There is no shortage of such options.

But these programs are limited in their ability to be customized. Certainly, they provide nothing like the flexibility of Mosaic in setting up user environments complete with annotations, personally selected hotlists, user-defined home pages and full control over the kinds of files—image, sound, moving video—that they can manipulate. In this way, Mosaic is truly *sui generis*.

Of course, you don't have to customize Mosaic. Having set the program up in Chapter 3, we found that it was possible to be up and running on the Internet almost immediately. This is because the program is almost preposterously easy to use—you point at what you want to see and click on it with your mouse to retrieve it. But a little experience, particularly if you are approaching Mosaic from a SLIP/PPP account over a telephone line, will convince you of the benefits to be gained by tweaking this program. Changing Mosaic's menus is but one way to do this. In this chapter, we examine some of the other possibilities.

Changing Your Home Page

As provided by the NCSA, Mosaic is configured to load a default home page. Which one you see will depend upon which version of Mosaic you are using. The NCSA home pages are useful to the novice because they provide background information, announcements about the latest versions of the program, and news of ongoing developments at NCSA. But because interest in Mosaic has become so great, the number of Mosaic programs out there trying to access the same server has grown to alarming proportions.

Our first step in this chapter, then, is to configure Mosaic to take the load off the NCSA servers. There are various ways to do this. We can disable the loading of a home page altogether by making changes to the **mosaic.ini** file, or we can change the default home page to a different document; both actions lighten the NCSA's traffic burden. The latter choice, changing the default, can be handled in two different ways. We can choose an existing home page as our default, or we can actually build a home page of our own. Let's run through all these scenarios.

A New Default Home Page

The first thing to try is choosing a different home page as the default. Before you can do this, you must have a home page in mind as a substitute for the NCSA home page. Any document will do, but it makes sense to find one that fits in with your own interests and work habits. Once you have located one (and you might consider looking through Chapter 10, which lists a number of interesting sites), you will need to procure the URL for this page. By now you know how to take the URL for the current document right off the Mosaic screen.

Once you have the URL, you will need to open the **mosaic.ini** file with any text editor. Just remember that you want to be able to open the file and save it as an ASCII file. And as an additional reminder, recall that in Chapter 3, we moved a copy of the **mosaic.ini** file to the *c:\windows* directory. This is the copy of the file that Mosaic uses as it works. But don't forget, we kept a clean backup copy of the file in the *\mosaic* directory, so make sure that the file you edit is the **mosaic.ini** file in the *\windows* directory. Changes you make to the other one will have no effect.

Move to the [Main] section of the **mosaic.ini** file, and look for a line that looks like this:

```
Home Page=http://www.ncsa.uiuc.edu/SDG/Software/WinMosaic/HomePage.html
```

You can see that the **mosaic.ini** file is pointing to the URL of the NCSA home page; this is the default. You will need to change this in your text editor to show the URL of the document you wish to use instead. Therefore, remove the NCSA URL and substitute the URL of your choice. Then save **mosaic.ini** in ASCII format. The next time you launch Mosaic, it will automatically load the document you have chosen.

Macintosh users can perform the same action by choosing the Preferences . . . item in the Options menu. In the Home Page: field, they can insert the URL of their choice, clicking on Apply to complete the action. Then the new home page will load whenever Mosaic is launched.

Disabling Home Page Autoloading

Turning off the automatic loading of any home page is the simplest of the home page options. Again, you will make a modification to the **mosaic.ini** file to accomplish it. Look in the [Main] section of the file once more. The line you are after reads as follows:

```
Autoload Home Page=yes
```

Simply edit the line, changing the yes to no:

```
Autoload Home Page=no
```

Now you can close the file, saving it as an ASCII file. When you launch Mosaic the next time, the program will load but without anything visible in the document view area. You can then choose whichever site you would like to visit by dropping down the File menu and taking the Open URL . . . option. Or you can use the Starting Points menu or any other menu you may have configured on your own to move from site to site. Remember that you can always go to the NCSA's Mosaic home page by using Starting Points.

Creating Your Own Home Page

Although it sounds intimidating, creating a home page of your own with HTML is not all that difficult. HyperText Markup Language, you'll recall, contains the commands that **World Wide Web** tools like Mosaic use to present their information. An HTML document thus contains the necessary information about formatting and the positioning of hyperlinks. Take a look at an HTML document, as shown in Figure 8.1.

I created this screen by pulling down the File menu and choosing the Document Source . . . option in Mosaic. You are looking at the HTML document that creates NCSA's home page for the Microsoft Windows version of Mosaic.

Yes, it looks like an extremely dicey proposition to create such a page. But note a critical fact: This is simply an ASCII text file, just like the **mosaic.ini** file. We can create something similar in any text editor (we're also beginning to see HTML editors like HTML Edit for the Macintosh and various programs for Microsoft Windows; expect the number of these to increase quickly, making the job even easier). Out of this jumble of straight text come all the graphical niceties of Mosaic. It should be clear that we don't have to master every

Figure 8.1   A basic HTML document as seen through Mosaic.

HTML trick to create a home page of our own. And the advantages of creating one are obvious. Such a page would place no strain on the NCSA server when we fired up Mosaic, and we could design a home page that pointed to the most common destinations in our own work. Let's consider how to go about this.

A Sample HTML Document

We can use a simple set of commands to set up a sample HTML document. Take a look at the following:

<title>A Sample Home Page</title>
<h1>Frequent World Wide Web Destinations</h1>
On this home page, we will locate a set of hyperlinks to
information we most frequently access.<p>
The best way to learn HTML is by example.<p>

Again, we're dealing with nothing but ASCII text. We have specified how that text should look on screen through the use of tags, known in HTML parlance as *mark-up tags.*

Thus, in the example above, <title> specifies the title of a document. Notice the end of the line, which closes the title section with another tag, </title>. We've also used the <h1> and corresponding </h1> tags to specify information that should appear as a level-one header, and the <p> tag to show where a paragraph ends. The text we are trying to format appears between the tags. Most, but not all, tags are paired. When they are, the ending tag includes the slash shown in </title> and </h1> in this example. The <p> tag is an exception to this rule; it has no pairing requirement. Inline images provide another exception to the rule.

HTML functions entirely through these formatting tags. You can enter spaces or tabs in the original HTML document but they will not appear when that document is displayed in Mosaic. Similarly, word wrap isn't a factor. Where the lines break on the Mosaic display screen will be determined by the placement of the tags in the HTML text. A lengthy line that wraps in your text editor will appear as a complete line in Mosaic's display. Your job as an HTML designer, then, is to thoroughly master the various tags available to the language.

For practice, why not set up the example shown several paragraphs above as an HTML document yourself? To do so, simply open a text editor and copy the material exactly as shown. Case is not significant. Save the file in ASCII format. Its name should end in an **.htm** (for Windows documents) or **.html** (for the Macintosh) suffix. You could call this document, then, **test.htm** or **test.html**. To view it in Mosaic, pull down the File menu and choose the Open Local File . . . option. This will open a dialog box that allows you to choose the file you want to see.

The Basic HTML Commands

The preceeding example gives us a glimpse of how to construct an HTML document. Of course, this one is "read-only"—there are no hyperlinks, no graphics, and very little text. To make a home page, and an interesting one, at that, we need to learn some other HTML commands. These will allow us to add a wide variety of features to our documents. Here, then, are the basic markup tags.

Title   When you create a title with the <title> tag and corresponding </title> tag at the end, you have created text that is displayed at the top of the screen. Choose your titles with care to reflect, accurately and concisely, what is contained on your home page.

Here is another example of a title:

<title>My Personal Home Page</title>

Notice that there is no space between the tags and the text that immediately follows or precedes them.

Headings   Six degrees of headers are available in HTML. Header 1 is the most prominent, header 6 the least. You can experiment with an HTML document to see how the different headings look on-screen. The basic syntax for creating them is shown in the following example

<h1>Headings help you separate levels of content</h1>

Substitute any number between 2 and 6 in the above example to vary the size of the font in the heading.

Paragraph Tags   You can separate paragraphs by ending a paragraph with the <p> tag. This inserts a carriage return and a line feed. An example follows.

This line will be separated as a paragraph<p>

An important point: Carriage returns within HTML files have no significance. The <p> tag, and the <br> tag in the next entry, are critical for setting up textual divisions within your document. Otherwise, word wrap can occur anywhere within the HTML document.

Line Breaks   You can force a line break with no extra space between the lines by using the <br> tag. I could set up an address this way:

John Gower
123 Confessio Lane
Amantis, ME 12345

Hyperlinks   The hyperlink tag is critical; it allows you to set up the relationship between the text and the servers it connects to on the **World Wide Web**. You use an <a> as the tag to show hypertext; it stands for anchor. Following is what a hyperlink looks like in HTML.

<a href="http://gnn.interpath.net/gnn/gnn.html">Global Network Navigator</a>

Take a close look at the preceding example. We have followed the opening tag with the href= statement, which is used to point to the document we wish to access. We use the URL of the resource to which we want the link to apply, enclosing it in quotation marks. We follow it with the name of the hyperlink, which is what we will see on the screen. The statement closes with the final </a> tag.

Now, when we activate the document, we will find that the words Global Network Navigator appear as a standard hyperlink; that is, they will be in color (if we're using a color monitor) and underlined. We use URLs according to the rules specified in Chapter 5; they allow us to link to a wide variety of file types, from **Gophers** to Telnet destinations, **World Wide Web** pages, and FTP sites.

You can also set up links to files on your own computer, in which case, the tag should simply point to the name of the file and, if it is in a different directory than the current document, the path from the current document to the linked document. Here is an example of a link to a file that resides in the same directory as the current document:

<a href="basic.htm">Tips</a>

The reference tells the browser to link to the file **basic.htm** and to call the hyperlink **Tips**.

If we were pointing to a file in a different directory, we would set up the link this way:

<a href="c:\web\basic.htm">Tips</a>

Now the same file is set up as the link, even though it resides in a different directory from the current document; we have provided a complete path so that Mosaic can find it. The link to the file is still called Tips.

Inline Images   Including an inline image within a document is a matter of pointing to the image file. To do this, we use HTML in the following format:

<img src="image.gif">

This example assumes that the image is in the same directory as the HTML document. If it is not, we can point to a file in a different directory, or on a different server. When we do this, we need to specify the URL of the image. Next, for example, is a tag pointing to an image that is located on a different directory on our own machine:

<img src="file:///c:\astro\mars.gif">

Notice that I have specified the URL using the file:// statement, showing that I am dealing with a file rather than a Web server or other type of resource. There is a third slash following file://; this is an indication that I have left blank the space that would have been filled by a machine address. In this case, I don't need one, because the file resides on my own computer.

And here is a tag pointing to a different server:

<img src="http://www.hydroplane.com/vintage/mitchell.gif">

Notice that, in this example, the URL contains an http:// statement, followed immediately by a machine address, and then the path to the image in question.

External Images   Perhaps you would rather open an image as a separate document, using whichever viewer you have set up within Mosaic. A reference to an external image takes the following format:

<a href="http://www.hydroplane.com/vintage/mitchell.gif">The B-25 in Flight</a>

In this case, we are pointing to the URL of the image, and including the name of the anchor that will appear on our document, *The B-25 in Flight.* The anchor statement will appear underlined and with the appropriate color change to indicate a hyperlink in the Mosaic document window.

If you point to an image located on your own computer this way, don't forget that you are not dealing with a **Web** server but with a file on your own machine. Thus the following statement inserts the URL with the file:// statement, rather than using http://. Always consider the nature of the resource to which you are pointing:

<a href="file:///c:\images\mosaic\jupiter.gif"

Lists   It is frequently useful in terms of clarity to set up lists in an HTML document. These can be displayed either with numbering or bullets. The <ol> tag is used to begin an ordered list; an unordered list uses the <ul> tag. In both cases, you then use a <li> tag to distinguish between the various items on the list. Examine the following example, and note that the list ends with a paired tag.

<ol>
<li>Wordsworth
<li>Coleridge
<li>Keats
<li>Shelley
<li>Byron
</ol>

An unordered, or bulleted, list would end with a <ul> tag.

Bold Text   You can cause text to appear in bold by using the <b> and </b> tags. Thus, the following line would appear in bold:

<b>Mosaic Formatting Commands</b>

Italics   To set up text in italics, use the <i> and </i> tags. The following will appear in italics:

<i>The Use of Markup Tags</i>

Nesting Formatting Tags

Mosaic allows you to enclose text within more than one formatting tag. Let's say, for example, that I would like to show a header and also place it in italics. To do so, I can use two sets of tags, as follows:

<h1><i>An Essential Guide to the Web</h1></i>

The text will appear as a regular header but in italics.

Table 8.1 summarizes the basic HTML formatting commands. Note again that most (though not all) of the tags come in pairs, and most use a slash to signify the end pair.

Table 8.1   The Basic HTML Formatting Commands

Design Element	Lead Tag	End Tag
Title	<title>	</title>
Headings	<h1> through <h6>	</h1>, </h2>, etc.
Paragraphs	<p>	No tag applicable
Line breaks	 	No tag applicable
Hyperlinks	<a href="*URL_of_link*">	</a>
Inline Images	<img src="*URL_of_link*">	No tag applicable
Ordered List	<ol>	</ol>
Bulleted list	<ul>	</ul>
Bold text	<b>	</b>
Italics	<i>	</i>

A Sample Home Page

Only you can decide what you would like to see in a home page. But I've included for your edification a simple home page that can be edited and expanded as you choose. I also have included an image for fun; you can do the same. Just choose a file in GIF format and either place it in the same directory as your HTML file or else show a path statement that allows Mosaic to find it. And, of course, change the name of the image to reflect your choice.

```
<title>Mosaic s Links to the World Wide Web</title>
<h1>A List of Frequent Destinations</h1>
<img src="file:///c:\mosaic\home\monet.gif">
<h2>Mosaic Information</h2>
<ul>
<li><a href="http://www.ncsa.uiuc.edu/SDG/Software/Mosaic/NCSAMosaicHome.html">Mosaic Home Page</a>
<li><a href="http://www.ncsa.uiuc.edu/SDG/Software/Mosaic/Docs/whats-new.html">What s New
with Mosaic</a>
<li><a href="http://www.ncsa.uiuc.edu/SDG/Software/Mosaic/MetaIndex.html">NCSA
MetaIndex</a>
</ul>
<p>
<h2>Internet Resources</h2>
<ul>
<li><a href="http://www.internic.net/infoguide.html">InterNIC InfoGuide</a>
<li><a href="http://www.rpi.edu/Internet/Guides/decemj/text.html">Internet Web Sources</a>
<li><a href="http://www.clark.net/pub/journalism/awesome.html">The Awesome List of
Resources</a>
<li><a href="http://slacvx.slac.stanford.edu:80/misc/internet-services.html">Internet
Services List</a>
</ul>
```

The home page created from this is shown in Figure 8.2. Naturally, your own choice of image file will differ from mine (I have a taste for Monet), but

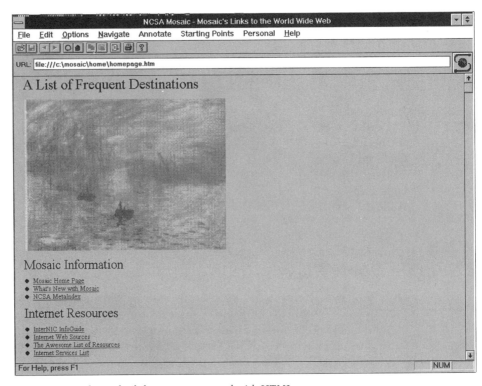

Figure 8.2 A home-built home page created with HTML.

note the construction. There is an image directly under the title, followed by two headers, each of which contain lists of Internet sites. The sites are underlined, indicating hyperlinks. Clicking on them will take you directly to the site of your choice.

You now need to set up the new home page as your default. To do so, open the **mosaic.ini** file again. As before, you are looking for this line:

```
Home Page=http://www.ncsa.uiuc.edu/SDG/Software/WinMosaic/HomePage.html
```

But you have to be careful when you change it. Assuming you are trying to load your home page from your own computer, you now need to specify that the home page must access a local file. In my case, for example, I have put the home page HTML document is a subdirectory of my \mosaic directory; the path is *c:\mosaic\home\homepage.htm*. To show this in the **mosaic.ini** file, I edit it as follows:

```
Home Page=file:///c:\mosaic\home\homepage.htm
```

I have replaced the http:// statement with a file:// statement, because I am not accessing a **WWW** server (which is what HTTP refers to), but rather an individual HTML file on my own computer. Note that I have named the page file **homepage.htm**. Since I am using Microsoft Windows, I must obey MS-DOS file conventions, and cannot have an extension that is longer than three letters.

Macintosh users have it easier. They can pull down the Options menu and select Use this URL for Home. The next time they call up Mosaic, it will go directly to this home page on the local hard drive. And both Macintosh and Microsoft Windows Mosaic users will find it easy to get back to their home pages whenever they choose by clicking on the small house icon at the top of the screen. (This, remember, takes you back to whatever home page you have established.)

Being able to create your own home page is quite a powerful capability. And although I'm fond of the home page I just created for you, I have to admit that it barely begins to tap the full formatting power of HTML. After all, you may want to add links to audio files or to MPEG or QuickTime movies. Or perhaps you'd like to explore the entire range of HTML formatting options, such as setting up addresses or preparing quotations for display.

If you get interested in exploring these issues further (who knows, you may become a home page designer—I have a hunch their numbers are about to grow significantly), then you will want to set up links to several sites that specialize in HTML. Either add them to your menus or set them up as hyperlinks on your own home page. As mentioned in Chapter 5, these sites are:

```
http://www.ncsa.uiuc.edu/demoweb/html-primer.html
http://www.ucc.ie/info/net/htmldoc.html
http://melmac.harris-atd.com/about_html.html
```

Also consider Dan Connolly's *HTML Design Notebook;* Connolly is one of the original developers of HTML. The URL is:

```
http://www.hal.com/~connolly/drafts/html-design.html
```

Master these sites and you will have quite an authoritative background in HTML.

Home Pages vs. Menus

As you work toward customizing your Mosaic environment to suit your needs, a question inevitably arises. Is it better to focus on manipulating the program's pull-down menus, inserting your favorite destinations there, or would it make more sense to construct a home page with references to these sites, perhaps connecting as well to other pages of your own devising? It's a call only you can make, but the advantage of taking the extra time to master HTML is that you can construct a graphical environment entirely suited to your own purposes. Menus, on the other hand, are easier to customize and provide a shortcut to much of the same functionality.

In my case, a combination of the two seems the best policy. I have constructed a home page with links to the resources I use most frequently in my writing, changing them as necessary when new projects arise. I also maintain basic Internet destinations on the menus, frequently adding new ones, and (sometimes) new menus to accommodate the rapidly expanding world of **Web** servers. It is instructive to look through the wide variety of home pages out there to see if there are any that particularly take your fancy.

If you like what you see at a certain site, remember that you can call up the HTML document behind that page to study it, thus learning how certain effects were achieved. Just pull down the File menu and choose the Document Source . . . item. The most complex of home pages yields its secrets quickly with this method, allowing you to duplicate its effects. There is no better way to improve your HTML skills than to occasionally study other people's work.

Design Issues When Building a Home Page

In the days of typewriters and, indeed, character-based computers, graphic design was an issue left in the hands of the experts. No one had the requisite tools on the desktop. When it came time to construct a new brochure for the company, someone in the office would create the copy, edit it for clarity and style, and pass it along to, perhaps, an art department, which would create an appropriate design. The whole brochure would then be placed in the hands of a printer, who would use various tools to lay out each page and produce a final document. With each segment of the operation handled by different people, printed projects were both harder to accomplish and more appropriately styled.

This is not to disparage the countless fine design tools now in the hands of the individual; indeed, the ability to create a document from top to bottom, including graphics of various kinds and employing a host of formatting tools, has never been so democratically distributed. But anyone who sees as many product announcements, sales presentations and company brochures as I do knows that the quality of their layout has suffered as the result of the new-found power made available throughout the company. If the boss doesn't need to hire an artist to create the new logo, he or she will save money. On the other hand, the logo probably won't look like it was created by a professional, no matter how fine the tools used to design it. We face many of the same issues with Mosaic.

A stroll through a variety of **World Wide Web** sites with Mosaic is enough to convince anyone of the proposition that some home pages are artfully conceived and beautifully executed. Others come up woefully short in terms of aesthetics and leave logic behind in terms of organization. The sites you tend to create slots for in your own menus are those with the most intelligence behind them, so why not apply the same principles to the creation of your own home page? Even if no one but you is likely to use it, a well-designed home page will pay off by ordering your **Web** sessions and providing an environment you're not unhappy to look at day after day.

Here are some key design principles to think about as you set about this process:

Go Easy On the Images.   This sounds like heresy, given the nature of Mosaic's appeal; after all, it's spectacular imagery that most people use to show off Mosaic's power. But now that you've constructed a home page of your own, the price for the images becomes obvious. The larger the image you add to your home page, the longer it takes Mosaic to load it; the greater the number of images, the more that factor becomes multiplied. There are home pages on the **Web** so stuffed with inline images that using them over a SLIP connection is all but precluded; many people simply throw the appropriate toggle in the Options menu so as not to see them.

Remember this principle: Inline images don't have to be large to be effective. If you do want to link to larger image files, set them up as external images so you'll have the option of not loading them. Then, when you do want to see them, it's simply a matter of clicking on the appropriate hyperlink.

Avoid Frequent Font Changes.   HTML allows you great control over the fonts you use; you can set up six levels of headers and use italics and boldface to good effect. But the key in working with fonts is moderation. A document that changes fonts every paragraph or so is one that distracts the eye, rather than enhancing the text. Soon readers find themselves wondering what's going to happen next. The attempt to beautify a document has become an exercise in pointless decoration.

The key, then, is moderation. Use font changes to emphasize key elements of your home page, and to draw attention to useful divisions between the information you are making available. Use italics and boldface sparingly. Both can be effective, but they rely on scarcity for their effect; otherwise, what you thought you were emphasizing simply becomes one in a series of type changes, incapable of catching the jaded eye of the reader.

And don't forget that you have a variety of settings available in the Options menu (following the Choose Font . . . option) that control how Mosaic formats the various style elements. You can do quite a lot to change settings to meet your own specifications using these settings, giving you control over your screen display. Elements from the various headers to bulleted lists, definitions, tables, block quotes, directories, addresses, menus, and forms can be manipulated through the pull-down menus.

Less Is More.   A cluttered home page is not only difficult to read; it also makes it almost impossible to find the information you need. Mosaic makes it possible to scroll through long home pages looking for information, but it's all too easy to lose the hyperlinks you're looking for if you have to page through an interminable document to find them.

The alternative? Consider breaking your hyperlinks into categories that can then be moved to separate pages. Suppose I have developed a series of hyperlinks to sites specializing in astronomy. Rather than scattering them over my home page, or even grouping them together on a home page that already contains multiple groups, I might choose to set up one hyperlink from the home page to a separate page containing astronomical information. Let your imagination roam here. Your new astronomy page could contain all of the astronomy links you prefer; you might also add a nice inline image of a NASA planetary flyby, or perhaps one of Chesley Bonestell's superb works of astronomical art (for the latter, see Chapter 10, where site references are given).

I tend to think in terms of simple pages, no more than two screens long, with multiple, organized links to other pages, which in turn break out the information I need. This way, research and information gathering is done in a logical manner, and I have a ready place to drop links to new sites as they develop. On the home page itself, I keep as my major hyperlinks a set of sites that specialize in news about both Mosaic and the **World Wide Web**. I am more interested in building hyper-environments than in creating single home pages. As you play with HTML, you may well develop a similar enthusiasm.

Keep Your Links Up to Date. A little net surfing will drive one point home forcefully—if you click on a hyperlink only to be told that it has been moved, the value of the hyperlink is lost. What happened? Somebody at the site in question has done some tinkering with the files being accessed; along the line, whoever built the home page you're using didn't keep up with events at the remote site and is not aware that what used to be a workable hyperlink no longer functions.

Mosaic didn't create the problem of out-of-date information on the Internet. Alas, it is an all too familiar situation. What you as a home page designer need to do is to periodically check your links. Your home page may look lovely, incorporating all the careful design and judicious use of graphics that you set out to create, but its hyperlinks may be defunct. Periodically try out each one of them, to see if anything has changed. Then, keep your eyes open for the new location. One way to track such changes is through the *net-happenings* mailing list put out by the InterNIC. Numerous **Web** sites are listed there. You can subscribe by sending e-mail to this address:

majordomo@is.internic.net

Your message should contain the statement:

subscribe net-happenings *your_name*

If you prefer to read the same material through a USENET newsgroup, you can access it through a brand new group:

comp.internet.net-happenings

The other way of keeping up with additions or changes to sites is through the three newsgroups already mentioned. Use your USENET reader to subscribe to:

comp.infosystems.www.users
comp.infosystems.www.providers
comp.infosystems.www.misc

Be Sparing with Audio Files.   There is a site in Peru that contains an audio link to a lovely Andean folk melody. The file is approximately 440 K long and takes some time to download, but the music is worth the wait. It would be wonderful if more sites used Mosaic's built-in audio capabilities as satisfyingly as this one, but unfortunately, much of the audio material now available over the **World Wide Web** is more or less experimental in nature. You can see how audio works by checking in with the NCSA's demonstration page (available through the Starting Points menu). The small speaker symbols are hyperlinked to underlying audio files which can be transferred to your system and played there.

The first few times you try it, moving audio over a network connection is a thrill. But the static nature of this material soon becomes apparent. In many cases, an audio link consists of someone reading text to you that is already present on the screen. It takes the person longer to read the text aloud than it takes you to read it on-screen, not to mention the length of time it takes to download the audio file in the first place. Considering how much bandwidth is taken up by the audio file you're moving, ask yourself whether it's really necessary to hear what is presented therein. And in terms of your own audio links, consider that once the thrill of making it work is gone, the real reason for having any kind of hyperlink is to impart information. Too many home pages on the **Web** use audio just to show off.

Label Page Elements Clearly.   With both audio and visual files, you will want to make it clear what each link refers to; no one likes to click on an image only to find that the file is more than a megabyte in length and the download will be a lengthy one. You can avoid this problem by labeling each image or audio file, describing not only what it is, but how big a file it involves. This is simply good HTML design, even if your home page is not destined to be used by anyone but yourself. If you get into MPEG or QuickTime movies, where file lengths are truly gigantic, the need for this caution will be all the more obvious.

Keep Your Home Page Flexible.   If only because you need to keep updating your hyperlinks, you don't want any home page to become a static entity. But beyond this maintenance issue is a broader question. As you work your way through site after site using Mosaic, you will encounter some that strike you as particularly pleasing. We all learn HTML one step at a time, and it may be that a particular effect is one you had never thought of implementing. If so, consider looking at the source HTML document and then trying to duplicate the effect on your own home page. Be alert for these kinds of ideas, which can benefit your own work and make you a better HTML author.

I think of Mosaic home pages as works in progress; the goal is not to complete them but to move them continuously toward greater utility and beauty.

That interesting snippet of art you ran across at a particular site might be transplanted to a page at your site, given a new context, and used to enhance an otherwise dull-looking document. Why not strive to improve your home page every time you open it, looking for ways to make it more attractive and more useful to you in your work? With more than 3,900 **Web** sites available at the time of this writing, there is no shortage of material to give you ideas.

Use the Tools You Have Available.   This cryptic advice simply refers to such easily used programs as spell checkers, which can avoid embarrassment. There is a prominent page on the **Web** in which the HTML authors have mis-spelled several words in major headers. Given the quality of the design we can create with HTML, it seems a shame to let the content side of the equation down so badly. A quick run through with a spell checker would have solved this problem, but the page's designers didn't think to do it. If the **Web** is all about making information available, then surely one of our goals must be to ensure that that information is of high quality.

Using (and Removing) Inline Images

What exactly do we mean by *inline images* anyway? An inline image is one that a **Web** browser like Mosaic can display next to text. We've just seen how to set up inline images on a home page, and we've considered as well how we can set up links to external images. The sparing use of inline images allows a **Web** page to be a visually exciting place. Unfortunately, not everyone is sparing about their use of imagery. As with any graphical tool, it is all too easy to abuse HTML, creating home pages with so many images on them that they take a long time to load. Images load one at a time, after all, and a particularly large image can make you wish you had never called up Mosaic in the first place.

Whether or not you experience Mosaic this way depends on the speed of your connection. Anyone working with a high-speed connection will doubtless keep all of Mosaic's imagery turned on; the processing time will not be that great. But those working on a SLIP connection have to deal with slower speeds, and anyone using less than a 14,400 bps modem may well find it preferable to turn off the inline images altogether. In this way, you can zip back and forth between Mosaic pages with little delay. Only the text will be trans-ferred, dramatically reducing the wait.

To turn off inline images, simply pull down the Options menu and click on Display Inline Images, thus causing the check mark by this item to disappear. Macintosh users will also use their Options menu, choosing the Auto-Load Images item. From this point on, when Mosaic transfers a document, you will see an icon instead of any inline image.

A document transferred with the inline images turned off looks like what you see in Figure 8.3. Note the icons. To see the image represented by any of these icons, all you need do is to click on the icon with the right mouse button.

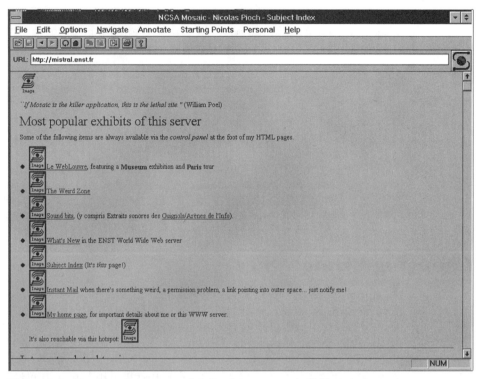

Figure 8.3   Viewing a document with inline images turned off. Note the image icons.

The linked image will then appear. If you click on the icon with the left mouse button, Mosaic will cause it to be transferred to your system, where it can be viewed with an external viewer. (This assumes that the inline image provides a hyperlink to an underlying, larger image. If it does not, then clicking on the left mouse button will have no effect, but clicking on the right one will still activate the inline image.)

Generally, I recommend that people leave their inline images on for as long as they enjoy them. If your connection is slow enough that you begin to feel frustrated by time lags (and this is particularly irritating when you return again and again to the same site), then it is probably time to turn off the images to speed up your work. You can always switch them back on again at any time.

Breaking Out of Long Transfers

You can interrupt the transfer of a lengthy document by clicking on the Mosaic symbol at the upper right of the screen. This will abort the process and allow you to get on with your work. Sometimes **Web** documents fail to specify how large a particular file is, which makes this a fairly common situation. If you are designing your own home page, be sure to remember to include the length of any particularly long files as a warning to possible users.

 Note: Clicking on the Mosaic symbol works only some of the time. In other cases, it can cause the program to crash, in which case there may be no choice but to exit Mosaic and start from scratch. In extreme cases, your entire system may freeze, necessitating a reboot. Because of this possibility, always be sure that any documents you are working on in simultaneously running software programs are saved to disk or closed completely before starting Mosaic. This advice applies largely to the latest, experimental versions of the program, where stability is still a problem.

Changing Window Size

If you don't like the size or placement of your Mosaic window, it's easy to customize. Simply resize by dragging the window with the cursor to the location desired. The entire window can be moved without altering its size by clicking on the title bar and dragging the window to the place of your choice. The new placement of the window can be saved by pulling down the File menu and choosing the Save Preferences item. All current window settings will be saved.

Fine-Tuning with the mosaic.ini File

We've already made several changes to the **mosaic.ini** file, starting with Chapter 3, when we downloaded Mosaic and began to run our initial sessions. Now let's return to this critical file to consider a few of its less obvious options. Remember that when you edit this file, you can use any text editor, but the file must be saved as straight ASCII. Also remember that, if you set up Mosaic the way we specified it in Chapter 3, you have a copy of the original **mosaic.ini** file in your *mosaic* subdirectory. This is your backup copy, in case you need to restore any of the original settings. Herewith a look at some **mosaic.ini** options.

Background Colors

As configured by NCSA, Mosaic is set up to show gray as its background window color; many **Web** documents assume this background, and their colors are designed to harmonize with it. But if you choose, you can change the background to white. Look for this statement in the [Main] section of the **mosaic.ini** file:

Grey Background=yes

If you would prefer a white background (I don't advise it), change the statement to read as follows:

Grey Background=no

Change Your Bullets

When we constructed a sample home page, we used a bulleted list which looks quite attractive on the screen. However, the process of drawing bullets does slow down Mosaic. You can turn on an option that shows bullets as lines instead of round figures by looking in the [Main] section of the **mosaic.ini** file and finding this statement:

Round List Bullets=yes

Change it as follows to see line bullets:

Round List Bullets=no

Removing Underlining

The underlining of hypertext links also slows performance. Those with monochrome monitors have no choice, nor do those who are printing documents to a black-and-white printer; for them, the underlining is necessary to reveal the presence of a hyperlink. But if you have a color monitor and would prefer not to use underlining, look in the [Settings] section of the **mosaic.ini** file. Find the following statement:

Anchor Underline=yes

Set it as follows:

Anchor Underline=no

The default setting is yes.

Specifying a News Server

As distributed by NCSA, Mosaic uses the network news server at the University of Illinois. However, you can change to a local news server if one is available. Look for the following line in the [Services] section of the **mosaic.ini** file:

NNTP Server="news.cso.uiuc.edu"

Change it to reflect the address of your local server.

Changing Mail Servers

Mosaic uses a Simple Mail Transfer Protocol (SMTP) server to send mail back to the NCSA developers. This is done by pulling down the Help menu and choosing the Mail to Developers . . . option. The copy of Mosaic we downloaded from NCSA is set up to use the NCSA FTP server for this task. However, you can insert the name of a local SMTP server if you choose. Look for the following entry:

SMTP Server="ftp.ncsa.uiuc.edu"

Change the name of the server to the local server address.

Group Annotations

We've already discussed how to create personal annotations, which attach comments to documents and are saved on your personal machine. But it is also possible to create group annotations that can be saved on a network machine and made accessible to all the members of a group whenever they access a particular URL. You have the option of using either personal or group annotations, but you cannot use both simultaneously.

There are two ways to control which kind of annotation you use. First, you can pull down the Options menu and take the Show Group Annotations item, clicking on it to activate group annotations. You must then tweak the **mosaic.ini** file to reflect several entries. For example, you will need to look for the line in the [Annotations] section that looks like this one (already set with the NCSA default):

Group Annotation Server=hoohoo.ncsa.uiuc.edu:8001

You will need to change the server to reflect your own group annotation server. Further, this entry:

Directory="c:\ncsa\annotate"

will need to be changed to point to the directory on your local hard disk where annotations are stored. Also look for this entry:

Default Title="Personal Annotation by Mosaic User"

You can change the default title to the title of your choice, which will appear on your personal annotations.

Finally, you can change the **mosaic.ini** setting for the following directly if you choose not to use the menus to do it:

Group Annotations=no

Change it to:

Group Annotations=yes

to enable the group annotation function.

What Not to Edit in mosaic.ini

Some sections of **mosaic.ini** are definitely hands-off. DO NOT EDIT ANY OF THE FOLLOWING:

- Any parts of the [User Menu] sections. These are handled by the Menu Editor.
- Any parts of the HotList section. As with the [User Menu] areas, this section is manipulated by using the Menu Editor.
- Any parts of the [Font] sections. Font changes must be made through the Mosaic menus, by pulling down the Options menu and taking the Choose Font . . . option.
- Any parts of the [Main Window] section. Window size and location can be adjusted with the mouse. Use the File menu, and take the Save Preferences option to save the changed window location.

Document Caching

Mosaic places some documents into a memory cache. This means that you don't have to go back to the network to retrieve a document you have just viewed. You can find the settings for this caching operation in the [Document Caching] section of the **mosaic.ini** file. Look for the following lines:

Type=Number

Number=2

As you can see, the default setting allows Mosaic to cache two documents. If your system has a great deal of memory, you can add to the cache number. It can also be reduced; setting it to 0 turns off caching altogether. Reducing the cache number is recommended for those using less than 8 MB of memory. Make no change to the Type= setting.

9

Robots, Wanderers, and the Future of Mosaic

Using Mosaic immediately transports us into a new realm, one for which all previous, character-based Internet tools could scarcely have prepared us. It's easy to understand why the program has elicited such a positive response from the Internet community, not to mention the near euphoria it has occasioned from the popular press. Mosaic seems to say that hitherto difficult to access network tools from now on are available to a new class of user, those people just learning about the benefits of the Internet and anxious to tap its potential.

While there is an element of hucksterism in some of the publicity, it is nonetheless true that Mosaic has galvanized the network community as no previous tool has done. HTML is the language of the moment, as new electronic pages appear in their legions. Many of them are poorly constructed and make more demands upon the reader/viewer than anyone has a right to expect, but some show a real flair for design. We can expect the process of evolving home page standards to be lengthy; this is, after all, a new medium, one that forces us to pause and consider how best to convey information within the context of hyperlinked networked data.

Commerce has also reared its head on the **World Wide Web**, just as it has emerged on the Internet in general. Any tool with the potential of Mosaic for making the network accessible will immediately attract developers, so it is no surprise to see that NCSA has begun licensing Mosaic to various commercial operations, some of which have already introduced their own readings on an improved Mosaic. One of these, Mosaic Communications Corporation, includes some of the developers of the original Mosaic. We can expect a fierce battle to loom over whose Mosaic is best, as each firm jockeys for position in the corporate marketplace.

But before we discuss these issues, there remain two areas that deserve our attention. The first of these is searching: How can we use Mosaic to home in on the information we need? A new breed of program attempts to mine the **Web** for data, and we begin this chapter with a look at what these programs are and how you can use them. We also will have a look at Mosaic's forms feature, which allows home page builders to create documents that can process information supplied by the user. The latter has implications for the commercial development of both Mosaic and the Internet.

Automated Searching of the World Wide Web

The Internet has always gloried in diversity, which is the natural result of linking more than 3.5 million computers into a worldwide network. The proliferation of FTP sites means that thousands of system administrators can choose which software programs and data files to place into public access areas on their servers, while the number of Telnet-accessible computers continues to grow. If it's possible to put something on a computer and make it available to the public, it's probably out there somewhere.

But the Internet's sheer diversity is also a source of confusion. In the past several years, we have seen the emergence of two kinds of software to handle this situation: *browsers* and *search engines.* The **World Wide Web** is an example of the first; it is a browser, a tool that allows us to go from place to place on the network through hyperlinks. We can uncover quite a bit of information as we follow logical (and sometimes not so logical) linkages to related collections of information. **Gopher** is another browsing engine. It uses menus and submenus to allow us to point to what we want and go straight to it.

The other kind of Internet tool is the search engine. Here we think of systems like **WAIS** (**W**ide **A**rea **I**nformation **S**ervers). **WAIS** allows us to enter search terms and search databases of information that are widely distributed on the Internet. **archie** is another system that permits searching; we enter a keyword and **archie** searches FTP holdings around the world (though only from a particular set of sites; not all FTP servers are searched by **archie**). **Veronica**, which is tightly integrated with **Gopher**, provides a way for us to search for all **Gopher** menus containing our search term.

Both systems—browsers and search engines—help us to find our way around the Internet and in many cases locate the information we're looking for. But both have their drawbacks. **Veronica** sites are vastly overloaded with requests as word of their usefulness spreads; it can take quite a while to run a **Veronica** search if we attempt it during a period of peak traffic. The **WAIS** engine is powerful but quirky, and as a system still undergoing early development, it remains in need of a wider selection of databases. At present, we only skim over the technological side of the Internet when we query the **WAIS** servers.

As for browsers, both **Gopher** and the **World Wide Web** can be frustrating in the extreme. **Gopher** requires us to run through its menus and submenus to find what we want; only its built-in bookmark system takes off the pressure by allowing us to mark items for future reference. The **World Wide Web** demands that we follow its hyperlinks to get to our destination. That means starting off in a known location and working our way, sometimes slowly, through a labyrinth of information. Although we often find what we want, the process can take quite some time.

Let's be clear on the reason why. Although the **Web**'s advocates speak of it as the ultimate information engine, it nonetheless possesses the same limitations as any network tool. Hyperlinks are, indeed, a wonderful way to connect to related information, but they must be built by hand. That means a human being must decide where the hyperlinks go and how to place them logically so that the reader can draw maximum utility out of the information space they create.

And even if we know where the good sites are, the entire system rests upon its connections to other information; the **Web** is meant to be a seamless whole. Choose a particular hyperlink and we may easily wind up on a home page half a continent away, one that has been built by someone whose sense of order and relationships differs substantially from our own. Then, too, following even the best of links to get to what we need often means starting with the general—archaeology as a subject, say—and working our way inexorably to the particular—the Incan ruins at Machu Picchu. It is this forced narrowing, requiring us to start with the broad and move to the narrow, that so frustrates the long-time user of the **Web**.

What we need is something that brings the focus of a search engine into the browsing environment. We need to be able to specify exactly what we need and let computers do our searching for us. They would then return a list of sites, **World Wide Web** pages that conform to our specifications. At that point, we could use Mosaic to access these pages and find, we hope, the promised data. The good news is that such search engines are beginning to appear on the **Web**'s horizon. In this chapter, we examine several, and consider where, in consequence, the **Web** is heading. Once you've used one of the **Web** search engines considered here, you'll probably want to create links to one or more on your home page, or add them to your menus.

A New Breed of Search Engine

Can a software tool be thought of as a *robot*? Evidently so, if it goes out on the network and harvests information. The new **Web** search engines are called *robots*, *wanderers*, or *spiders*, and they are all gifted with the ability to find information in this widely distributed environment. And while development of these engines is in its infancy, their number has grown surprisingly large. I counted twenty-five projects active in September 1994, and by the time you read this, there may be several others.

Some of these programs are exceedingly tight in their specifications. The Repository Based Software Engineering Project Spider (RBSE), for example, consists of a program that creates an Oracle database of HTML documents on the **Web**, feeding them into an index searchable by freeWAIS, the noncommercial version of the **WAIS** engine (RBSE is sponsored by NASA). Lycos, from Carnegie Mellon University, provides an extensive database of abstracts of **World Wide Web** documents. The MacWWWWorm, developed in Montreal, is a keyword-searching robot apparently created in a French context (news on this one is still scarce). SG-Scout runs as an internal Xerox research project. The list could be extended, but perhaps this is enough to give you an idea of the activity in this field. For now, we'll look at several of the better tools to see how they work.

Be aware that robots are not without their share of controversy. They put a strain on the network in the course of their activities (after all, the **Web** is one big place to search!). Some robots, in addition, are better behaved than others. There are stories of robots that continuously retrieve documents from the same site, over and over again, and there is no clue as to the source of the robot. Some system administrators, tired of the activity, have put up barriers so that robots will have a harder time working at their site. Get enough robots visiting enough sites and you have created a situation that results in network congestion for all, with limited return on the resources employed. A well-designed robot makes clear where it is from, what its purpose is, and how to contact its creators. We are seeing standards for robot activity evolve as the **Web** grows.

If you are intrigued by these issues, you may want to examine the following URL:

```
http://web.nexor.co.uk/mak/doc/robots/guidelines.html
```

This is a document called *Guidelines for Robot Writers* which explains what the issues are and how robot development can be guided for the benefit of all. The work of Martijn Koster at NEXOR, a technology company in Nottingham in the United Kingdom, it makes interesting reading within the context of an overall discussion of **Web** search engines. The World Wide Web Robots, Wanderers, and Spiders home page is at this URL:

```
http://web.nexor.co.uk/mak/doc/robots/robots.html
```

If you put only one URL on your menu in connection with robots, it should be this one. Links to all known **Web** wanderers and robots are provided at the site, which is shown in Figure 9.1.

The WebCrawler

Run by Brian Pinkerton at the University of Washington, the WebCrawler builds indices for the documents it finds on the **Web** and allows you to search

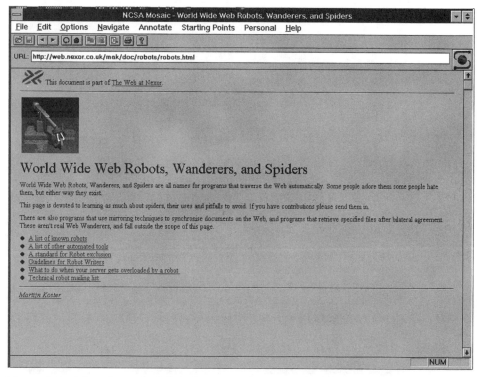

Figure 9.1 A key place to look for information about **World Wide Web** search tools.

for documents of interest. Using the WebCrawler, Pinkerton has been able to create a list of the twenty-five most frequented documents on the **Web**, which in itself is an interesting resource. Its URL is:

```
http://www.biotech.washington.edu/WebCrawler/Top25.html
```

The search screen for the WebCrawler is shown in Figure 9.2. As you can see, the screen makes searching easy. You simply type in the search term, clicking on the Search button when you are ready, and let the WebCrawler do its work. In Figure 9.3, you see the results of my entering the search term **television** in the dialog box.

You can see that this page consists of a series of services, each of which is itself a hyperlink. I can click on any of them to go directly to the site. In Figure 9.4, I have selected the third item on the hit list, *Science Fiction TV Series Guides,* and clicked on it.

You can see how much the WebCrawler's search capability has helped in cutting down my time on the **Web**. To find the site otherwise might have involved going to a directory of subjects, such as the one maintained by CERN, and working my way from general to specific until I found this page. With a

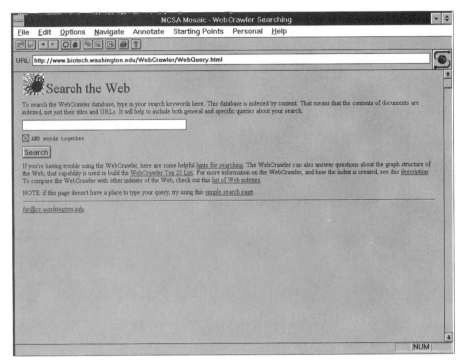

Figure 9.2 The search screen for the WebCrawler.

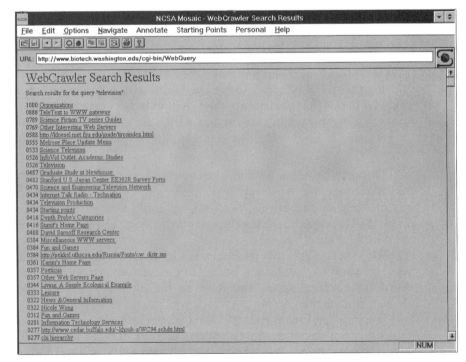

Figure 9.3 Results of a WebCrawler search under the term **television**.

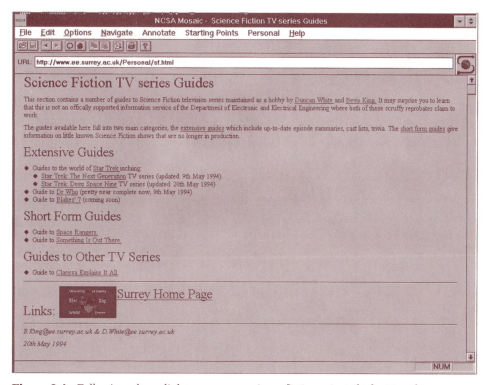

Figure 9.4   Following a hyperlink to a page on science fiction-oriented television shows.

search engine like this one, I simply enter the term and quickly receive a list of applicable sites. To reach the WebCrawler, you can use the following URL:

```
http://www.biotech.washington.edu/WebCrawler/WebQuery.html
```

The World Wide Web Wanderer

Matthew Gray at MIT runs the World Wide Web Wanderer, or W4 as it is more familiarly known. Gray's interest was to determine how big the **World Wide Web** really is. His first run with W4 in June 1993 found about 100 HTTP sites; a rerun in September of that year showed that the number had doubled. By March 1994, W4 was finding more than 1,200 sites. By June 1994, the number had reached 3,100. Figure 9.5 shows W4's site list.

As you can see, the World Wide Web Wanderer is not designed as a search tool as much as it is a tracker of **Web** growth. Anyone interested in **Web** statistics will be interested in checking into this URL:

```
http://www.mit.edu:8001/afs/sipb/user/mkgray/ht/comprehensive.html
```

Figure 9.5   The World Wide Web Wanderer site list.

The World Wide Web Worm

Developed by Oliver McBryan at the University of Colorado, the World Wide Web Worm uses forms to help you search. The search screen for the Worm is shown in Figure 9.6.

Remember that HTML documents contain title information; this is data that can be searched by a **Web** tool like the World Wide Web Worm. The Worm can also search for hyperlinks within HTML documents and by the names of HTML home pages and their accompanying URLs. If you wanted, for example, to search for sites in Colorado, the Worm would be able to find all sites with **colorado** in the machine name. Similarly, it could search by country, looking for URLs with particular country designations, or for types of links.

Notice that you can search in titles or by names within the URLs in HTML documents. In Figure 9.7 you can see the results of searching by title under the term **exhibit**.

I entered the search term and then clicked on the Start Search button. Again, we are presented with a list of hyperlinks, each of which can be accessed by clicking on it. The URL for the World Wide Web Worm is:

`http://www.cs.colorado.edu/home/mcbryan/WWWW.html`

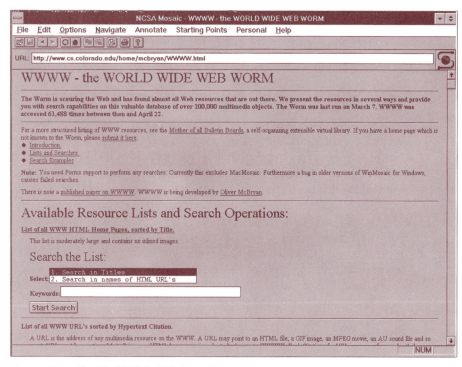

Figure 9.6 The World Wide Web Worm's search screen.

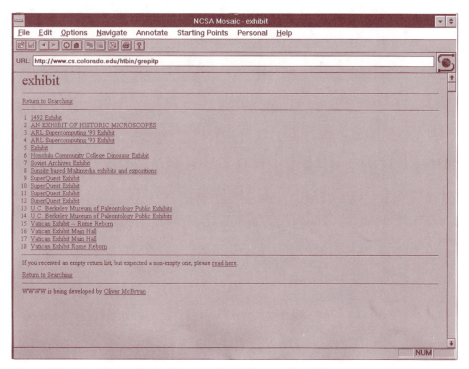

Figure 9.7 Searching with the Worm under the keyword **exhibit**.

The JumpStation

Like other **Web** wanderers, the JumpStation allows users to query a database of information by keyword; answers are supplied with hyperlinks for easy access to the resources needed. Documents can be searched by title header and subject; in addition, servers can be found by using a partial address (for those moments when you remember part but not all of a URL). Jonathon Fletcher at the University of Stirling in the United Kingdom is the power behind the JumpStation, and he has currently brought development up to a beta implementation of version 2. Figure 9.8 shows the search screen.

As you can see, I have inserted the search term **chemistry** in the Enter Subject Word: box. I also could have selected other options by checking the appropriate box (and note that, by combining options, you can create up to seven different ways to use the JumpStation to search).

Although you can't see it on the screen in Figure 9.8, the Submit button (which I clicked to get the search running) can be found by scrolling down just slightly in the document. Here is the URL for the JumpStation:

```
http://www.stir.ac.uk/jsbin/js/
```

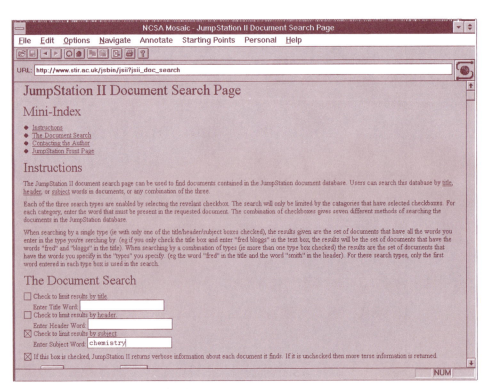

Figure 9.8 The search screen for the JumpStation.

Where Robots and Wanderers Are Headed

Figure 9.9 shows the home page for the SG-Scout robot, developed at the Xerox Palo Alto Research Center (this is the famous PARC where so many seminal computer developments took place, including the development of intuitive user interfaces of the kind that later appeared on the Macintosh).

The only way to keep up with a field in such a rapid state of transition is to monitor places like this. And as mentioned, the best place to track the development and location of new home pages for robots and wanderers is through the site maintained by Martijn Koster. Koster does a wonderful job at keeping up with robot developments on his *World Wide Web Robots, Wanderers, and Spiders* page.

Be advised, however, that the entire field of **Web** wanderers and robots is highly experimental and, as we've seen, controversial. You can expect many changes in addresses as new **Web** wanderers come on the scene and old ones disappear. We're also seeing a movement toward developing standards for robot activity that should result in more efficient **Web** searching with fewer hassles for system administrators and less workload on individual sites.

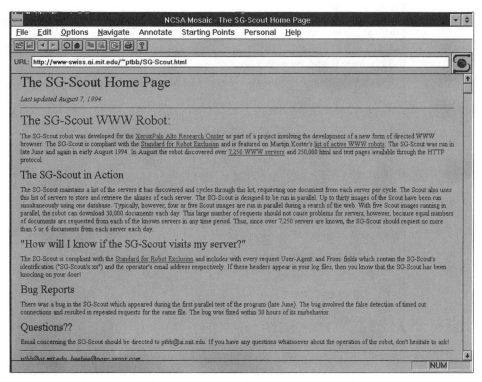

Figure 9.9   The home page for SG-Scout, a **Web** robot.

For those interested in following the issues raised by **Web** robots, a mailing list exists. You can join it by sending e-mail to the following address.

robots-request@nexor.co.uk

The body of your message should contain the words **subscribe**, **help**, and **stop** on separate lines. Be aware that this is a technical list intended for the authors, administrators, and maintainers of **WWW** robots; it is not a general discussion list about the **Web**.

And, if you've ever doubted that search tools are becoming more and more available on the **World Wide Web**, look no further than this Swiss URL:

`http://cui_www.unige.ch/meta-index.html`

You can see this home page in Figure 9.10. Notice what you have here. A wide variety of search tools are accessible from this page, from **World Wide Web** catalogs to search engines ranging from WebCrawler, the World Wide Web Worm, **Veronica**, **Jughead**, and **WAIS**. You can only see a fraction of them from this screen, but scrolling down through the page would reveal the rest. It's quite a site, and one you'll want to add to your menus or home page.

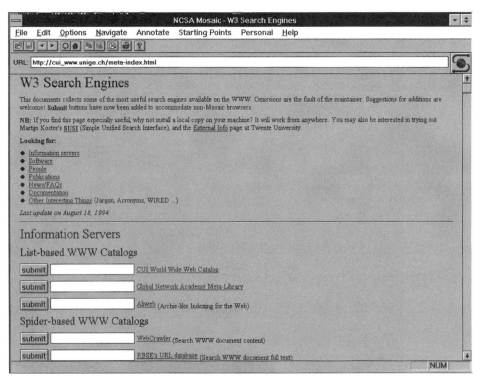

Figure 9.10   A home page tracking search engines on the **Web**.

Other Forms of Web Searching

Not all **Web** searching is handled through automated tools. In fact, the over-head caused by these tools has many developers wondering whether there isn't some better way to produce the information needed. Here are two alternatives to the automated approach. Both contain databases that you can search to generate interesting **Web** sites.

ALIWEB

ALIWEB is a way for people to personally generate information about the ser-vices they provide. ALIWEB gathers this information into a searchable data-base, which is updated every few days. The service, which stands for Archie-like indexing for the **Web**, is theoretically as up to date as any **Web** wanderer, but does not cause the overhead created by setting up automatic search routines on the net. Figure 9.11 shows the search page for ALIWEB. The URL for this site is:

```
http://web.nexor.co.uk/aliweb/doc/form-search.html
```

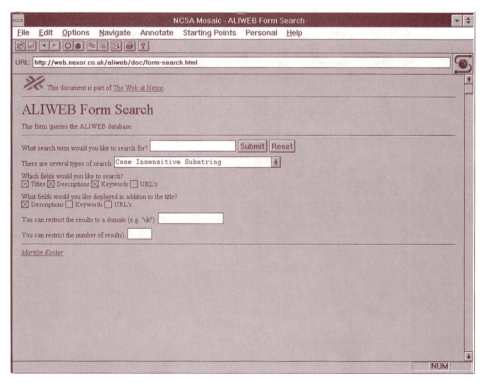

Figure 9.11   ALIWEB's search form.

The CUI W3 Catalog

The W3 Catalog is built up from lists available on the **World Wide Web**. A variety of useful documents, including Scott Yanoff's *Internet Services List,* and John December's *Computer-Mediated Communication and Internet Tools Summary,* are used to provide material. These sources are consulted on a daily basis to keep the catalog up to date. Figure 9.12 shows the search page for this catalog.

The Form and the Function

Forms are a natural for Mosaic. By allowing designers to create home pages supplying fields that can be filled in by readers, they make the tool interactive as well as graphical. Without forms, Mosaic is strictly a one-way operation, allowing you to read what someone else has decided to put on-line. With forms, the program accepts feedback. You can drop an e-mail note to a developer commenting on his or her home page. You can fill out a request for information or enter a password to gain access to a commercial database. If you are a system administrator, you can set up a screening process to restrict access to

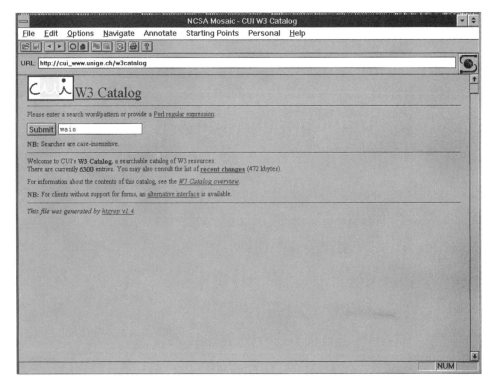

Figure 9.12 Using the W3 Catalog to set up a search under the keyword **wais**.

your site, or if you're in business, you can use forms to promote on-line ordering of products from your catalog.

We have already looked at a few forms on-line; we filled in information to use some of the **Web** wanderer programs discussed, using fields created by the programs' authors. Any time you fill in a blank you are filling out a form of some kind. You may also see forms that use buttons that require you click on them to make them work, and that contain Send buttons that cause your request to be sent to the server. Figure 9.13 shows an example of a typical form for sending electronic mail.

This figure shows a page provided by Tyler Jones as part of a project he has created to teach Spanish on-line. Users can work through one or more of his Spanish lessons (they contain audio links to help you pronounce the vocabulary words), and then send e-mail commenting on the course work and including an e-mail return address for reply. As forms become more widespread, we will see this kind of page proliferate.

We have mastered elementary creation of an HTML document, learning how to build our own home pages and where to look for further information. Forms are more complicated, but if you would like to learn more about how to create them, you will want to examine the following URL:

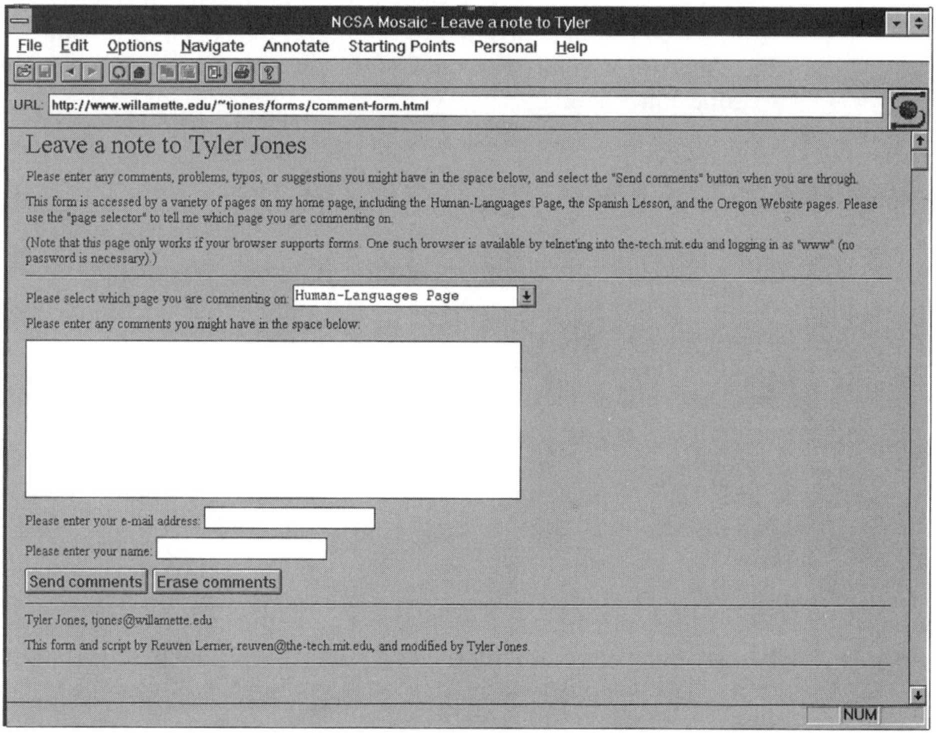

Figure 9.13   Filling in a form to send electronic mail.

http://south.ncsa.uiuc.edu/forms.html

Keep an eye on this page for further developments in forms.

And further developments there will be. Imagine yourself as the owner of a small specialty store with a printed catalog of products. Perhaps you would like to put your catalog on-line using the **World Wide Web**. You know that with Mosaic, a potential customer could look at selected images of your products, check prices, and make buying decisions. With a properly designed form, that customer could also send a request for information to you or actually place an order on-line. So many businesses are getting involved in the Internet these days that we can expect form creation to become a major growth industry.

Commercial Development of Mosaic

There is every reason to believe that the entry of commerce onto the Internet will have a profound impact upon the development of Mosaic. Given the ongoing nature of the program's development, and the fact that users of the NCSA product are working with essentially experimental software, it is natural that users will find particular areas they think should be improved (indeed, NCSA actively solicits opinions on these matters). And it is natural, too, that the people who worked so hard to create Mosaic in the first place would begin to see the potential for their product in the marketplace. Once business caught on to what the **Web** was all about, an explosion of interest in its capabilities was a foregone conclusion.

Mosaic Communications Corporation

And so we come to Mosaic Communications Corporation. Based in Mountain View, California, the company has set its sights on providing services and software to businesses interested in setting up operations on the Internet. Silicon Graphics founder James Clark is one of the new firm's guiding lights; so is Marc Andreessen, perhaps the key figure in early Mosaic development. And while it would be an overstatement to say that Mosaic Communications Corporation has pulled the entire original development team away from NCSA, it is nonetheless true that many key players on that team—Eric Bina, Jon Mittelhauser, Chris Houck and others—have opted to sign on with the new firm. So has Lou Montulli, the author of **lynx**, a fine, VT-100 based **World Wide Web** browser.

What can a company like this offer that NCSA can't? Commercializing Mosaic gives the firm the ability to add features specifically designed for the business environment, and to couple them with technical support beyond the ability of NCSA to provide; at least, these are the intentions of the company's founders as conveyed in recent press materials. And according to the same press release, they intend to provide consulting and support for companies hoping to go out onto the net, as well as running their own **Web** server, which will act as a kind of cyberspace business development for those companies that choose to lease space on it. All the while, of course, the firm intends to develop what it considers to be the next-generation, commercial-grade product based on Mosaic, to be made available in the first half of 1995. Rather than licensing the system from NCSA, Mosaic Communications Corporation plans to develop its version of the product from the ground up.

These are ambitious plans, and if they interest you, here is the address of the company:

Mosaic Communications Corporation
650 Castro Street, Suite 500
Mountain View, CA 94041
Voice: 415-254-1900
Fax: 415-254-0239

A call to the company will doubtless provide updated information on its products and services.

But wait. Mosaic Communications Corporation is hardly alone in the new and burgeoning field of Mosaic development and consulting. A host of other firms have decided to license the Mosaic engine from NCSA and bring their own reading of the product to market. Software developer Quarterdeck Office Systems (developers of DESQview), for example, is aiming at a Mosaic of its own, to be introduced some time in late 1994. The Santa Cruz Operation, a developer of UNIX software, is incorporating Mosaic into a product called SCO Global Access. The Electric Power Research Institute in Palo Alto is planning to use Mosaic to make multimedia reports available to its membership.

Quadralay, a marketer of software tools, is working on a product called Global-Wide Help & Information System that will include Mosaic. O'Reilly & Associates uses Mosaic as the front end to its *Global Network Navigator,* an on-line magazine and testbed for new network concepts. Both Spyglass and Spry Inc. are designing their own Mosaics, as is Enterprise Integration Technologies.

In a field so young, it is far too early to pick any winners. All we can do is to look at some of the early front runners. It is safe to say that each version of Mosaic that makes it to market will offer some kind of proprietary enhancements while preserving the core NCSA engine. It is also safe to assume that, as with most market-saturating phenomena, the rash of new Mosaics will settle into a stable few, as companies and their products gradually drop out of the competition. Mosaic Communications Corporation appears to have the stamina—and the resources—to stay a major player, but the firms competing with it are just as determined to push their products into the forefront.

Spry's AirMosaic

Spry Incorporated has already made a name for itself through its joint venture with publisher O'Reilly & Associates called *Internet In A Box* (we discussed the product in Chapter 2). The Seattle-based developer already offers a series of Internet applications including electronic mail, a USENET news reader, a **Gopher** client and more. It was only natural that the firm should turn its attention to Mosaic at a time when SLIP accounts were making the program available to a much broader audience.

Spry's AirMosaic offers a series of modifications to the NCSA product. These include:

- The ability to configure AirMosaic from within the program using pull-down menus. You are thus able to avoid editing the **mosaic.ini** file by hand.

- A redesigned toolbar with larger, customizable buttons.

- An enhanced hotlist that simplifies management of URLs.

- Full print capabilities including print preview and the ability to print graphics.

These and other features are available for testing, because Spry has made a demonstration version of AirMosaic available over the Internet. You can download it from the following URL:

```
ftp://ftp.spry.com/vendor/spry/demo/
```

According to a recent press release, the company is encouraging people to download this demonstration version and e-mail comments with suggestions for improvements. You can also reach Spry at the following address:

Spry Inc.
316 Occidental Avenue South
Suite 200
Seattle, WA 98104
Voice: 800-777-9638
Fax: 206-447-9008
E-mail: **info@spry.com**
URL: **http://www.spry.com**

Spyglass's Enhanced NCSA Mosaic

Spyglass Inc. is a developer of data analysis tools for engineering and scientific applications, with support for platforms ranging from Windows to the Macintosh and UNIX. Based in Savoy, Illinois, the company moved quickly to license Mosaic from the NCSA, and has turned its attention to developing a version of Mosaic that can be incorporated within other company's products for distribution. Customers targeted in this effort include communications vendors, publishers, and on-line information providers. Versions are to be made available for all three of the platforms Spyglass supports—Microsoft Windows, X Windows and the Macintosh—and should be on the market by the time you read this.

What has Spyglass added to its Enhanced NCSA Mosaic that was missing from the original NCSA version? According to a summer 1994 press release, the enhancements include:

- Better memory management.
- Improved installation options.
- New forms options, thus enlarging the product's commercial potential.
- A developed, hypertext help system (recall that NCSA, at least at the time of this writing, had yet to install the help system into Mosaic for Microsoft Windows).
- Support for multiple windows and other interface improvements.
- Filters that will allow Mosaic to read widely distributed document formats like PostScript. At present, you must use an external viewer program like GhostScript to accomplish this.

Spyglass also says it intends to add security features to enable credit card transactions to be managed through the Internet; the integration of the product with a variety of existing editing tools is also in the works. For more information, you can contact Spyglass at the following address:

Spyglass, Inc.
1800 Woodfield Dr.
Savoy, IL 61874
Voice: 217-355-6000
Fax: 217-355-8925
E-mail: **info@spyglass.com**
URL: **http://www.spyglass.com**

In addition to the aforementioned O'Reilly & Associates, Spyglass's venture into the commercial Mosaic marketplace has already landed such clients as IBM's Networking Software Division, FTP Software Inc. (North Andover, Massachusetts), Firefox Inc. (San Jose, California), and Digital Equipment Corporation, which plans to add the program into its base systems platforms, thus bundling it with most of the major computer systems DEC delivers. Spyglass says it has licensed more than five million copies of Enhanced NCSA Mosaic to these companies and others, all of whom are integrating the product into their own software for distribution to their customers. Interestingly, the company intends to provide to NCSA a number of its own improvements to Mosaic so that they can be incorporated back into the NCSA version of the software. In August 1994, Spyglass announced that it had signed a deal with NCSA to take over licensing arrangements for the software.

Enterprise Integration Technologies

The spread of Mosaic into the commercial arena places demands upon developers to offer a product that can be safely used for commercial transactions.

Facing into this problem is Enterprise Integration Technologies Corporation (EIT), a Palo Alto, California-based developer that is now working with another firm, RSA Data Security Inc., to find ways of making Mosaic secure. RSA is a major player in the field of cryptography, marketing software and performing research and development on the issues involved in keeping data safe.

The plan is to integrate EIT's secure software with RSA's public key cryptography into NCSA Mosaic and the **World Wide Web** servers behind it. These enhancements are to be made available to NCSA for subsequent public distribution as well as commercial licensing. A key to placing these agreements in context is to examine CommerceNet, a trial run at electronic marketing on the Internet which will use EIT's Secure NCSA Mosaic software starting in the fall of 1994.

CommerceNet is the first large-scale attempt at commerce on the Internet. A consortium of companies—Apple Computer, Sun Microsystems, BankAmerica, Hewlett-Packard and Lockheed—are building it, with funding from consortium members and a $6 million grant from the U.S. government. Companies going on-line through CommerceNet will offer products to consumers, everything from on-line banking to brokerage and notary services. Security concerns are obviously critical when you are dealing with financial transactions and similar services; data authentication and privacy of information are paramount.

Secure NCSA Mosaic will provide the ability to add signatures and time stamps to electronic contracts, making them both legally binding and subject to standard auditing procedures. At the same time, credit card information can be encrypted, allowing for the safe transaction of business. EIT and RSA intend to develop licensing programs for the commercial use of this technology in **World Wide Web** servers. By making security features available to NCSA on a royalty-free basis, the firms will allow the public version of Mosaic to be enhanced, thus spreading security capabilities into the broader audience of users. It will be intriguing to see how these features fare as CommerceNet develops.

For more information about Secure NCSA Mosaic, you can contact EIT at the following address:

Enterprise Integration Technologies, Inc.
800 El Camino Real, Fourth Floor
Menlo Park, CA 94025
Voice: 415-617-8000
Fax: 415-617-8019
E-mail: **info@eit.com**
URL: **http://www.eit.com**

Enterprise Integration Technologies and RSA Data Security have also formed a new company specializing in Internet security. The firm, called Terisa, will develop toolkits for developers creating services within the **World Wide Web**. The company combines the efforts of the two firms in developing a secure Mosaic product, but as of this writing, the distinction between Terisa's work and that ongoing between EIT and RSA has not firmly been established.

The Best Mosaic for You

The growth of commerce on the Internet and, by extension, on the **World Wide Web** as mediated through Mosaic and other browsers, forces us to examine the fate of Mosaic as a commercial product, and to compare that fate to its history as a free, though copyrighted, program from NCSA. What do all these maneuvers mean for you, the user, and how will they affect your decision about which version of Mosaic to use? What is the best course of action as the marketplace fights out the issue of which Mosaic will be the standard? Or will there even be a single standard?

The situation is murky at present, but certain outlines are beginning to emerge. We know, for example, that the attempt to commercialize Mosaic is in its infancy. The team with the greatest number of original Mosaic hands (and also, it seems, the youngest development staff) is clearly Mosaic Communications Corporation. These are the people who, having built it, presumably understand Mosaic's core engine best, and their product should contain numerous enhancements that have been suggested through long familiarity with the program. Unfortunately, the Mosaic Communications version of Mosaic isn't out as we go to press, so we are left to speculate about what it will include. Remember that theirs will not be a licensed Mosaic from NCSA but rather a new Mosaic built from scratch.

Spyglass, on the other hand, is licensing NCSA Mosaic with a vengeance, and is marketing itself aggressively (and in high volume) toward publishers and other information companies that may want to incorporate the product in their own offerings. We can expect this attempt to enjoy considerable success, thanks to Spyglass's good working relationship with NCSA. The last thing on the mind of a research-minded institution is handling the commercialization of a product like Mosaic, and Spyglass has obviously struck a sympathetic chord with NCSA's leaders.

We mustn't, however, discount the rest of the field. Spry is a developer with a proven track record and an ability to market itself well. Spry AirMosaic will win converts, particularly since it is available in a demonstration model over the Internet. Nor should we discount companies like Quarterdeck Office Systems, which has proven that it can take an innovative route toward technology, as it did with DESQview, and create a market niche of considerable interest. And needless to say, we can expect other licensees to be scrambling to find the kind of Mosaic improvements that will win market share.

Finally, keep in mind that NCSA is determined to continue to develop its own version of Mosaic. Never forget that, while commercial concerns are adding features, the development team at NCSA is doing the same thing, and that individual users can take advantage of the benefits of each new revision *for free*. It is also significant that some of the technologies being developed by other firms, such as Enterprise Integration Technologies, are to be folded back into the NCSA version of Mosaic. It appears that the individual user will enjoy an increasing range of options no matter which Mosaic he or she chooses to use.

The sensible Mosaic user will, then, be wary of market hype and exaggeration. We live in an overheated age, one in which claim follows counterclaim so rapidly that determining the truth can be challenging. Numerous versions of Mosaic are to become available in the year following the publication of this book. But the key benefits of the program—its ability to use hyperlinks between data and to present that data in an aesthetically pleasing way—will be present in all of them.

I think of NCSA Mosaic as the generic product; it contains the engine that became the Internet's hottest access tool. The latest versions of the program are experimental—we've already seen that by examining some of the features that are not yet implemented, such as the help system and the Save and Save As options in the Microsoft Windows versions, which are only now becoming operational. But the heart of the program is intact and workable.

My advice, then, is to master NCSA Mosaic. If you're an individual user, it will probably prove adequate for every task you can imagine on the net. If you are hoping to introduce Mosaic into a commercial setting, then examine the commercial products with care, looking for the one with the features that best fit your plan of business. Because the new Mosaic marketplace has not begun to reach maturity, there will be plenty of time to make a final decision.

One way or another, you are going to be using Mosaic and other graphical tools as the Internet opens up to individuals and small businesses alike. The excitement of watching a product evolve, and the ability to participate in that process through suggestions to its developers, will probably keep me in the NCSA camp. But whichever version you wind up with, Mosaic's key attributes—its menus, its hyperlinks, its graphical sophistication—will bring new tools to your desktop. Properly used, they can turn the Internet into a place of exploration and discovery.

What Mosaic Needs

Mosaic is evolving beautifully without help from me. But it's clear that there are two things that the program needs before it can become the kind of access tool some enthusiasts are already proclaiming it to be. Neither, it turns out, is an addition to the program itself; rather, the necessary additions have to do with the nature of the net.

Mosaic needs wider bandwidth to work well. Large businesses already have this, but the average desktop user does not, nor does the average small business. A wide bandwidth connection, of the kind promised by all the talk of digital highways and infobahns, would allow users to move quickly between images, sound and text, rather than waiting out interminable delays as huge hypermedia files flow through the network. Mosaic in a wide bandwidth environment is truly a joy to behold.

The other thing Mosaic needs is content. This superb access tool must be able to reach into home pages that are packed with information and hyperlinks to yet more information. Many of the resources available on the **World Wide Web** today do little more than hint at the possibilities. We need digitized libraries of information, searchable by the Mosaic engine. We need text, text, and more text—images need the supporting envelope of writing to convey high-quality information. We also need more editors, more journals, more people willing to take publishing into the Internet realm and make it go. And we need more private individuals willing to take the time and effort to create innovative, content-rich home pages.

For the Internet to become the great highway of information it is promised to be, we must enter the era of the content provider. My hope is that the commercial impulse will drive firms with useful databanks of information into the network arena. If they can make the network succeed as a business proposition and still support the net's great democratizing presence as a propagator of data across national and cultural boundaries, then Mosaic may become familiar in households around the world in coming years. It is the kind of interface that people of all ages can use to find things, and thus the ideal format for engaging the minds of a technologically enriched culture.

10

A Travelogue of Interesting Sites

There was a time, not too long ago, when compiling a list of intriguing sites on the **World Wide Web** would have been the work of an afternoon, with time out for a coffee break and a long walk with my Border Collie. Today, the World Wide Web Wanderer reports well more than 3,000 sites. And a check at CERN, the cradle of the **World Wide Web** project, reveals a remarkable bounty. There, **Web** servers are listed by geographical area, as shown in Figure 10.1.

The figure shows just a sampling of a lengthy document with links all over the world. There is no better way to obtain an overview of the **Web**'s spread than to spend some time prowling around this document. Its URL is:

```
http://info.cern.ch/hypertext/DataSources/ByAccess.html
```

Don't be surprised if the home page takes a while to load. At the time of this writing, it was well over 400 K.

Newcomers often assume that the sheer number of sites available through the Internet guarantees an inexhaustible store of information. In fact, what we frequently discover is that the information falls into areas of greater and lesser concentration. We will certainly find plentiful information about the Internet and the **World Wide Web**, along with resources in the areas of computing that range from on-line newsletters to vast collections of software. The hard sciences are well represented; certainly we can access many a site specializing in chemistry or biology, and even the so-called "soft" sciences—psychology, sociology—are becoming more and more available. A glance through this chapter will likewise reveal strengths in geographical information, as developers use the **Web** to highlight the resources of a particular country or to energize further networking within its borders.

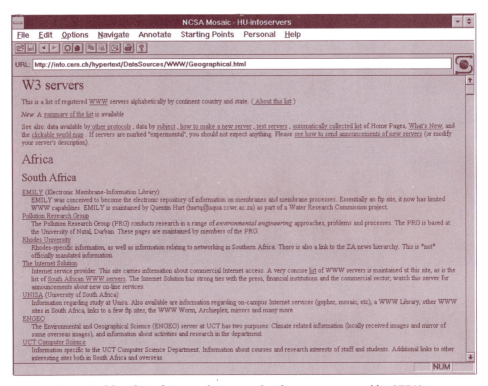

Figure 10.1   World Wide Web servers by geographical area, as presented by CERN.

Unfortunately, we also find great gaps in our searching. Because the Internet is only beginning to accommodate itself to the growing presence of commercial companies, the number of sites specializing in proprietary information is vanishingly small. The new InfoSeek project addressed earlier is an attempt to create a search tool that can be used by Internet users, one that must inevitably lead to a commercial model for database access with user authentication and billing features. We will see more of these as products like the Enterprise Integration Technologies secure Mosaic make it feasible for companies to perform credit card charges over the net. At that point, a convergence between commercial databases like DIALOG and BRS and the Internet, as a means of access, is all but inevitable.

Users will also note and appreciate, by their very rarity, the museum exhibits listed here. Nothing gets across the power of Mosaic better than the ability to click on a hyperlink and see a full-screen image of a painting or an artifact from a distant museum, supported by text and audio links. Thus far, however, the few projects that provide these features, while famous on the net, have attracted few competitors. It will be interesting to observe what the second generation of museum and educational exhibits may provide, and how they may be supported by other attempts to make public information more widely accessible.

Exploring with Mosaic

The sites that follow represent the wanderings of one person over a network that facilitates eccentric travel. You can use these sites as a means of introduction to the entire range of **World Wide Web** activities. And don't forget that you now have abundant means at your disposal for customizing Mosaic, so that it can reflect your own set of interests. My home page is laden with links to information in my own fields, while my menus likewise break into categories that take me quickly to places I have discovered.

If you want to get the most out of HTTP sites on the **World Wide Web**, you must cultivate a patient, nondemanding frame of mind. And that, I think, is the key to using Mosaic. Your best sites will be those you discover after you examine the ones in this chapter; they're the places you blunder into while following up a link somewhere else, the out-of-the-way destinations you would probably never find again if you didn't have an easy way to add them to a menu. Because making directories of an entity as fluid as the Internet is a task that leaves you constantly trying to catch up, you should consider any directory as merely a starting point. Keeping up with the net means using it.

The WWW Virtual Library

URL: http://info.cern.ch/

An essential page for Mosaic browsing is the **Web** index by subject provided by CERN. Here, information is broken into convenient categories in a list that is frequently updated. You can go straight to chemistry, for example, calling up a separate list of servers, or choose landscape architecture for a similar sublist. As you can see from Figure 10.2, the catalog is wide-ranging and provides plenty of jumping off places for your browsing.

Notice, too, that there is a convenient summary of the information available through hyperlink, as well as a link to other catalogs of network information. As ever, when it comes to information about the **Web**, CERN is a key resource. The subject areas even contain ratings, as shown by the number of stars following the item. New material is shown with an exclamation point.

The list of virtual libraries is shown in Figure 10.3. Here we have a compendium of sites specializing in information by subject, catalogs, and various forms of searchable information. You can learn a great deal about the Internet by browsing through some of these pages.

Nova-Links

URL: http://alpha.acast.nova.edu/start.html

Nova-Links is the work of Rob Kabacoff, an associate professor at the Center for Psychological Studies at Nova Southeastern University in Fort Lauderdale,

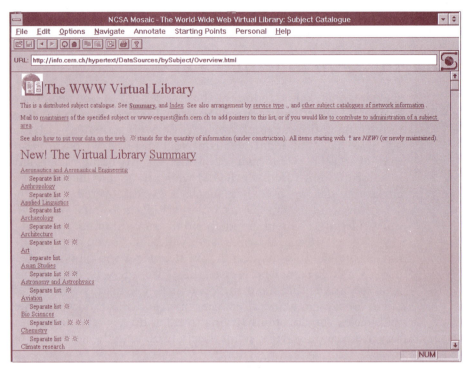

Figure 10.2 A list of information by category from CERN.

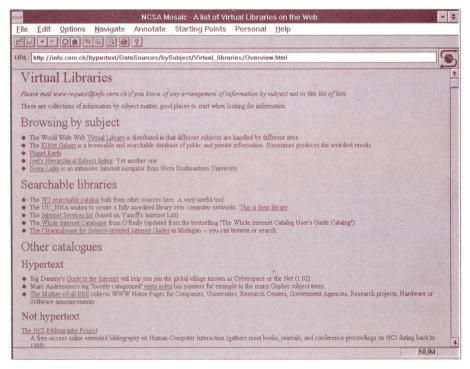

Figure 10.3 The **Web**'s Virtual Library.

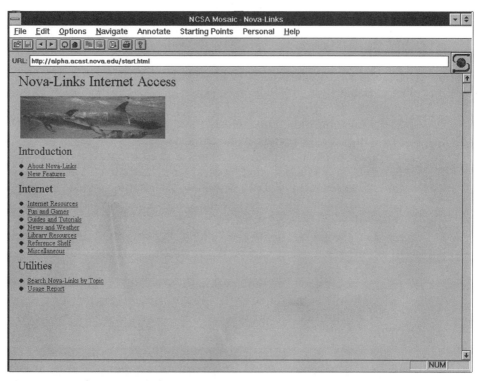

Figure 10.4 The Nova-Links home page.

Florida. It is designed as an Internet navigation tool with links to core documents about the **Web** and the broader range of Internet information servers. Begun as a hobby, Nova-Links now consumes a great deal of Kabacoff's time; he reports that the fast growth of the net has him tinkering with the system on a daily basis. Figure 10.4 shows its home page.

Of particular interest here are the usage reports. Nova-Links as of late August 1994 had received more than two million accesses from 70,000-plus sites, averaging close to 10,000 calls per day. Following the trend of most Internet tools, the site is clearly being discovered by searchers worldwide. It is valuable for its logical approach to finding information. Note that you can enter a keyword to search titles, text, and URLs around the **Web**.

The Awesome List

URL: http://www.clark.net/pub/journalism/awesome.html

John Makulowich has put together a page with links of considerable value; the emphasis is on sites that would be useful to Internet trainers and journalists. The Awesome List includes a variety of non-HTTP sites as well as **Web** pages; the sites are presented in alphabetical order rather than by topic.

EINet Galaxy

URL: http://www.einet.net/galaxy.html

Enterprise Integration Network provides Galaxy, a directory service with searchable index to help you locate Internet information. Its home page is shown in Figure 10.5. Here again we have information broken down by topic; at the bottom of the page, out of view in the figure, is a search field in which you can enter the term of your choice.

Sponsored by Microelectronics and Computer Technology Corporation, EINet Galaxy is a polished, professional take on **Web** access. EINet, incidentally, produces a variety of software tools for Internet use, including clients like EINet MacWeb and EINet winWAIS. Some versions of these products are released as shareware or freeware.

You should check out the Galaxy site; its abundant links to business organizations show what can be done with product information in a seamlessly organized hypertext environment. Note, too, from the HTML design side of things, how efficiently the developers have laid out their pages. Images in particular, while enhancing the various documents, are never cumbersome; their use is sparing and effective.

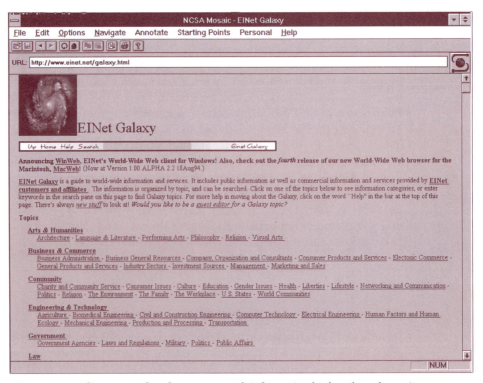

Figure 10.5 The EINet Galaxy home page, with information broken down by topics.

Net Happenings (IU Local Archive)

URL: http://www-iub.indiana.edu/cgi-bin/nethaps/

Net Happenings is a newsletter maintained by Gleason Sackman and circulated under the auspices of the InterNIC (Internet Network Information Center). At the time of this writing, it was also about to become established as a USENET newsgroup. This site is useful because it provides a way for you to search back postings of *Net Happenings* under whatever topic you're interested in. By entering the term **painting** as my search term, I uncovered the Bonestell Gallery presented later in the chapter. If you're looking for new sites, this is an easy way to search for them.

The Mother-of-all BBS

URL: http://www.cs.colorado.edu/homes/mcbryan/public_html/bb/summary.html

Here is a useful collection of **World Wide Web** home pages for business, government, research projects, and other related announcements. Its home page is shown in Figure 10.6. The Mother-of-all BBS is the work of Oliver McBryan at

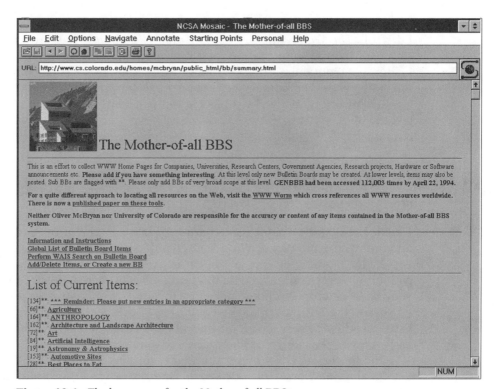

Figure 10.6   The home page for the Mother-of-all BBS.

the University of Colorado. Using its built-in support for **WAIS**, you can key in a search term and let the system find pointers to a variety of information sources.

The Clearinghouse for Subject-Oriented Internet Guides

URL: http://http2.sils.umich.edu/~lou/chhome.html

Here's a site you won't want to miss, even if it doesn't specialize in HTTP pages per se. The Clearinghouse contains collections of information by subject matter, with abundant links to **Gopher** servers and other sources of Internet data. Its **WAIS** engine allows you to search the text of any of these guides in the humanities, sciences and social sciences. The Clearinghouse is part of the Internet Resource Discovery project, which is a joint effort of the University of Michigan's School of Information and Library Studies and the University Library. Its goal is to provide a comprehensive guide to information by subject on the net. I have found it particularly strong in the humanities, an area where most **Web** servers could use improvement.

The Whole Internet Catalog

URL: http://nearnet.gnn.com/wic/newrescat.toc.html

Ed Krol's *The Whole Internet User's Guide and Catalog* has proven a popular source of Internet information for a new generation of users. This is a hypermedia site containing the Whole Internet Catalog, Krol's compilation of intriguing sites. The home page is shown in Figure 10.7.

Krol's work is divided by subject and is frequently updated. It forms part of O'Reilly & Associates' *Global Network Navigator,* an on-line magazine we examine next.

Global Network Navigator

URL: http://www.wimsey.com/gnn/wel/sites.html

Global Network Navigator (GNN) attained fame as one of the earliest serious attempts to use the **World Wide Web** to publish information for general audiences, and it remains one of the most interesting **Web** sites in existence. Numerous servers are available to handle its ever-increasing access load, and you should attempt to choose one close to you to avoid network congestion. To do so, use the URL given at the beginning of this section. It is an index page listing worldwide servers; an on-line, clickable map is also available. You can easily choose the site you'd like to use as your default.

Once accessed, GNN offers abundant features, including the Whole Internet Catalog, network news, financial features, a travel information section, and a focus on multimedia happenings wherever they occur on the net.

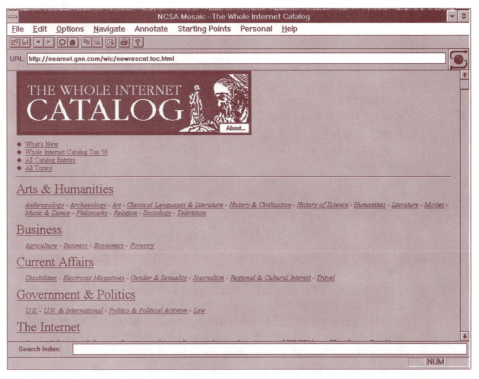

Figure 10.7 Ed Krol's The Whole Internet Catalog is a fine starting point to search for information by topic.

Global Network Academy

URL: http://uu-gna.mit.edu:8001/uu-gna/

Global Network Academy (GNA) is an attempt to build a fully accredited on-line university. Incorporated in the state of Texas, the Academy calls itself the "world's first virtual corporation." On-line courses have included an introduction to the Internet and a programming course in the C++ programming language. Both are supported through Internet archives, volunteer consulting on-line for questions, and a GNA Virtual Library designed to provide course materials.

The **Web** has generated little in terms of on-line education, so the Global Network Academy will be a project worth watching. While still in its infancy, it serves as a unique testbed for new concepts. The idea of absorbing on-line sites through the **Web**'s hyperlinks into a virtual library is limited by the hit-and-miss nature of on-line information, but could prove useful in modeling the kind of virtual environments that future computer educators will deal with as we move toward a broader information highway.

Views of the Solar System

URL: http://www.c3.lanl.gov/~cjhamil/SolarSystem/homepage.html

And speaking of education, here we have a guided tour of the solar system, sure to arouse the interest of any astronomy buff. The tour was created and compiled by Calvin J. Hamilton at Los Alamos National Laboratory. Click on one of these planetary images and both text and graphics about that planet appear on the screen. A glossary page provides background information on the terminology used. There are also abundant links to other sites of astronomical data and imagery.

Britannica Online

URL: http://www.eb.com/about.html

I am lucky enough to own not one but two sets of the *Encyclopedia Britannica's* Eleventh Edition, widely considered to be the greatest encyclopedia ever created. The *Britannica,* in production since 1768, set the standard for encyclopedia production from the beginning, although recent editions have broken the text into confusing sections, causing you to hunt through multiple volumes in searches that once could be accomplished by pulling one book off the shelf. Perhaps the **World Wide Web** can change that, because the *Encyclopedia Britannica* is moving on-line.

Although the project is only in its planning stages, the goal is to put 44 million words on-line, along with related graphics and sounds in the **World Wide Web** environment, and links to extraneous sources on the Internet. The on-line encyclopedia was originally conceived as straight ASCII text, but when its developers took a look at Mosaic, they realized they could use it to draw together various forms of media (the encyclopedia, after all, contains 23,000 maps, figures, and drawings). You can examine this site to monitor the progress of the project, but getting into the encyclopedia itself involves being on a subscriber list that, for the time being, is limited to university and library use.

A Tourist Expedition to Antarctica

URL: http://http2.sils.umich.edu/Antarctica/Story.html

Mosaic as an educational tool is thus far at its best when it is used to acquaint us with diverse cultures and regions. This is a site that specializes in perhaps the remotest area on earth, Antarctica. Its home page is shown in Figure 10.8.

The work of Lee Liming at the University of Michigan, the on-line tour is based on the author's experiences aboard the MV Marco Polo, which completed an Antarctic circumnavigation in February 1994. Audio and photographs from the journey are made available here, along with Liming's

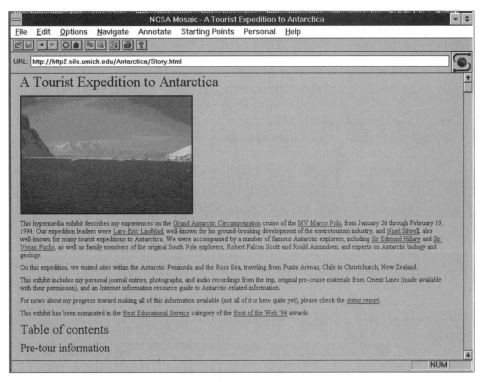

Figure 10.8 Taking a tour of Antarctica through Mosaic.

journal notes about the voyage. Liming also provides a booklist and guide to further information on the Internet. All told, this is one of the most comprehensive geographical guides available through the **Web** (check out the satellite imagery of Antarctica for starters).

The Scottish Highlands and Islands Server

URL: http://nsa.bt.co.uk/nsa.html

The Network Services Agency, a subsidiary of British Telecom, has created another geographical server of interest, this one based in the highlands of Scotland. BT's interest in the area is as a site for telecommuting; after all, this is a rugged, rural landscape, low in population but an obvious test site for telecommunications projects. This page is new and very much under construction, but it will be a good one to remember for those interested in Scotland and the Celtic cultures of the British Isles.

University of California Museum of Paleontology

URL: http://ucmp1.berkeley.edu/

Here's an intriguing take on an on-line museum. Figure 10.9 illustrates how the home page provides links to museum exhibits and catalogs through an artfully designed logo. The large image is taken from a sculpture showing two saber-tooth tigers attacking a bison. Notice how the buttons to proceed into the exhibit are worked into the image; this is artful HTML work!

Currently, the museum's exhibits include a family tree of living organisms, a study of geological time frames, and a history of evolutionary thought.

Latin America/Spanish Speaking Countries Page

URL: http://edb518ea.edb.utexas.edu/html/LatinAmerica.html

Lengthy URLs like this one are the reason we need Mosaic's ability to add items to our own menus; heaven forbid that we should have to type in such addresses every time we want to visit a site. And if you have an interest in Latin

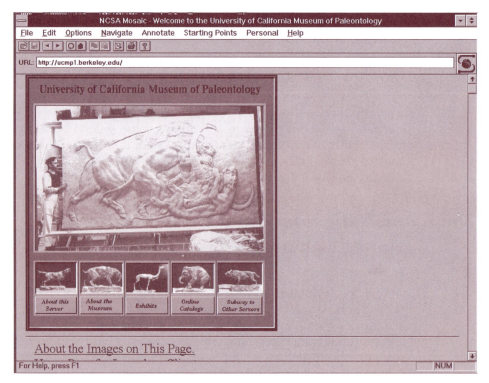

Figure 10.9 A museum of paleontology moves on-line.

America, this site is ideal for you. It contains Internet information broken down by country and by resource; thus you can quickly examine the various **Gophers** in Mexico, or look for **World Wide Web** sites in Chile (there are several). Organizing information by geographical regions, with links to the various countries represented, is a quick way to find your way to data about various cultures.

Red Cientifica Peruana (The Internet Network of Peru)

URL: http://www.rcp.net.pe/peru/peru_ingles.html

This is one of the sites listed on the Latin America page, of particular interest because of its wealth of information about one of South America's most fascinating cultures, Peru. The home page here is available in both English and Spanish, and includes a clickable map for quick access to information about specific sites within the country. There are also some nice audio clips of Peruvian music. Wisely, the developers have provided the length of each sound file along with its name, to help you avoid getting stuck with a massive download when you didn't expect it. El Condor Pasa is still beautiful music.

Map Viewer

URL: http://pubweb.parc.xerox.com/map/

Remarkably, this project from Xerox's Palo Alto Research Center is an HTTP tool that allows you to click on a world map to generate an image of the area you've chosen. Steve Putz, its author, includes a Frequently Asked Questions document on-line that explains how the system works. By pointing to a site and clicking repeatedly, it is possible to zoom in on a specific country or landmass. In Figure 10.10, I have zoomed in on the North Atlantic to view Iceland, Greenland, and the northern part of the UK.

You have a variety of ways of manipulating the image, including showing borders and rivers, adding color, and more. Be aware: This site can absorb plenty of your spare time!

Internet Computer Index

URL: http://ici.proper.com/

The Internet Computer Index is a free on-line reference service provided by Proper Publishing of Santa Cruz, California. You are able to search databases to find pointers to the information you need. Indices of product reviews and an index to sponsoring companies' products are particularly useful. Subheadings allow you to concentrate your search in the PC, Macintosh, or UNIX environments.

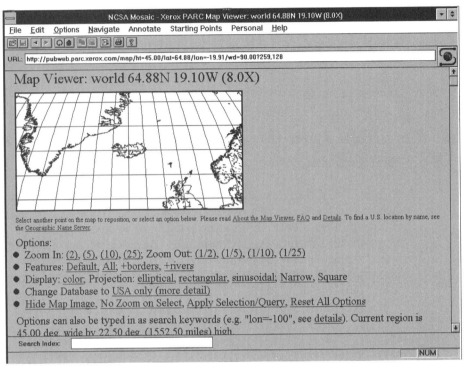

Figure 10.10   Using the Map Viewer to examine part of the North Atlantic.

Amateur Radio/Shortwave Listening

URL: http://buarc.bradley.edu/wwwvl-ham.html

Ham radio operators and interested parties will find this a useful page for background information. Links include documents like a ham radio Frequently Asked Questions list, searchable callbooks for the U.S., the United Kingdom, and Canada, and links to USENET newsgroups with radio connections. There is also a link to a useful shortwave listener page that includes broadcast schedules from major services like the BBC and Radio Canada. The latter deserves separate mention, for the quality of its information and the careful design of its home page:

URL: http://itre.uncecs.edu/radio/

And if you're a radio buff, don't miss this page:

URL: http://www.bbcnc.org.uk/bbctv/sched.html

Here you'll find the complete schedule for BBC World Service Radio, as well as BBC television shows. As one whose shortwave receiver spends a lot of time tuned to World Service, I can tell you what a valuable resource this is!

Library of Congress

URL: http://lcweb.loc.gov/homepage/lchp.html

The Library of Congress **Web** site shows considerable promise. Currently, it offers prints and photography from the American Memory project and links to its Global Electronic Library, a subject index to the **World Wide Web**. You can also tap the library's on-line catalogs and databases through the LOCIS service. Figure 10.11 shows you the home page.

WebWorld

URL: http://sailfish.peregrine.com/WebWorld/welcome.html

Here's a good way to occupy a rainy afternoon. WebWorld, developed by Ron Britvich of Peregrine Systems, is a virtual reality project that allows you to move through electronic cities and towns, and to build your own structures within them. You can link such structures to your own home page, your company's home page, or any other place on the **Web**.

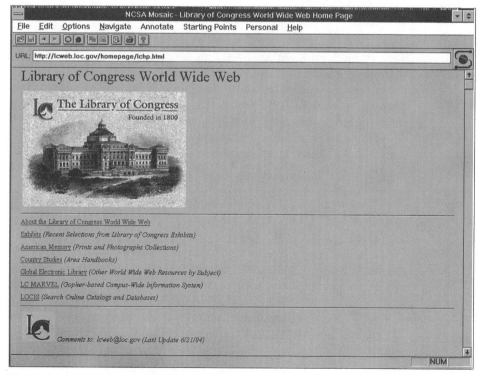

Figure 10.11   The home page at the Library of Congress.

With its graphical capabilities (you click on a square and it becomes your new view) and the elastic and growing nature of its contents, WebWorld is a fascinating experiment in group interaction. You are even alerted to the presence of other visitors to WebWorld, and can move your cursor to find out who is there. Be sure to read the introduction before proceeding.

GoldSite Europe

URL: http://www.3w.com/

This **Web** site contains information about more than 500 commercial organizations, along with Internet guides and directories. A link to the Guardian On-line Database allows you to search back issues of the publication. The developers claim more than half a million accesses per month. The service's Global On-line Newspage is a fascinating place to rummage for clues on how various kinds of businesses are using the net. Advertising here is free and the page is well traveled.

webNews: A "URL-Anchorized" USENET News Article Archive

URL: http://twinbrook.cis.uab.edu/hwebNews:80/

This is an archive of USENET news articles about the **Web** with inserted hypertext links. When a particular service is mentioned, along with its address, the material is set up as a link, so that you can click to go straight to the site. Many of us have had the experience of reading a USENET newsgroup and discovering an interesting **Web** site, only to have to enter a lengthy URL into Mosaic to go to it. This archive presents a clever way around that problem. This is how I discovered several of the sites discussed in this book, including the next one.

A Purgatory of Semiotics

URL: http://www.sonoma.edu/Exhibits/Semiotics/

Semiotics? My dictionary has it as semantics, the study of meaning in language; in formal logic, it also deals with the relationships between symbols and the things they represent. But don't be put off by the terminology. This site is actually a collection of poetry and interesting imagery. It contains the work of poet Michael Mollo, and holds implications for the display of art and text on a personalized basis. We can imagine the Internet being used to capture the ambiance of a small art gallery, or perhaps a coffee house where art and literature freely mingle.

Cardiff's Movie Database Browser

URL: http://www.cm.cf.ac.uk/Movies/

Movie lovers will want to check into this site, which offers a gateway to the USENET group **rec.arts.movies** and its database of cinema-related materials. You can search the database by title, character name, actors, or directors, and can call up lists of the top and bottom 40 films. The database itself is no small effort; it contains more than 31,000 movies at the time of this writing, with more than 370,000 entries on filmography—material on actors, directors, writers, and so on.

I searched the database for the relatively obscure but wonderful wartime drama *Five Graves to Cairo* (1943). I received not just a plot summary, but a complete breakdown of the cast and production company, with hypertext links to information about the careers of virtually everyone listed. The only missing item was the name of the costume designer. The database allows you to enter missing information, which I would have done had I known the answer. You can also vote on the film itself, on a scale of 1 to 10. I gave it an 8 (the ending was a bit mawkish, but what suspense!). The bulk of the voting, I noticed, regarded it less highly, with the largest number of votes assigning it a mere 5. The Cardiff's Movie Database Browser home page is shown in Figure 10.12.

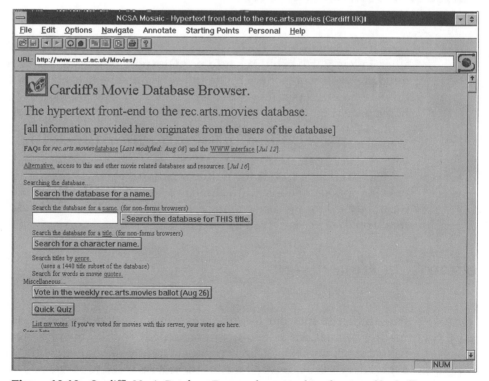

Figure 10.12 Cardiff's Movie Database Browser has something for every film buff.

What is particularly exciting about this site is that its extensive information has been assembled entirely by volunteers. We need more projects like this to exploit the interests and talents of people on the **Web**.

Chesley Bonestell Gallery

URL: http://www.secapl.com/bonestell/top.html

As a boy, I was captivated by the paintings of Chesley Bonestell, who captured astonishing views of astronomical objects based on sound scientific knowledge. The Bonestell gallery here divides his work into planetary views and scenes of various star systems. Bonestell, incidentally, led quite a full life, serving as an architect on the Golden Gate Bridge and the Chrysler Tower in New York; he also is responsible for the stunning special effects in such films as *When Worlds Collide* and *Destination Moon*. But it was as a painter whose work appeared in magazines like *Life* and *Scientific American* that he is best remembered. You can read all about him in the biographical article that accompanies the pictures at this site.

Space Activism Home Page

URL: http://muon.qrc.com/space/start.html

Here it is, 25 years after the first moon landing and we seem to be permanently stuck in low Earth orbit. What to do? One possibility is to check in with like-minded people who believe in the future of humans in space. You can do so at this site, where expanding the scope of manned spaceflight is the agenda. The home page (Figure 10.13) includes numerous links to information on political contacts and space organizations to help keep the pressure on Congress to act. You also receive updates on legislation as well as technology and links to a variety of other space sites.

The **Web** as a forum for political action? This site makes an interesting case for organizing those with similar ideas into a political force, especially as it can be used for updating contact information and informing users of events that would otherwise receive little publicity.

QuoteCom Home Page

URL: http://www.quote.com/

One thing the Internet has hitherto lacked has been sound financial information. QuoteCom is an attempt to remedy that. Some of its features, such as five stock quotes per day, are provided free of charge, while serious users are advised to subscribe to one of its more advanced services. The Basic Service, for example, costs $9.95 per month, and includes access to 100 quotes

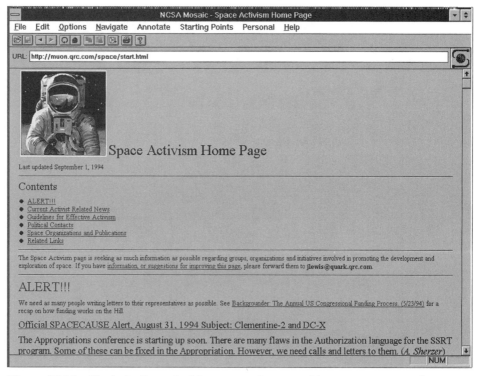

Figure 10.13   Check the Space Activism page to keep up with attempts to return humans to the moon.

per day, end of day portfolio updates, retrieval of basic balance sheet data including yield, price/earnings ratio and 52-week price history, and headline items for any news that pertains to your stocks. Various other services include access to such news sources as BusinessWire and S&P MarketScope Alert, a financial market information service. Figure 10.14 shows the Quote-com home page.

loQtus

URL: http://pubweb.ucdavis.edu/Documents/Quotations/homepage.html

loQtus stands for "Latticed On-line Quotations User Service," a system maintained by Jason Newquist at the University of California at Davis that gathers all the Internet resources concerning quotations in a single site. Included are interesting quotation archives and links to applicable USENET group databases, LISTSERVs, and FTP sites.

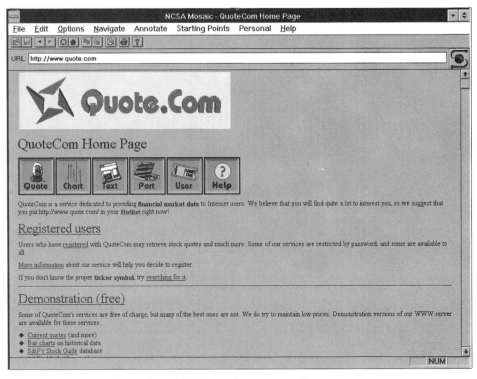

Figure 10.14   QuoteCom—financial information moves to the net.

The Internet Plaza

URL: http://storefront.xor.com/

Much has been made of the concept of the Internet as an on-line shopping center, where customers can find and buy what they need across the net. Take a look at The Internet Plaza if you want to get an early take on how this is developing. Figure 10.15 shows its home page. Companies that want to sell their products on-line or, at least, provide information about those products, can do so by signing up for space at this address. We'll see a sharp growth in on-line shopping activities as the net spreads in use, particularly as more and more home users sign on.

Russian and East European Studies Home Pages

URL: http://www.pitt.edu/~cjp/rees.html

The question of how to organize the **Web**'s banks of information remains with us. Take a look at the Russian and East European page to see how efficiently

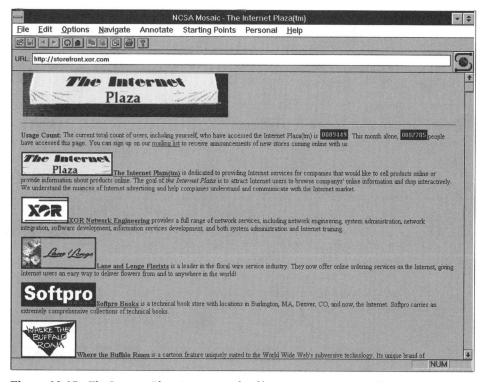

Figure 10.15   The Internet Plaza is an example of how commerce is spreading to the Internet.

the problem can be dealt with. Here you have links to resources by discipline, type, geographical origin and more. As the Internet spreads more broadly into eastern Europe, it will be fascinating to watch the activity. Pages like this can keep you close to the action.

Xanadu Home Page

URL: http://www.aus.xanadu.com:70/1/xanadu/

If you're interested in the history of hypertext and have thoughts about its future, you may want to connect with this server. Project Xanadu is the vision of Ted Nelson, who envisioned it as a worldwide hypertext implementation that would ultimately encompass the written word—not just a few written words but all of them. The goal was to make Xanadu the ultimate on-line library, containing the totality of human knowledge, all available through hyperlinks. The notion, too, was to make it a paying system; you would be charged for what you saw on a per-access basis. Abundant background information about it is available at this site.

Nelson, incidentally, is the person responsible for coining the terms hypertext and hypermedia. At work on Xanadu concepts as early as 1960, he can be considered a pioneer in the whole field of linked information. Recently, there has been movement toward implementing a version of Xanadu as a business publishing system. The long saga of Xanadu development continues.

Nova Scotia's Rest Stop on the Information Highway

URL: http://ttg.sba.dal.ca/nstour/

Planning a trip to Nova Scotia? Few lovelier places exist. Mosaic can help you with travel details if you know where to look. This well-designed page, shown in Figure 10.16, has been established to provide Nova Scotia tourism information.

Click on any of the items in the top box to move to a tour of the area, to a dining guide, or a list of top attractions. You can also click on individual cities and towns to retrieve background data on them. The server is still short on content but makes an interesting start. How long will it be before more chambers of commerce realize the tourism potential of the net and launch similar servers?

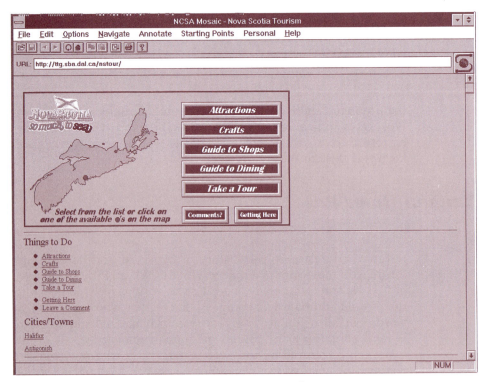

Figure 10.16   Using the **Web** as a repository of tourism information.

Downtown Anywhere

URL: http://www.awa.com/

Here's another take on transacting business on the Internet. Downtown Anywhere bills itself as a combination of library, laboratory, and place of business. Presented by AnyWare Associates and Softlock Services, this site offers links to services in a wide variety of fields, with a library, newsstand, sports arena, and post office designed to carry through the "network as small city" metaphor.

WiReD Magazine

URL: http://www.wired.com/

What a publishing phenomenon *WiReD Magazine* has turned out to be. Early copies of the magazine now command high prices among collectors, and the journal's focus on network activities coupled with a wild and irreverent sense of humor (check out the page layouts!) has won converts around the world. This is the WiReD **Web** site, and it's worth a look. The home page at WiReD is shown in Figure 10.17.

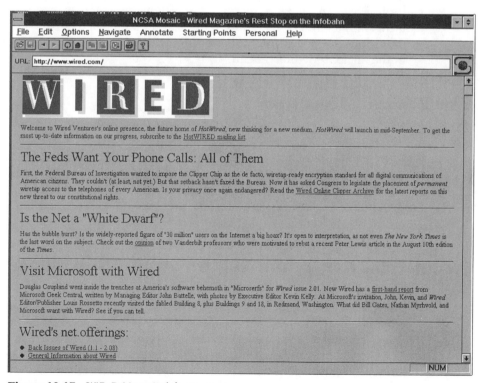

Figure 10.17   *WiReD Magazine*'s home page.

You can tap such interesting information as an archive of articles on the controversial Clipper Chip and look into back issues for further reading on a variety of subjects. The magazine offers an MPEG video if you're interested in checking out how your viewers are doing. Best of all is the ability to run full-text searches on back issues. More magazines should look at this page; these guys are doing it right.

PCWeek Best News Sources & On-line Magazines

URL: http://www.ziff.com/~pcweek/best_news.html

Looking for news on the net? This page can be of use. It contains links to a variety of news sources, including BBC radio, the Voice of America, the *San Francisco Examiner*, International Teletimes, and more.

ArtServe

URL: http://rubens.anu.edu.au/

Australian National University makes available a server specializing in the history of art. And what a server it is. Watch this page for exhibits on various facets of ancient art, including a tutorial on the palace of Diocletian. Literally thousands of images are available here, with a heavy emphasis on architecture in the ancient Mediterranean.

New Zealand/Aotearoa

URL: http://www.cs.cmu.edu:8001/Web/People/mjw/NZ/MainPage.html

Here is another useful site for tourists and anyone interested in New Zealand. The server includes the Frequently Asked Questions document from the USENET newsgroup **soc.culture.new-zealand**. It also makes recent New Zealand news stories available, and provides information on the history, government, and culture of the island nation.

Commercial Use (of the Net) Strategies Home Page

URL: http://pass.wayne.edu/business.html

Anyone hoping to transact business on the Internet should take a look at this page. The work of Andrew Dinsdale at Wayne State University in Michigan, it is an extensive article with hyperlinks dealing with the basic issues. You will find information about how to get connected, how to ensure security, and ways to use the Internet to your advantage. The abundant hyperlinks within this document to other sources of information make it helpful to any business person with questions about net access. Check out especially the link to other commercial sites on the **Web**.

Weather World

URL: `http://www.atmos.uiuc.edu/wxworld/html/top.html`

This site is managed by the Department of Atmospheric Sciences at the University of Illinois. Here you can find weather information ranging from infrared and visible satellite images to a whole range of surface weather maps. You may also want to investigate The Daily Planet, a server at the same location containing a variety of other weather resources and links to other weather services. You can reach it at this URL:

`http://www.atmos.uiuc.edu/`

Graphics, Visualization, and Usability Center

URL: `http://www.cc.gatech.edu/gvu/stats/NSF/merit.html`

If you follow the Internet's growth, you may be interested in accessing this page, which draws on data from NSFNET. Graphs showing network growth are provided, along with byte and packet counts for various kinds of Internet services.

MPEG Movie Archive

URL: `http://www.eeb.ele.tue.nl/mpeg/index.html`

This archive contains MPEG movies divided into categories like Animations, Music, Space, and others. It also provides links to other sites containing MPEG archives and background information about MPEG viewers. Under the Space category, I recently found movies showing the repair of the Hubble space telescope, the American flag being put on the moon, and animations of the Shoemaker-Levy 9 cometary impact on Jupiter. File sizes for these lengthy files are provided. The movie page is shown in Figure 10.18. Links to mirror sites are also provided; these help take the load off the main server.

The Legal Information Institute

URL: `http://fatty.law.cornell.edu/`

Cornell University makes this potpourri of legal information available, with both **Gopher**-based and **World Wide Web** offerings. You can check out recent

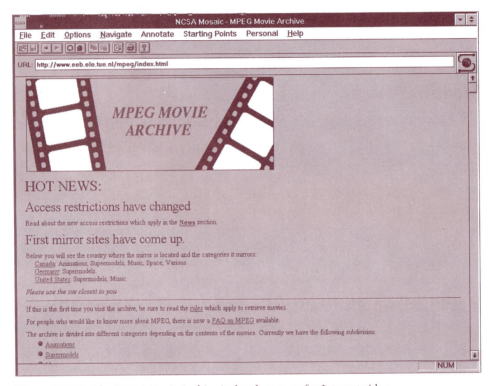

Figure 10.18   The MPEG Movie Archive is the place to go for Internet video.

Supreme Court decisions, directories of attorneys, and legal news on the state and federal level. The document also provides a menu that breaks down information by topics like constitutional law, environmental law, and disability issues. This site is quite thorough and is perhaps the most extensive database of legal materials available through the **Web**.

Kids Internet Delight

URL: http://www.clark.net/pub/journalism/kid.html

This site truly is a delight. John Makulowich (the power behind The Awesome List) has gathered pointers to every site he believes children would enjoy. What a great place to start a youngster out on Internet explorations. Here you find links to such sites as KidLink, MTV, and an exhibition on dinosaurs. If you can't seem to get your child interested in computers, a quick stop on this page just might do the trick. Makulowich is president of The Writers Alliance, a Maryland-based corporation specializing in Internet training.

The Internet Society

URL: http://info.isoc.org/home.html

If you plan to be around the Internet for long, you owe it to yourself and the net to join the Internet Society. The organization promotes cooperation and coordination for Internet activities of all kinds, and maintains a historical archive of Internet-related materials. To keep up with network developments, checking the links on this page is the best way to proceed. You'll also find the information you need to acquire your own membership in the Society.

HyperDOC: The National Library of Medicine

URL: http://www.nlm.nih.gov/

Here is a superb resource for anyone interested in medicine and health. Of particular interest to me was a searchable collection of almost 60,000 on-line images from the NLM's library of historical prints and photographs. Figure 10.19 shows what you will see when you access HyperDOC.

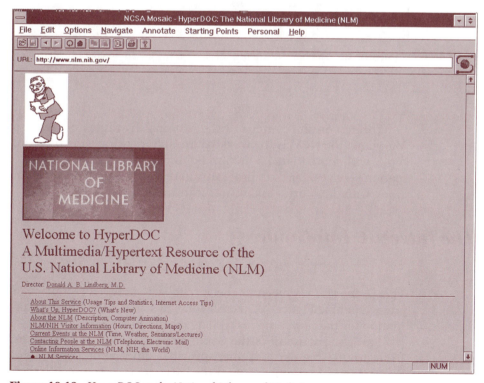

Figure 10.19 HyperDOC at the National Library of Medicine.

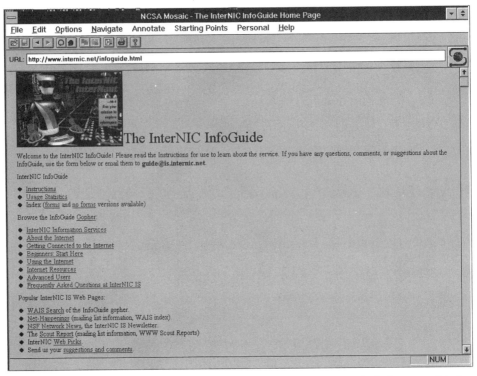

Figure 10.20 The InterNIC InfoGuide, a page you'll want to check regularly for network information.

Located on the campus of the National Institutes of Health in Bethesda, Maryland, the NLM is the world's largest library focusing on a single scientific topic, with more than 4.5 million holdings. It provides extensive on-line information services. Links to programs in research and development are provided along with directories and visitor information.

The InterNIC InfoGuide

URL: http://www.internic.net/

This is one site you need to check regularly; it deserves a place on your home page. Examine Figure 10.20, and you will see that the InterNIC provides information for the newcomer as well as the old hand.

Particularly useful is the Scout Report, which gives you the latest news from around the net and often provides clues about new sites to visit. The Scout Report is a reminder that the best way to keep up with the Internet is to use active, online resources.

Index

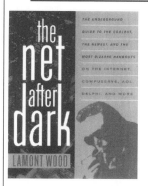
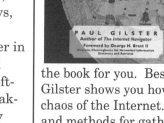